REA's Test Prep Books Are The Best!

(a sample of the <u>hundreds of letters</u> REA receives each year)

" This is the only book you will need to pass ... ed States I exam. [REA offers] an outstanding re ... ers contain supplemental information you will need for the ...

CLEP History of the United States I Test-Taking Student

" I found this book to be outstanding preparation for the CLEP [History of the United States I]. "

Student, Corpus Christi, TX

" This book enabled me to pass the CLEP [History of the United States I] test with flying colors. "

Student, Mequon, WI

" Your book was such a better value and was so much more complete than anything your competition has produced — and I have them all! "

Teacher, Virginia Beach, VA

" Compared to the other books that my fellow students had, your book was the most useful in helping me get a great score. "

Student, North Hollywood, CA

" Your book was responsible for my success on the exam, which helped me get into the college of my choice... I will look for REA the next time I need help. "

Student, Chesterfield, MO

(more on next page)

(continued from front page)

" I just wanted to thank you for helping me get a great score on the AP U.S. History exam... Thank you for making great test preps! "

Student, Los Angeles, CA

" Your *Fundamentals of Engineering Exam* book was the absolute best preparation I could have had for the exam, and it is one of the major reasons I did so well and passed the FE on my first try. "

Student, Sweetwater, TN

" I used your book to prepare for the test and found that the advice and the sample tests were highly relevant... Without using any other material, I earned very high scores and will be going to the graduate school of my choice. "

Student, New Orleans, LA

" What I found in your book was a wealth of information sufficient to shore up my basic skills in math and verbal... The practice tests were challenging and the answer explanations most helpful. It certainly is the *Best Test Prep for the GRE.* "

Student, Pullman, WA

" I really appreciate the help from your excellent book. Please keep up the great work. "

Student, Albuquerque, NM

" I am writing to thank you for your test preparation... your book helped me immeasurably and I have nothing but praise for your *GRE* preparation. "

Student, Benton Harbor, MI

THE BEST TEST PREPARATION FOR THE

CLEP

COLLEGE-LEVEL EXAMINATION PROGRAM

HISTORY OF THE UNITED STATES I

Early Colonizations to 1877

With CD-ROM for Windows
REA's Interactive TEST*ware*® for the
CLEP History of the United States I

Staff of Research & Education Association
Dr. M. Fogiel, Director

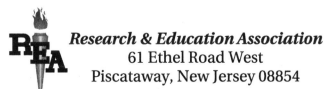

Research & Education Association
61 Ethel Road West
Piscataway, New Jersey 08854

The Best Test Preparation for the
CLEP HISTORY OF THE UNITED STATES I:
EARLY COLONIZATIONS TO 1877
With CD-ROM for Windows
REA's TESTware® for the CLEP History of the United States I

Printed in the United States of America

Library of Congress Control Number 2003106314

International Standard Book Number 0-87891-272-X

C-V-1-I

CONTENTS

About Research & Education Association

Research & Education Association (REA) is an organization of educators, scientists, and engineers specializing in various academic fields. Founded in 1959 with the purpose of disseminating the most recently developed scientific information to groups in industry, government, high schools, and universities, REA has since become a successful and highly respected publisher of study aids, test preps, handbooks, and reference works.

REA's Test Preparation series includes study guides for all academic levels in almost all disciplines. Research & Education Association publishes test preps for students who have not yet completed high school, as well as high school students preparing to enter college. Students from countries around the world seeking to attend college in the United States will find the assistance they need in REA's publications. For college students seeking advanced degrees, REA publishes test preps for many major graduate school admission examinations in a wide variety of disciplines, including engineering, law, and medicine. Students at every level, in every field, with every ambition can find what they are looking for among REA's publications.

Unlike most test preparation books—which present only a few practice tests that bear little resemblance to the actual exams—REA's series presents tests that accurately depict the official exams in both degree of difficulty and types of questions. REA's practice tests are always based upon the most recently administered exams, and include every type of question that can be expected on the actual exams.

REA's publications and educational materials are highly regarded and continually receive an unprecedented amount of praise from professionals, instructors, librarians, parents, and students. Our authors are as diverse as the fields represented in the books we publish. They are well-known in their respective disciplines and serve on the faculties of prestigious high schools, colleges, and universities throughout the United States and Canada.

Acknowledgments

In addition to our authors, we would like to thank Dr. Max Fogiel, President, for his overall guidance, which brought this publication to completion; Carl Fuchs, Director of Educational Software, for his guidance in the design and development of the software; John Paul Cording, Manager of Educational Software, for coordinating the design, development and testing of the software; Project Managers Amy Jamison and Reena Shah for their design contributions and tireless testing efforts; Larry B. Kling, Quality Control Manager, for his editorial direction; Craig Yetsko, Editorial Assistant, Paul Babbitt, Ph.D., John Chilton, Ph.D., and William Walker, Ph.D., for their editorial contributions; and Joanne Morbitt for typesetting the book.

CHAPTER 1
PASSING THE CLEP HISTORY OF THE UNITED STATES I CBT

Chapter 1

PASSING THE CLEP HISTORY OF THE UNITED STATES I CBT

ABOUT THIS BOOK & TEST*ware*®

This book provides you with complete preparation for the CLEP History of the United States I Computer-Based Test, or CBT. Inside you will find a concise review of the subject matter, as well as tips and strategies for test-taking. We also give you three practice tests—all based on the official CLEP History of the United States I CBT. Our practice tests contain every type of question that you can expect to encounter on the actual exam. Following each practice test you will find an answer key with detailed explanations designed to help you more completely understand the test material.

All 34 CLEP subject exams are computer-based. As you can see, the practice tests in our book are presented as paper-and-pencil exams. The content and format of the actual CLEP subject exams are faithfully mirrored. We detail the format of the CLEP History of the United States I CBT on pages 4–5.

The practice tests in this book and software package are included in two formats: in printed form in this book, and in TEST*ware*® format on the enclosed CD. **We recommend that you begin your preparation by first taking the practice exams on your computer.** The software provides timed conditions, automatic scoring, and scoring information that makes it easier to target your strengths and weaknesses.

ABOUT THE EXAM

Who takes the CLEP CBT and what is it used for?

CLEP (College-Level Examination Program) examinations are usually taken by people who have acquired knowledge outside the classroom and wish to bypass certain college courses and earn college credit. The CLEP Program is designed to reward students for learning—no matter where or how that knowledge was acquired. CLEP is the most widely accepted credit-by-examination program in the country, with more than 2,900 colleges and universities granting credit for satisfactory scores on CLEP exams.

Although most CLEP examinees are adults returning to college, many graduating high school seniors, enrolled college students, and international students also take the exams to earn college credit or to demonstrate their ability to perform at the college level. There are no prerequisites, such as age or educational status, for taking CLEP examinations. However, because policies on granting credits vary among colleges, you should contact the particular institution from which you wish to receive CLEP credit.

Most CLEP examinations include material usually covered in an undergraduate course with a similar title to that of the exam (e.g., History of the United States I). However, five of the exams do not deal with subject matter covered in any particular course but rather with material taken as general requirements during the first two years of college. These general exams are English Composition (with or without essay), Humanities, College Mathematics, Natural Sciences, and Social Sciences and History.

Who administers the exam?

The CLEP CBTs are developed by the College Board, administered by Educational Testing Service (ETS), and involve the assistance of educators throughout the United States. The test development process is designed and implemented to ensure that the content and difficulty level of the test are appropriate.

When and where is the exam given?

The CLEP History of the United States I CBT is administered each month throughout the year at more than 1,400 test centers in the United States and can be arranged for candidates abroad on request. To find the test center nearest you and to register for the exam, you should obtain a copy of the free booklets *CLEP Colleges* and *CLEP Information for Candidates and Registration Form.* They are available at most colleges where CLEP credit is granted, or by contacting:

CLEP Services
P.O. Box 6600
Princeton, NJ 08541-6600
Phone: (609) 771-7865
Fax: (609) 771-7088
Website: http://www.collegeboard.com

HOW TO USE THIS BOOK

What do I study first?

Read over the course review and the suggestions for test-taking, take the first practice test to determine your area(s) of weakness, and then go back and focus your study on those specific problems. Studying the reviews thoroughly will reinforce the basic skills you will need to do well on the exam. Make sure to take the practice tests to become familiar with the format and procedures involved with taking the actual exam.

To best utilize your study time, follow our Independent Study Schedule, which you'll find in the front of this book. The schedule is based on a four-week program, but can be condensed to two weeks, if necessary, by collapsing each two-week period into one.

When should I start studying?

It is never too early to start studying for the CLEP History of the United States I. The earlier you begin, the more time you will have to sharpen your skills. Do not procrastinate! Cramming is *not* an effective way to study, since it does not allow you the time needed to learn the test material. The sooner you learn the format of the exam, the more time you will have to familiarize yourself with it.

FORMAT AND CONTENT OF THE CLEP CBT

The CLEP History of the United States I covers the period of American History from the Spanish and French colonizations to the end of Reconstruction. The primary emphasis of the exam is on the English colonies and the early period of nationhood.

There are 120 multiple-choice questions, each with five possible answer choices, to be answered in 90 minutes.

The approximate breakdown of topics is as follows:

35%	Political institutions and behavior and public policy
25%	Social developments
10%	Economic developments
15%	Cultural and intellectual developments
15%	Diplomacy and international relations

Approximately one-third of the questions focus on the period from 1500 to 1789, while the rest deal with the period from 1790 to 1877.

ABOUT OUR COURSE REVIEW

The history review in this book covers all major events and historical figures from the early Spanish and French colonizations up to Reconstruction. The review is divided into seven major time periods:

1. *The Colonial Period* (1500–1763)
2. *The American Revolution* (1763–1787)
3. *The United States Constitution* (1787–1789)
4. *The New Nation* (1789–1824)
5. *Jacksonian Democracy and Westward Expansion* (1824–1850)
6. *Sectional Conflict and the Causes of the Civil War* (1850–1860)
7. *The Civil War and Reconstruction* (1860–1877)

SCORING YOUR PRACTICE TESTS vs. THE CLEP CBT

How do I score my practice tests?

The CLEP History of the United States I is scored on a scale of 20 to 80—just like our practice tests. To score your practice tests, count up the number of correct answers and enter the result on the scoring worksheet below. Next, total your incorrect answers, multiply this number by one-fourth, and enter the result on the scoring worksheet. As shown below, subtract the number of incorrect responses from the number of correct ones—this will yield your total raw score. Finally, convert your raw score to a scaled score using the conversion table that follows.

PRACTICE-TEST SCORING WORKSHEET

Raw Score: ________ – (1/4 x ________) = ________

 # correct *# incorrect**

Scaled Score: ________

(Caution: The conversion table on page 6 provides ***only an estimate*** *of your scaled score. Since scaled scores vary from one form of a test to another,* ***your score on the actual exam may be higher or lower*** *than what appears on the table. Your CLEP CBT score is based only on the number of items you answer correctly. You* ***will not be penalized*** *for incorrect answers, as you are on our printed practice tests.)*

PRACTICE-TEST RAW SCORE CONVERSION TABLE*

Raw Score	Scaled Score	Course Grade	Raw Score	Scaled Score	Course Grade
100 & up	80	A	48	54	B
99	80	A	47	53	B
98	80	A	46	52	B
97	79	A	45	51	B
96	79	A	44	51	B
95	78	A	43	50	B
94	78	A	42	50	B
93	77	A	41	50	B
92	77	A	40	50	B
91	76	A	39	50	B
90	76	A	38	49	B
89	75	A	37	48	B
88	74	A	36	48	B
87	74	A	35	47	B
86	73	A	34	46	B
85	72	A	33	46	B
84	72	A	32	45	C
83	71	A	31	45	C
82	71	A	30	45	C
81	70	A	29	45	C
80	69	A	28	45	C
79	69	A	27	44	C
78	68	A	26	44	D
77	67	A	25	43	D
76	67	A	24	42	D
75	66	A	23	41	D
74	66	A	22	41	D
73	65	A	21	40	F
72	64	A	20	40	F
71	64	A	19	40	F
70	63	A	18	40	F
69	62	A	17	39	F
68	62	A	16	39	F
67	61	A	15	38	F
66	61	A	14	37	F
65	60	A	13	36	F
64	60	A	12	35	F
63	60	A	11	34	F
62	60	A	10	33	F
61	59	B	9	32	F
60	58	B	8	31	F
59	58	B	7	30	F
58	57	B	6	29	F
57	57	B	5	28	F
56	56	B	4	26	F
55	56	B	3	24	F
54	55	B	2	23	F
53	55	B	1	22	F
52	55	B	0	21	F
51	55	B	–1	20	F
50	55	B	–2	20	F
49	54	B	and below	20	F

*This table is provided for scoring REA practice tests only. With the advent of computer-based testing, the College-Level Examination Program uses a single across-the-board credit-granting score of 50 for all 34 CLEP computer-based exams. Nonetheless, on account of the different skills being measured and the unique content requirements of each test, the actual number of correct answers needed to reach 50 will vary. A "50" is calibrated to equate with performance that would warrant the grade C in the corresponding introductory college course.

When will I receive my score report?

The test administrator will print out a full Candidate Score Report for you immediately upon your completion of the CBT (except for CLEP English Composition with Essay). Your scores are reported only to you, unless you ask to have them sent elsewhere. If you want your scores reported to a college or other institution, you must say so when you take the examination. Since your scores are kept on file for 20 years, you can also request transcripts from Educational Testing Service at a later date.

STUDYING FOR THE CLEP CBT

It is very important for you to choose the time and place for studying that works best for you. Some students set aside a certain number of hours every morning, while others may choose to study at night before going to sleep. Only you can determine when and where your study time will be most effective. But be consistent and use your time wisely. Work out a study routine and stick to it!

When you take the practice tests, try to make your testing conditions as much like the actual test as possible. Turn your television and radio off, and sit down at a quiet table free from distraction. Make sure to time yourself. Start off by setting a timer for the time that is allotted for each section, and be sure to reset the timer for the appropriate amount of time when you start a new section.

As you complete each practice test, score your test and thoroughly review the explanations to the questions you answered incorrectly; but don't review too much at once. Concentrate on one problem area at a time by reading over the question and explanation, and by studying germane portions of our review until you are confident that you understand the material.

Keep track of your scores and mark them on the Scoring Worksheet. By doing so, you will be able to gauge your progress and discover weaknesses in particular sections.

TEST-TAKING TIPS

Although you may not be familiar with computer-based standardized tests such as the CLEP History of the United States I, there are many ways to acquaint yourself with this type of examination and thus help alleviate your test-taking anxieties. Listed below are ways to help you become accustomed to the CLEP CBT, some of which may be applied to other computer-based standardized tests as well.

Know the format of the CBT. CLEP CBTs are not adaptive but rather fixed-length tests. In a sense, this makes them kin to the familiar paper-and-pencil exam in that you have the same flexibility to go back and review your work in each section. Moreover, the format hasn't changed a great deal from the paper-and-pencil CLEP.

Read all of the possible answers. Just because you think you have found the correct response, do not automatically assume that it is the best answer. Read through each choice to be sure that you are not making a mistake by jumping to conclusions.

Use the process of elimination. Go through each possible response to a question and eliminate as many of the answer choices as possible. By eliminating just two answer choices, you give yourself a better chance of getting the item correct, since there will be only three choices left from which to make your guess. Remember, your score is based only on the number of questions you answer *correctly*.

Work quickly and steadily. You will have only 90 minutes to work on 120 questions, so work quickly and steadily to avoid focusing on any one question too long. Taking the practice tests in this book will help you learn to budget your time.

Acquaint yourself with the CBT screen. Familiarize yourself with the CLEP CBT screen beforehand by logging on to the College Board website. Waiting until test day to see what it looks like in the pretest tutorial risks injecting needless anxiety into your testing experience. Also, familiarizing yourself with the directions and format of the exam will save you valuable time on the day of the actual test.

Be sure that your answer registers before you go on to the next item. Look at the screen to see that your mouse-click causes the pointer to darken the proper oval. This takes less effort than darkening an oval on paper, but don't lull yourself into taking less care!

THE DAY OF THE EXAM

Preparing for the CLEP CBT

On the day of the test, you should wake up early (after a decent night's rest, we hope) and have a good breakfast. Make sure to dress comfortably so that you are not distracted by being too hot or too cold while taking the test. Plan to arrive at the test center early. This will allow you to collect your thoughts and relax before the test, and will also spare you the anxiety that comes with being late. As an added incentive to make sure you arrive early, keep in mind that no one will be allowed into the test session after the test has begun.

Before you leave for the test center, make sure that you have your admission form and another form of identification, which must contain a recent photograph, your name, and signature (i.e., driver's license, student identification card, or current alien registration card). You will not be admitted to the test center if you do not have proper identification.

If you would like, you may wear a watch to the test center. However, you may not wear one that makes noise, because it may disturb the other test-takers. No dictionaries, textbooks, notebooks, briefcases, or packages will be permitted and drinking, smoking, and eating are prohibited.

Good luck on the CLEP History of the United States I CBT!

INDEPENDENT STUDY SCHEDULE
CLEP HISTORY OF THE UNITED STATES I

The following study schedule allows for thorough preparation for the CLEP History of the United States I Computer-Based Test. Although our timetable is designed for four weeks, it can be condensed into a two-week course by collapsing each two-week period into one. Be sure to set aside enough time—at least two hours each day—to study. But no matter which study schedule works best for you, the more time you spend studying, the more prepared, relaxed, and confident you will feel on the day of the exam.

Week	*Activity*
1	Carefully read and study the American History Review: 1500–1877 included in this book. We strongly recommend using a recognized textbook in conjunction with our study guide.
2	Read and study Chapter 1, which will introduce you to the CLEP History of the United States I CBT. Then take Practice Test 1 on TEST*ware*; determine your strengths and weaknesses by looking at the different sections on the score report. You can then determine the areas upon which you need to focus your efforts.
3	Take Practice Test 2 on TEST*ware* and, after reading your score report, carefully review detailed explanations for the items you answered incorrectly. If there are any types of questions or particular subjects that seem difficult to you, review those subjects by reading the appropriate section of this book's American History Review: 1500–1877.
4	Take Practice Test 3 on TEST*ware* and, after reading your score report, carefully review detailed explanations for the items you answered incorrectly. If there are any types of questions or particular subjects that prove difficult for you, review those subjects by reading over the appropriate sections of our American History Review: 1500–1877.

CHAPTER 2
AMERICAN HISTORY REVIEW: 1500 – 1877

Chapter 2

AMERICAN HISTORY REVIEW: 1500-1877

The following American History review covers the period of time from the earliest colonizations in America through 1877, the end of Reconstruction. The review is divided into seven time periods, as follows:

1: **The Colonial Period** (1500-1763)
2: **The American Revolution** (1763-1787)
3: **The United States Constitution** (1787-1789)
4: **The New Nation** (1789-1824)
5: **Jacksonian Democracy and Westward Expansion** (1824-1850)
6: **Sectional Conflict and the Causes of the Civil War** (1850-1860)
7: **The Civil War and Reconstruction** (1860-1877)

By thoroughly studying this course review, you will be well-prepared for the material on the CLEP History of the United States I exam.

1 THE COLONIAL PERIOD (1500-1763)

THE AGE OF EXPLORATION

The Treaty of Tordesillas

Excited by the gold Columbus had brought back from America (after Amerigo Vespucci, an Italian member of a Portuguese expedition to South America whose widely reprinted report suggested a new world had been found), Ferdinand and Isabella, joint monarchs of Spain, sought formal confirmation of their ownership of these new lands. They feared the interference of Portugal, which was at that time a powerful seafaring nation and had been active in overseas exploration. At Spain's urging the pope drew a "Line of Demarcation" 100 leagues west of the Cape Verde Islands dividing the heathen world into two equal parts—that east of the line for Portugal and that west of it for Spain.

Because this line tended to be unduly favorable to Spain, and because Portugal had the stronger navy, the two countries worked out the Treaty of Tordesillas (1494), by which the line was moved farther west. As a result, Brazil eventually became a Portuguese colony, while Spain maintained claims to the rest of the Americas. As other European nations joined the hunt for colonies, they tended to ignore the Treaty of Tordesillas.

The Spanish Conquistadores

To conquer the Americas the Spanish monarchs used their powerful army, led by independent Spanish adventurers known as *conquistadores*. At first the conquistadores confined their attentions to the Caribbean islands, where the European diseases they unwittingly carried with them devastated the local Indian populations, who had no immunities against such diseases.

After about 1510 the conquistadores turned their attention to the American mainland. In 1513 Vasco Nunez de Balboa crossed the isthmus of Panama and became the first European to see the Pacific Ocean. The same year Juan Ponce de Leon explored Florida in search of gold and a fabled fountain of youth. He found neither but claimed Florida for Spain. In 1519 Hernando (Hernan) Cortes led his dramatic expedition against the Aztecs of Mexico. Aided by the fact that the Indians at first mistook him for a god, and armed with firearms, armor, horses, and (unknown to him) smallpox germs, all previously unknown in America, Cortes destroyed the Aztec empire and won enormous riches. By the 1550s other such fortune seekers had conquered much of South America.

In North America the Spaniards sought in vain for riches. In 1528 Panfilio de Narvaez led a disastrous expedition through the Gulf Coast region from which only four of the original 400 men returned. One of them, Cabeza de Vaca, brought with him a story of seven great cities full of gold (the "Seven Cities of Cibola") somewhere to the north. In response to this, two Spanish expeditions explored the interior of North America. Hernando de Soto led a 600-man expedition (1539–1541) through what is now the southeastern United States, penetrating as far west as Oklahoma and discovering the Mississippi River, on whose banks de Soto was buried. Francisco Vasquez de Coronado led an expedition (1540–1542) from Mexico, north across the Rio Grande and through New Mexico, Arizona, Texas, Oklahoma, and Kansas. Some of Coronado's men were the first Europeans to see the Grand Canyon. While neither expedition discovered rich Indian civilizations to plunder, both increased Europe's knowledge of the interior of North America and asserted Spain's territorial claims to the continent.

New Spain

Spain administered its new holdings as an autocratic, rigidly controlled empire in which everything was to benefit the parent country. Tight control of even mundane matters was carried out by a suffocating bureaucracy run directly from Madrid. Annual treasure fleets carried the riches of the New World to Spain for the furtherance of its military-political goals in Europe.

As population pressures were low in sixteenth-century Spain, only about 200,000 Spaniards came to America during that time. To deal with the consequent labor shortages and as a reward to successful conquistadores, the Spaniards developed a system of large manors or estates (*encomiendas*) with Indian slaves ruthlessly managed for the benefit of the conquistadores. The *encomienda* system was later replaced by the similar but somewhat milder *hacienda* system. As the Indian population died from overwork and European diseases, Spaniards began importing African slaves to supply their labor needs. Society in New Spain was rigidly stratified, with the highest level reserved for natives of Spain (*peninsulares*) and the next for those of Spanish parentage born in the New World (*creoles*). Those of mixed (Mestizo) or Indian blood occupied lower levels.

English and French Beginnings

In 1497 the Italian John Cabot (Giovanni Caboto), sailing under the sponsorship of the king of England in search of a Northwest Passage (a water route to the Orient through or around the North American continent), became the first European since the Viking voyages more than four centuries earlier to reach the mainland of North America, which he claimed for England.

In 1524 the king of France authorized another Italian, Giovannia da Verrazzano, to undertake a mission similar to Cabot's. Endeavoring to duplicate the achievement of Portugal's Ferdinand Magellan, who had five years earlier found a way around the southern tip of South America, Verrazzano followed the American coast from present-day North Carolina to Maine.

Beginning in 1534, Jacques Cartier, also authorized by the king of France, mounted three expeditions to the area of the St. Lawrence River, which he believed might be the hoped-for Northwest Passage. He explored up the river as far as the site of Montreal, where rapids prevented him—or so he thought—from continuing to China. He claimed the area for France before abandoning his last expedition and returning to France in 1542. France made no further attempts to explore or colonize in America for 65 years.

England showed little interest in America as well during most of the sixteenth century. But when the English finally did begin colonization, commercial capitalism in England had advanced to the point that the English efforts were supported by private rather than government funds, allowing the English colonists to enjoy a greater degree of freedom from government interference.

Partially as a result of the New World rivalries and partially on account of differences between Protestant and Catholic countries, the sixteenth century was a violent time both in Europe and in America. French Protestants, called Huguenots, who attempted to escape persecution in Catholic France by settling in the New World were massacred by the Spaniards. One such incident led the Spaniards, nervous about any possible encroachment on what they considered to be their exclusive holdings in America, to build a fort that became the beginning of a settlement at St. Augustine, Florida, the oldest European settlement in what is now the United States. Spanish priests ventured north from St. Augustine, but no permanent settlements were built in the interior.

French and especially English sea captains made great sport of and considerable profit from plundering the Spaniards of the wealth they had first plundered from the Indians. One of the most successful English captains, Francis Drake, sailed around South America and raided the Spanish settlements on the Pacific coast of Central America before continuing on to California, which he claimed for England and named Nova Albion. Drake then returned to England by sailing around the world. England's Queen Elizabeth, sister and Protestant successor to Mary, had been quietly investing in Drake's highly profitable voyages. On Drake's return from his round-the-world voyage, Elizabeth openly showed her approval.

Angered by this as well as by Elizabeth's support of the Protestant cause in Europe, Spain's King Philip II in 1588 dispatched a mighty fleet, the Spanish Armada, to conquer England. Instead, the Armada was defeated by the English navy and largely destroyed by storms in the North Sea. This victory established England as a great power and moved it a step closer to overseas colonization, although the war with Spain continued until 1604.

Gilbert, Raleigh, and the Roanoke Settlers

English nobleman Sir Humphrey Gilbert believed England should found colonies and find a Northwest Passage. In 1576 he sent English sea captain Martin Frobisher to look for such a passage. Frobisher scouted along the inhospitable northeastern coast of Canada and brought back large amounts of a yellow metal that turned out to be fool's gold. In 1578 Gilbert obtained a charter allowing him to found a colony with his own funds and guaranteeing the prospective colonists all the rights of those born and residing in England, thus setting an important precedent for future colonial charters. His attempts to found a colony in Newfoundland failed, and while pursuing these endeavors he was lost at sea.

With the queen's permission, Gilbert's work was taken up by his half-brother, Sir Walter Raleigh. Raleigh turned his attention to a more southerly portion of the North American coastline, which he named Virginia, in honor of England's unmarried queen. He selected as a site for the first settlement Roanoke Island, just off the coast of present-day North Carolina.

After one abortive attempt, a group of 114 settlers—men, women, and children—were landed in July 1587. Shortly thereafter, Virginia Dare became the first English child born in America. Later that year the expedition's leader, John White, returned to England to secure additional supplies. Delayed by the war with Spain he did not return until 1590, when he found the colony deserted. It is not known what became of the Roanoke settlers. After this failure, Raleigh was forced by financial constraints to abandon his attempts to colonize Virginia. Hampered by unrealistic expectations, inadequate financial resources, and the ongoing war with Spain, English interest in American colonization was submerged for 15 years.

THE BEGINNINGS OF COLONIZATION

Virginia

In the first decade of the 1600s, Englishmen, exhilarated by the recent victory over Spain and influenced by the writings of Richard Hakluyt (who urged American colonization as the way to national greatness and the spread of the gospel), once again undertook to plant colonies.

Two groups of merchants gained charters from James I, Queen Elizabeth's successor. One group of merchants was based in London and received a charter to North America between what are now the Hudson and the Cape Fear rivers. The other was based in Plymouth and was granted the right to colonize in North America from the Potomac to the northern border of present-day Maine. They were called the Virginia Company of London and the Virginia Company of Plymouth, respectively. These were joint-stock companies, which raised their capital by the sale of shares of stock. Companies of this sort had already been used to finance and carry on English trade with Russia, Africa, and the Middle East.

The Plymouth Company, in 1607, attempted to plant a colony in Maine, but after one winter the colonists became discouraged and returned to Britain. Thereafter, the Plymouth Company folded.

The Virginia Company of London, in 1607, sent out an expedition of three ships with 104 men to plant a colony some 40 miles up the James River from Chesapeake Bay. Like the river on which it was located, the new settlement was named Jamestown in honor of England's king. It became the first permanent English settlement in North America, but for a time it appeared to be going the way of the earlier attempts. During the early years of Jamestown, the majority of the settlers died of starvation, various diseases, or hostile action by Indians. Though the losses were continuously replaced by new settlers, the colony's survival remained in doubt for a number of years.

There were several reasons for these difficulties. The entire colony was owned by the company, and all members shared the profits regardless of how much or how little they worked; thus, there was a lack of incentive. Many of the settlers were gentlemen, who considered themselves too good to work at growing the food the colony needed to survive. Others were simply unambitious and little inclined to work in any case. Furthermore, the settlers had come with the expectation of finding gold or other quick and easy riches and wasted much time looking for these while they should have been providing for their survival.

For purposes of defense, the settlement had been sited on a peninsula formed by a bend in the river; but this low and swampy location proved to be a breeding ground for all sorts of diseases and, at high tide, even contaminated the settlers' drinking supply with sea water. To make matters worse, relations with Powhatan, the powerful local Indian chief, were at best uncertain and often openly hostile, with disastrous results for the colonists.

In 1608 and 1609 the dynamic and ruthless leadership of John Smith kept the colony from collapsing. Smith's rule was, "He who works not, eats not." After Smith returned to England in late 1609, the condition of the colony again became critical.

In 1612, a Virginia resident named John Rolfe discovered that a superior strain of tobacco, native to the West Indies, could be grown in Virginia. There was a large market for this tobacco in Europe, and Rolfe's discovery gave Virginia a major cash crop.

To secure more settlers and boost Virginia's shrinking labor force, the company moved to make immigration possible for Britain's poor who were without economic opportunity at home or financial means to procure transportation to America. This was achieved by means of the indenture system, by which a poor worker's passage to America was paid by an American planter (or the company itself), who in exchange, was indentured to work for the planter (or the company) for a specified number of years. The system was open to abuse and often resulted in the mistreatment of the indentured servants.

To control the workers thus shipped to Virginia, as well as the often lazy and unruly colonists already present, the company gave its governors in America dictatorial powers. Governors such as Lord De La Warr, Sir Thomas Gates, and Sir Thomas Dale made use of such powers, imposing a harsh rule.

For such reasons, and its well-known reputation as a death trap, Virginia continued to attract inadequate numbers of immigrants. To solve this, a reform-minded faction within the company proposed a new approach, and under its leader Edwin Sandys made changes designed to attract more settlers. Colonists were promised the same rights they had in England. A representative assembly, the House of Burgesses, was founded in 1619—the first in America. Additionally, private ownership of land was instituted.

Despite these reforms, Virginia's unhealthy reputation kept many Englishmen away. Large numbers of indentured servants were brought in, especially young, single men. The first Africans were brought to Virginia in 1619 but were treated as indentured servants rather than slaves.

Virginia's Indian relations remained difficult. In 1622 an Indian massacre took the lives of 347 settlers. In 1644 the Indians struck again, massacring some 300 more. Shortly thereafter, the coastal Indians were subdued and no longer presented a serious threat.

Impressed by the potential profits from tobacco growing, King James I determined to have Virginia for himself. Using the high mortality and the 1622 massacre as a pretext, in 1624 he revoked the London Company's charter and made Virginia a royal colony. This pattern was followed throughout colonial history; both company colonies and proprietary colonies tended eventually to become royal colonies. Upon taking over Virginia, James revoked all political rights and the representative assembly—he did not believe in such things—but 15 years later his son, Charles I, was forced, by constant pressure from the Virginians and the continuing need to attract more settlers, to restore these rights.

New France

Shortly after England returned to the business of colonization, France renewed its interest in the areas previously visited by such French explorers as Jacques Cartier. The French opened with the Indians a lucrative trade in furs, plentiful in America and much sought after in Europe.

The St. Lawrence River was the French gateway to the interior of North America. In 1608 Samuel de Champlain established a trading post in Quebec, from which the rest of what became New France eventually spread.

Relatively small numbers of Frenchmen came to America, and partially because of this they were generally able to maintain good relations with the Indians. French Canadians were energetic in exploring and claiming new lands for France.

French exploration and settlement spread through the Great Lakes region and the valleys of the Mississippi and Ohio rivers. In 1673 Jacques Marquette explored the Mississippi Valley, and in 1682 Sieur de la Salle followed the river to its mouth. French settlements in the Midwest were not generally real towns, but rather forts and trading posts serving the fur trade.

Throughout its history, New France was handicapped by an inadequate population and a lack of support by the parent country.

New Netherlands

Other countries also took an interest in North America. In 1609 Holland sent an Englishman named Henry Hudson to explore for them in search of a Northwest Passage. In this endeavor Hudson discovered the river that bears his name.

Arrangements were made to trade with the Iroquois Indians for furs, especially beaver pelts for the hats then popular in Europe. In 1624 Dutch trading outposts were established on Manhattan Island (New Amsterdam) and at the site of present-day Albany (Fort Orange). A profitable fur trade was carried on and became the main source of revenue for the Dutch West India Company, the joint-stock company that ran the colony.

To encourage enough farming to keep the colony supplied with food, the Dutch instituted the patroon system, by which large landed estates would be given to wealthy men who transported at least 50 families to New Netherlands. These families would then become tenant farmers on the estate of the patroon who had transported them. As Holland's home economy was healthy, few Dutch felt desperate enough to take up such unattractive terms.

New Netherlands was, in any case, internally weak and unstable. It was poorly governed by inept and lazy governors; and its population was a mixture of people from all over Europe as well as many African slaves, forming what historians have called an "unstable pluralism."

The Pilgrims at Plymouth

Many Englishmen came from England for religious reasons. For the most part, these fell into two groups, Puritans and Separatists. Though similar in many respects to the Puritans, the Separatists believed the Church of England was beyond saving and so felt they must separate from it.

One group of Separatists, suffering government harassment, fled to Holland. Dissatisfied there, they decided to go to America and thus became the famous Pilgrims.

Led by William Bradford, they departed in 1620, having obtained from the London Company a charter to settle just south of the Hudson River. Driven by storms, their ship, the *Mayflower*, made landfall at Cape Cod in Massachusetts; and they decided it was God's will for them to settle in that area. This, however, put them outside the jurisdiction of any established government; and so before going ashore they drew up and signed the *Mayflower Compact*, establishing a foundation for orderly government based on the consent of the governed. After a difficult first winter that saw many die, the Pilgrims went on to establish a quiet and modestly prosperous colony. After a number of years of hard work, they were able to buy out the investors who had originally financed their voyage and thus gain greater autonomy.

The Massachusetts Bay Colony

The Puritans were far more numerous than the Separatists. Contrary to stereotype, they did not dress in drab clothes and were not ignorant or bigoted. They did, however, take the Bible and their religion seriously and felt the Anglican church still retained too many unscriptural practices left over from Roman Catholicism.

King James I had no use for the Puritans but refrained from bringing on a confrontation with their growing political power. His son, Charles I, determined in 1629 to persecute the Puritans aggressively and to rule without the Puritan-dominated Parliament. This course would lead eventually (ten years later) to civil war, but in the meantime some of the Puritans decided to set up a community in America.

To accomplish their purpose, they sought in 1629 to charter a joint-stock company to be called the Massachusetts Bay Company. Whether because Charles was glad to be rid of the Puritans or because he did not realize the special nature of this joint-stock company, the charter was granted. Further, the charter neglected to specify where the company's headquarters should be located. Taking advantage of this unusual omission, the Puritans determined to make their headquarters in the colony itself, 3,000 miles from meddlesome royal officials.

Under the leadership of John Winthrop, who taught that a new colony should provide the whole world with a model of what a Christian society ought to be, the Puritans carefully organized their venture and, upon arriving in Massachusetts in 1630, did not undergo the "starving time" that had often plagued other first-year colonies.

The government of Massachusetts developed to include a governor and a representative assembly (called the General Court) selected by the "freemen"—adult male church members. As Massachusetts' population increased (20,000 Puritans had come by 1642 in what came to be called the Great Migration), new towns were chartered, each town being granted a large tract of land by the Massachusetts government. As in European villages, these towns consisted of a number of houses clustered around the church house and the village green. Farmland was located around the outside of the town. In each new town the elect—those who testified of having experienced saving grace—covenanted together as a church.

Rhode Island, Connecticut, and New Hampshire

Puritans saw their colony not as a place to do whatever might strike one's fancy, but as a place to serve God and build His kingdom. Dissidents would only be tolerated insofar as they did not interfere with the colony's mission.

One such dissident was Roger Williams. A Puritan preacher, Williams was received warmly in Massachusetts in 1631; but he had a talent for carrying things to their logical (or sometimes not so logical) extreme. When his activities became disruptive he was asked to leave the colony. To avoid having to return to England—where he would have been even less welcome—he fled to the wilderness around Narragansett Bay, bought land from the Indians, and founded the settlement of Providence (1636), soon populated by his many followers.

Another dissident was Anne Hutchinson, who openly taught things contrary to Puritan doctrine. Called before the General Court to answer for her teachings, she claimed to have had special revelations from God superseding the Bible. This was unthinkable in Puritan theology and led to Hutchinson's banishment from the colony. She also migrated to the area around Narragansett Bay and with her followers founded Portsmouth (1638). She later migrated still farther west and was killed by Indians.

In 1644 Roger Williams secured from Parliament a charter combining Providence, Portsmouth, and other settlements that had sprung up in the area into the colony of Rhode Island. Through Williams' influence the colony granted complete religious toleration. Rhode Island tended to be populated by such exiles and troublemakers as could not find welcome in the other colonies or in Europe. It suffered constant political turmoil.

Connecticut was founded by Puritans who had slight religious disagreements with the leadership of Massachusetts. In 1636 Thomas Hooker led a group of settlers westward to found Hartford. Hooker, though a good friend of Massachusetts Governor John Winthrop, felt he was exercising somewhat more authority than was good. Others also moved into Connecticut from Massachusetts. In 1639 the *Fundamental Orders of Connecticut*, the first written constitution in America, were drawn up, providing for representative government.

In 1637 a group of Puritans led by John Davenport founded the neighboring colony of New Haven. Davenport and his followers felt that Winthrop, far from being too strict, was not being strict enough. In 1662 a new charter combined both New Haven and Connecticut into an officially recognized colony of Connecticut.

New Hampshire's settlement did not involve any disagreement at all among the Puritans. It was simply settled as an overflow from Massachusetts. In 1677 King Charles II chartered the separate royal colony of New Hampshire. It remained economically dependent on Massachusetts.

Maryland

By the 1630s, the English crown was taking a more direct interest in exercising control over the colonies, and therefore turned away from the practice of granting charters to joint-stock companies, and towards granting such charters to single individuals or groups of individuals known as proprietors. The proprietors would actually own the colony and would be directly responsible for it to the king, in an arrangement similar to the feudalism of medieval Europe. Though this was seen as providing more opportunity for royal control and less for autonomy on the part of the colonists, in practice proprietary colonies turned out much like the company colonies because settlers insisted on self-government.

The first proprietary colony was Maryland, granted in 1632 to George Calvert, Lord Baltimore. It was to be located just north of the Potomac River and to be at the same time a reward for Calvert's loyal service to the king as well as a refuge for English Catholics, of which Calvert was one. George Calvert died before the colony could be planted, but the venture was carried forward by his son Cecilius.

From the start more Protestants than Catholics came. To protect the Catholic minority, Calvert approved an Act of Religious Toleration (1649) guaranteeing political rights to Christians of all persuasions. Calvert also allowed a representative assembly. Economically and socially Maryland developed as a virtual carbon copy of neighboring Virginia.

The Carolinas

In 1663 Charles II, having recently been restored to the throne after a 20-year Puritan revolution that had seen his father beheaded, moved to reward eight of the noblemen who had helped him regain the crown by granting them a charter for all the lands lying south of Virginia and north of Spanish Florida.

The new colony was called Carolina, after the king. In hopes of attracting settlers, the proprietors came up with an elaborate plan for a hierarchical, almost feudal, society. Not surprisingly, this proved unworkable, and despite offers of generous land grants to settlers, the Carolinas grew slowly.

The area of North Carolina developed as an overflow from Virginia with similar economic and cultural features. South Carolina was settled by English planters from the island of Barbados, who founded Charles Town (Charleston) in 1670. These planters brought with them their black slaves; thus, unlike the Chesapeake colonies of Virginia and Maryland, South Carolina had slavery as a fully developed institution from the outset. South Carolina eventually found rice to be a staple crop.

New York and New Jersey

Charles II, though immoral and dissolute, was cunning and had an eye for increasing Britain's power. The Dutch colony of New Netherlands, lying between the Chesapeake and the New England colonies, caught his eye as a likely target for British expansion. In 1664 Charles gave his brother, James, Duke of York, title to all the Dutch lands in America, provided James conquered them first. To do this James sent an invasion fleet under the command of Colonel Richard Nicols. New Amsterdam fell almost without a shot and became New York.

James was adamantly opposed to representative assemblies and ordered that there should be none in New York. To avoid unrest Nicols shrewdly granted as many other civil and political rights as possible; but residents, particularly Puritans who had settled on Long Island, continued to agitate for self-government. Finally, in the 1680s, James relented, only to break his promise when he became king in 1685.

To add to the confusion in the newly renamed colony, James granted a part of his newly acquired domain to John Lord Berkeley and Sir George Carteret (two of the Carolina proprietors) who named their new proprietorship New Jersey. James neglected to tell Colonel Nicols of this, with the result that both Nicols, on the one hand, and Carteret and Berkeley, on the other, were granting title to the same land—to different settlers. Conflicting claims of land ownership plagued New Jersey for decades, being used by the crown in 1702 as a pretext to take over New Jersey as a royal colony.

THE COLONIAL WORLD

Life in the Colonies

New England grew not only from immigration but also from natural increase during the seventeenth century. The typical New England family had more children than the typical English or Chesapeake family, and more of those children survived to have families of their own. A New Englander could expect to live 15 to 20 years longer than his counterpart in the parent country and 25 to 30 years longer than his fellow colonist in the Chesapeake. Because of the continuity provided by these longer life spans, because the Puritans had migrated as intact family units, and because of the homogeneous nature of the Puritan New England colonies, New England enjoyed a much more stable and well-ordered society than did the Chesapeake colonies.

Puritans placed great importance on the family, which in their society was highly patriarchal. Young people were generally subject to their parents' direction in the matter of when and whom they would marry. Few defied this system, and illegitimate births were rare. Puritans also placed great importance on the ability to read, since they believed everyone should be able to read the Bible, God's word, himself. As a result, New England was ahead of the other colonies educationally and enjoyed extremely widespread literacy.

Since New England's climate and soil were unsuited to large-scale farming, the region developed a prosperous economy based on small farming, home industry, fishing, and especially trade and a large shipbuilding industry. Boston became a major international port.

Life in the Chesapeake colonies was drastically different. The typical Chesapeake colonist lived a shorter, less healthy life than his New England counterpart and was survived by fewer children. As a result the Chesapeake's population steadily declined despite a constant influx of settlers. Nor was Chesapeake society as stable as that of New England. Most Chesapeake settlers came as indentured servants; and since planters desired primarily male servants for work in the tobacco fields, men largely outnumbered women in Virginia and Maryland. This hindered the development of family life. The short life spans also contributed to the region's unstable family life as few children reached adulthood without experiencing the death of one or both parents. Remarriage resulted in households that contained children from several different marriages.

The system of indentured servitude was open to serious abuse, with masters sometimes treating their servants brutally or contriving through some technicality to lengthen their terms of indenture. In any case, 40 percent of Chesapeake region indentured servants failed to survive long enough to gain their freedom.

By the late seventeenth century, life in the Chesapeake was beginning to stabilize, with death rates declining and life expectancies rising. As society stabilized, an elite group of wealthy families such as the Byrds, Carters, Fitzhughs, Lees, and Randolphs, among others, began to dominate the social and political life of the region. Aping the lifestyle of the English country gentry, they built lavish manor houses from which to rule their vast plantations. For every one of these, however, there were many small farmers who worked hard for a living, showed deference to the great planters, and hoped someday they, or their children, might reach that level.

On the bottom rung of Southern society were the black slaves. During the first half of the seventeenth century, blacks in the Chesapeake made up only a small percentage of the population and were treated more or less as indentured servants. In the decades between 1640 and 1670 this gradually changed and blacks came to be seen and treated as life-long chattel slaves whose status would be inherited by their children. Larger numbers of them began to be imported and with this and rapid natural population growth they came by 1750 to compose 30 to 40 percent of the Chesapeake population.

While North Carolina tended to follow Virginia in its economic and social development (although with fewer great planters and more small farmers), South Carolina developed a society even more dominated by large plantations and chattel slavery. By the early decades of the eighteenth century, blacks had come to outnumber whites in that colony. South Carolina's economy remained dependent on the cultivation of its two staple crops, rice and, to a lesser extent, indigo.

Mercantilism and the Navigation Acts

Beginning around 1650, British authorities began to take more interest in regulating American trade for the benefit of the mother country. A key idea that underlay this policy was the concept of mercantilism. Mercantilists believed the world's wealth was sharply limited, and therefore one nation's gain was automatically another nation's loss. Each nation's goal was to export more than it imported (i.e., to have a "favorable balance of trade"). The difference would be made up in gold and silver, which, so the theory ran, would make the nation strong both economically and militarily. To achieve their goals, mercantilists believed economic activity should be regulated by the government. Colonies could fit into England's mercantilist scheme by providing staple crops, such as rice, tobacco, sugar, and indigo, and raw materials, such as timber, that England would otherwise have been forced to import from other countries.

To make the colonies serve this purpose Parliament passed a series of Navigation Acts (1651, 1660, 1663, and 1673). These were the foundation of England's worldwide commercial system and some of the most important pieces of imperial legislation during the colonial period. They were also intended as weapons in England's running struggle against its chief seventeenth-century maritime rival, Holland. The system created by the Navigation Acts stipulated that trade with the colonies was to be carried on only in ships made in Britain or America and with at least 75 percent British or American crews. Additionally, when certain "enumerated" goods were shipped from an American port, they were to go only to Britain or to another American port. Finally, almost nothing could be imported to the colonies without going through Britain first.

Mercantilism's results were mixed. Though ostensibly for the benefit of all subjects of the British Empire, its provisions benefited some at the expense of others. It boosted the prosperity of New Englanders, who engaged in large-scale shipbuilding (something Britain's mercantilist policymakers chose to encourage), while it hurt the residents of the Chesapeake by driving down the price of tobacco (an enumerated item). On the whole, the Navigation Acts, as intended, transferred wealth from America to Britain by increasing the prices Americans had to pay for British goods and lowering the prices Americans received for the goods they produced. Mercantilism also helped bring on a series of three wars between England and Holland in the late 1600s.

Charles II and his advisors worked to tighten up the administration of colonies, particularly the enforcement of the Navigation Acts. In Virginia tempers grew short as tobacco prices plunged as a result. Virginians were also angry at Royal Governor Sir William Berkeley, whose high-handed, high-taxing ways they despised and whom they believed was running the colony for the benefit of himself and his circle of cronies.

In 1674, Nathaniel Bacon, an impoverished nobleman with a shady past, came to Virginia and failed to gain admittance to Berkeley's inner circle, whose financial advantages he coveted. Bacon then began to oppose Berkeley at every turn and came to head a faction of like-minded persons. In 1676 disagreement over Indian policy brought the matter to the point of armed conflict. Bacon and his men burned Jamestown, but then the whole matter came to an anticlimactic ending when Bacon died of dysentery.

The British authorities, hearing of the matter, sent ships, troops, and an investigating commission. Berkeley, who had 23 of the rebels hanged in reprisal, was removed; and thenceforth Virginia's royal governors had strict instructions to run the colony for the benefit of the mother country. In response, Virginia's gentry, who had been divided over Bacon's Rebellion, united to face this new threat to their local autonomy. By political means they consistently obstructed the governors' efforts to increase royal control.

The Half-Way Covenant

By the latter half of the seventeenth century, many Puritans were coming to fear that New England was drifting away from its religious purpose. The children and grandchildren of the first generation were displaying more concern for making money than creating a godly society.

To deal with this, some clergymen in 1662 proposed the "Half-Way Covenant," providing a sort of half-way church membership for the children of members, even though those children, having reached adulthood, did not profess saving grace as was normally required for Puritan church membership. Those who embraced the Half-Way Covenant felt that in an increasingly materialistic society it would at least keep church membership rolls full and might preserve some of the church's influence in society.

Some communities rejected the Half-Way Covenant as an improper compromise, but in general the shift toward secular values continued, though slowly. Many Puritan ministers strongly denounced this trend in sermons that have come to be referred to as "jeremiads."

King Philip's War

As New England's population grew, local Indian tribes felt threatened, and conflict sometimes resulted. Puritans endeavored to convert Indians to Christianity. The Bible was translated into Algonquian; four villages were set up for converted Indians, who by 1650 numbered over a thousand. Still, most Indians remained unconverted.

In 1675 a Wampanoag chief named King Philip (Metacomet) led a war to exterminate the whites. Some 2,000 settlers lost their lives before King Philip was killed and his tribe subdued. New England continued to experience Indian troubles from time to time, though not as severe as those suffered by Virginia.

The Dominion of New England

The trend toward increasing imperial control of the colonies continued. In 1684 the Massachusetts charter was revoked in retaliation for that colony's large-scale evasion of the restrictions of the Navigation Acts.

The following year Charles II died and was succeeded by his brother, James II. James was prepared to go even farther in controlling the colonies, favoring the establishment of a unified government for all of New England, New York, and New Jersey. This was to be called the Dominion of New England, and the fact that it would abolish representative assemblies and facilitate the imposition of the Church of England on Congregationalist (Puritan) New England made it still more appealing to James.

To head the Dominion, James sent the obnoxious and dictatorial Sir Edmond Andros. Arriving in Boston in 1686, Andros quickly alienated the New Englanders. When news reached America of England's 1688 Glorious Revolution, replacing the Catholic James with his Protestant daughter Mary and her husband William of Orange, New Englanders cheerfully shipped Andros back to England.

Similar uprisings occurred in New York and Maryland. William and Mary's new government generally accepted these actions, though Jacob Leisler, leader of Leisler's Rebellion in New York, was executed for hesitating to turn over power to the new royal governor. This unfortunate incident poisoned the political climate of New York for many years.

The charter of Massachusetts, now including Plymouth, was restored in 1691, this time as a royal colony, though not as tightly controlled as others of that type.

The Salem Witch Trials

In 1692 Massachusetts was shaken by an unusual incident in which several young girls in Salem Village (now Danvers) claimed to be tormented by the occult activities of certain of their neighbors. Before the resulting Salem witch trials could be stopped by the intervention of Puritan ministers such as Cotton Mather, some 20 persons had been executed (19 by hanging and one crushed under a pile of rocks).

Pennsylvania and Delaware

Pennsylvania was founded as a refuge for Quakers. One of a number of radical religious sects that had sprung up about the time of the English Civil War, the Quakers held many controversial beliefs. They believed all persons had an "inner light" which allowed them to commune directly with God. They believed human institutions were, for the most part, unnecessary and, since they believed they could receive revelation directly from God, placed little importance on the Bible. They were also pacifists and declined to show customary deference to those who were considered to be their social superiors. This and their aggressiveness in denouncing established institutions brought them trouble in both Britain and America.

William Penn, a member of a prominent British family, converted to Quakerism as a young man. Desiring to found a colony as a refuge for Quakers, in 1681 he sought and received from Charles II a grant of land in America as payment of a large debt the king had owed Penn's late father.

Penn advertised his colony widely in Europe, offered generous terms on land, and guaranteed a representative assembly and full religious freedom. He personally went to America to set up his colony, laying out the city of Philadelphia. He succeeded in maintaining peaceful relations with the Indians.

In the years that followed settlers flocked to Pennsylvania from all over Europe. The colony grew and prospered, and its fertile soil made it not only attractive to settlers, but also a large exporter of grain to Europe and the West Indies.

Delaware, though at first part of Pennsylvania, was granted by Penn a separate legislature, but until the American Revolution, Pennsylvania's proprietary governors also functioned as governors of Delaware.

THE EIGHTEENTH CENTURY

Economy and Population

British authorities continued to regulate the colonial economy, though usually without going so far as to provoke unrest. An exception was the Molasses Act of 1733, which would have been disastrous for New England merchants. In this case trouble was averted by the customs agents wisely declining to enforce the act stringently.

The constant drain of wealth from America to Britain, created by the mother country's mercantilistic policies, led to a corresponding drain in hard currency (gold and silver). The artificially low prices that this shortage of money created for American goods was even more advantageous to British buyers. When colonial legislatures responded by endeavoring to create paper money, British authorities blocked such moves. Despite these hindrances, the colonial American economy remained for the most part extremely prosperous.

America's population continued to grow rapidly, both from natural increases due to prosperity and a healthy environment, and from large-scale immigration, not only of English but also of such other groups as Scot-Irish and Germans.

The Germans were prompted to migrate by wars, poverty, and religious persecution in their homeland. They found Pennsylvania especially attractive and they settled fairly close to the frontier, where land was more readily available. They eventually came to be called the "Pennsylvania Dutch."

The Scotch-Irish, Scottish Presbyterians who had been living in northern Ireland for several generations, left their homes because of high rent and economic depression. In America they settled even farther west than the Germans, on or beyond the frontier in the Appalachians. They spread southward into the mountain valleys of Virginia and North Carolina.

The Early Wars of the Empire

Between 1689 and 1763 Britain and its American colonies fought a series of four wars with Spain, France, and France's Indian allies, in part to determine who would dominate North America.

Though the first war, known in America as King William's War (1689–1697) but in Europe as the War of the League of Augsburg, was a limited conflict involving no major battles in America, it did bring a number of bloody and terrifying border raids by Indians. It was ended by the Treaty of Ryswick, which made no major territorial changes.

The second war was known in America as Queen Anne's War (1702–1713), but in Europe as the War of the Spanish Succession, and brought America 12 years of sporadic fighting against France and Spain. It was ended by the Treaty of Utrecht, the terms of which gave Britain major territorial gains and trade advantages.

In 1739 war once again broke out with France and Spain. Known in America as King George's War, it was called the War of Jenkin's Ear in Europe and later the War of the Austrian Succession. American troops played an active role, accompanying the British on several important expeditions and suffering thousands of casualties. In 1745 an all New England army, led by William Pepperrell, captured the powerful French fortress of Louisbourg at the mouth of the St. Lawrence River. To the Americans' disgust, the British in the 1748 Treaty of Aix-la-Chapelle gave Louisbourg back to France in exchange for lands in India.

Georgia

With this almost constant imperial warfare in mind, it was decided to found a colony as a buffer between South Carolina and Spanish-held Florida. A group of British philanthropists, led by General James Oglethorpe, in 1732 obtained a charter for such a colony, to be located between the Savannah and Altamaha rivers and to be populated by such poor as could not manage to make a living in Great Britain.

The philanthropist trustees, who were to control the colony for 21 years before it reverted to royal authority, made elaborate and detailed rules to mold the new colony's society as they felt best. As a result, relatively few settlers came, and those who did complained endlessly. By 1752 Oglethorpe and his colleagues were ready to acknowledge their efforts a failure. Thereafter, Georgia came to resemble South Carolina, though with more small farmers.

The Enlightenment

As the eighteenth century progressed, Americans came to be more or less influenced by European ways of thought, culture, and society. Some Americans embraced the European intellectual movement known as the "Enlightenment."

The key concept of the Enlightenment was rationalism—the belief that human reason was adequate to solve all of mankind's problems and, correspondingly, much less faith was needed in the central role of God as an active force in the universe.

A major English political philosopher of the Enlightenment was John Locke. Writing partially to justify England's 1688 Glorious Revolution, he strove to find in the social and political world the sort of natural laws Isaac Newton had recently discovered in the physical realm. He held that such natural laws included the rights of life, liberty, and property; that to secure these rights people submit to governments; and that governments which abuse these rights may justly be overthrown. His writings were enormously influential in America though usually indirectly, by way of early eighteenth century English political philosophers. Americans tended to equate Locke's law of nature with the universal law of God.

The most notable Enlightenment man in America was Benjamin Franklin. While Franklin never denied the existence of God, he focused his attention on human reason and what it could accomplish. His renown spread to Europe both for the wit and wisdom of his *Poor Richard's Almanac* and for his scientific experiments.

The Great Awakening

Of much greater impact on the lives of the common people in America was the movement known as the Great Awakening. It consisted of a series of religious revivals occurring throughout the colonies from the 1720s to the 1740s. Preachers such as the Dutch Reformed Theodore Frelinghuysen, the Presbyterians William and Gilbert Tennent, and the Congregationalist Jonathan Edwards—best known for his sermon "Sinners in the Hands of an Angry God"—proclaimed a message of personal repentance and faith in Jesus Christ for salvation from an otherwise certain eternity in hell. The most dynamic preacher of the Great Awakening was the Englishman George Whitefield, who traveled through the colonies several times, speaking to crowds of up to 30,000.

The Great Awakening had several important results. America's religious community came to be divided between the "Old Lights," who rejected the great Awakening, and the "New Lights," who accepted it—and sometimes suffered persecution because of their fervor. A number of colleges were founded (many of them today's "Ivy League" schools), primarily for the purpose of training New-Light ministers. The Great Awakening also fostered a greater readiness to lay the claims of established religious authority alongside a fixed standard—in this case the Bible—and to reject such claims it found wanting.

The French and Indian War

The Treaty of Aix-la-Chapelle (1748), ending King George's War, provided little more than a breathing space before the next European and imperial war. England and France continued on a collision course as France determined to take complete control of the Ohio Valley and western Pennsylvania.

British authorities ordered colonial governors to resist this; and Virginia's Robert Dinwiddie, already involved in speculation on the Ohio Valley lands, was eager to comply. George Washington, a young major of the Virginia militia, was sent to western Pennsylvania to request the French to leave. When the French declined, Washington was sent in 1754 with 200 Virginia militiamen to expel them. After success in a small skirmish, Washington was forced by superior numbers to fall back on his hastily built Fort Necessity and then to surrender.

The war these operations initiated spread to Europe two years later, where it was known as the Seven Years' War. In America it later came to be known as the French and Indian War.

While Washington skirmished with the French in western Pennsylvania, delegates of seven colonies met in Albany, New York, to discuss common plans for defense. Delegate Benjamin Franklin proposed a plan for an intercolonial government. While the other colonies showed no support for the idea, it was an important precedent for the concept of uniting in the face of a common enemy.

To deal with the French threat, the British dispatched Major General Edward Braddock with several regiments of British regular troops. Braddock marched overland toward the French outpost of Fort Duquesne, at the place where the Monongahela and Allegheny rivers join to form the Ohio. About eight miles short of his goal he was ambushed by a small force of French and Indians. Two-thirds of the British regulars, including Braddock himself, were killed. However, Britain bounced back from this humiliating defeat and several others that followed, and under the leadership of its capable and energetic prime minister, William Pitt, had by 1760 taken Quebec and Montreal and virtually liquidated the French empire in North America.

By the Treaty of Paris of 1763, which officially ended hostilities, Britain gained all of Canada and all of what is now the United States east of the Mississippi River. France lost all of its North American holdings.

Americans at the end of the French and Indian War were proud to be part of the victorious British Empire and proud of the important role they had played in making it so. They felt affection for Great Britain, and thoughts of independence would not have crossed their minds.

2 THE AMERICAN REVOLUTION (1763-1787)

THE COMING OF THE AMERICAN REVOLUTION

Writs of Assistance

While Americans' feelings toward Great Britain were pride and affection, British officials felt contemptuous of Americans and anxious to increase imperial control over them beyond anything that had previously been attempted. This drive to gain new authority over the colonies, beginning in 1763, led directly to American independence.

Even before that time the Writs of Assistance cases had demonstrated that Americans would not accept a reduction of their freedom.

In 1761 a young Boston lawyer named James Otis argued before a Massachusetts court that Writs of Assistance (general search warrants issued to help royal officials stop evasion of Britain's mercantilist trade restrictions) were contrary to natural law. He made his point though he lost his case, and others in the colonies joined in protesting against the Writs.

Grenville and the Stamp Act

In 1763 the strongly anti-American George Grenville became prime minister and set out to solve some of the empire's more pressing problems. Chief of these was the large national debt incurred in the recent war.

Of related concern was the cost of defending the American frontier, recently the scene of a bloody Indian uprising led by an Ottawa chief named Pontiac. Goaded by French traders, Pontiac had aimed to drive the entire white population into the sea. While failing in that endeavor, he had succeeded in killing a large number of settlers along the frontier.

Grenville created a comprehensive program to deal with these problems and moved energetically to put it into effect. He sent the Royal Navy to suppress American smuggling and enforce vigorously the Navigation Acts. He also issued the Proclamation of 1763, forbidding white settlement west of the crest of the Appalachians, in hopes of keeping the Indians happy and the settlers close to the coast and thus easier to control.

In 1764, Grenville pushed through Parliament the Sugar Act (also known as the Revenue Act) aimed at raising revenue by taxes on goods imported by the Americans. It lowered by one-half the duties imposed by the Molasses Act but was intended to raise revenue rather than control trade. Unlike the Molasses Act, it was stringently enforced, with accused violators facing trial in admiralty courts without benefit of jury or the normal protections of due process.

Grenville determined to maintain up to 10,000 British regulars in America to control both colonists and Indians and secured passage of the Quartering Act, requiring the colonies in which British troops were stationed to pay for their maintenance. Americans had never before been required to support a standing army in their midst.

Grenville also saw through the passage of his Currency Act of 1764, which forbade once and for all any colonial attempts to issue currency not redeemable in gold or silver, making it more difficult for Americans to avoid the constant drain of money that Britain's mercantilist policies were designed to create in the colonies.

Most important, however, Grenville got Parliament to pass the Stamp Act (1765), imposing a direct tax on Americans for the first time. The Stamp Act required Americans to purchase revenue stamps on everything from newspapers to legal documents and would have created an impossible drain on hard currency in the colonies. Because it overlooked the advantage already provided by Britain's mercantilist exploitation of the colonies, Grenville's policy was shortsighted and foolish; but few in Parliament were inclined to see this.

Americans reacted first with restrained and respectful petitions and pamphlets, in which they pointed out that "taxation without representation is tyranny." From there resistance progressed to stronger and stronger protests that eventually became violent and involved intimidation of those Americans who had contracted to be the agents for distributing the stamps.

Resistance was particularly intense in Massachusetts, where it was led first by James Otis and then by Samuel Adams who formed the organization known as the Sons of Liberty.

Other colonies copied Massachusetts' successful tactics while adding some of their own. In Virginia, a young Burgess named Patrick Henry introduced seven resolutions denouncing the Stamp Act. Though only the four most moderate of them were passed by the House of Burgesses, newspapers picked up all seven and circulated them widely through the colonies, giving the impression all seven had been adopted. By their denial of Parliament's authority to tax the colonies, they encouraged other colonial legislatures to issue strongly worded statements.

In October 1765, delegates from nine colonies met as the Stamp Act Congress. Called by the Massachusetts legislature at the instigation of James Otis, the Stamp Act Congress passed moderate resolutions against the act, asserting that Americans could not be taxed without their consent, given by their representatives. They pointed out that Americans were not, and because of their location could not practically be, represented in Parliament and concluded by calling for the repeal of both the Stamp and Sugar Acts. Most important, however, the Stamp Act Congress showed that representatives of the colonies could work together and gave political leaders in the various colonies a chance to become acquainted with each other.

Most effective in achieving repeal of the Stamp Act was colonial merchants' nonimportation (boycott) of British goods. Begun as an agreement among New York merchants, the boycott spread throughout the colonies and had a powerful effect on British merchants and manufacturers, who began clamoring for the act's repeal.

Meanwhile, the fickle King George III had dismissed Grenville over an unrelated disagreement and replaced him with a cabinet headed by Charles Lord Rockingham. In March 1766, under the leadership of the new ministry, Parliament repealed the Stamp Act. At the same time, however, it passed the Declaratory Act, claiming power to tax or make laws for the Americans "in all cases whatsoever."

Though the Declaratory Act denied exactly the principle Americans had just been at such pains to assert—that of no taxation without representation—the Americans generally ignored it in their exuberant celebration of the repeal of the Stamp Act. Americans eagerly proclaimed their loyalty to Great Britain.

The Townshend Acts

The Rockingham ministry proved to be even shorter lived than that of Grenville. It was replaced with a cabinet dominated by Chancellor of the Exchequer Charles Townshend. Townshend had boasted that he could successfully tax the colonies, and in 1766 Parliament gave him his chance by passing his program of taxes on items imported into the colonies. These taxes came to be known as the Townshend Duties. Townshend mistakenly believed the Americans would accept this method while rejecting the use of direct internal taxes.

The Townshend Acts also included the use of admiralty courts to try those accused of violations, the use of writs of assistance, and the paying of customs officials out of the fines they levied. Townshend also had the New York legislature suspended for noncompliance with the Quartering Act.

American reaction was at first slow. Philadelphia lawyer John Dickinson wrote an anonymous pamphlet entitled "Letters from a Farmer in Pennsylvania," in which he pointed out in moderate terms that the Townshend Acts violated the principle of no taxation without representation and that if Parliament could suspend the New York legislature it could do the same to others. At the same time he urged a restrained response on the part of his fellow Americans.

In February 1768 the Massachusetts legislature, at the urging of Samuel Adams, passed the Massachusetts Circular Letter, reiterating Dickinson's mild arguments and urging other colonial legislatures to pass petitions calling on Parliament to repeal the acts. Had the British government done nothing, the matter might have passed quietly.

Instead, British authorities acted. They ordered that if the letter was not withdrawn, the Massachusetts legislature should be dissolved and new elections held. They forbade the other colonial legislatures to take up the matter, and they also sent four regiments of troops to Boston to prevent intimidation of royal officials and to intimidate the populace instead.

The last of these actions was in response to the repeated pleas of the Boston customs agents. Corrupt agents had used technicalities of the confusing and poorly written Sugar and Townshend Acts to entrap innocent merchants and line their own pockets. Mob violence had threatened when agents had seized the ship *Liberty*, belonging to Boston merchant John Hancock. Such incidents prompted the call for troops.

The sending of troops, along with the British authority's repressive response to the Massachusetts Circular Letter aroused the Americans to resistance. Nonimportation was again instituted, and soon British merchants were calling on Parliament to repeal the acts. In March 1770, Parliament, under the new prime minister, Frederick Lord North, repealed all of the taxes except that on tea, which was retained to prove Parliament had the right to tax the colonies if it so desired.

By the time of the repeal, however, friction between British soldiers and Boston citizens had led to an incident in which five Bostonians were killed. Although the British soldiers had acted more or less in self-defense, Samuel Adams labeled the incident the "Boston Massacre" and publicized it widely. At their trial the British soldiers were defended by prominent Massachusetts lawyer John Adams and were acquitted on the charge of murder.

In the years that followed, American orators desiring to stir up anti-British feeling often alluded to the Boston Massacre.

The Return of Relative Peace

Following the repeal of the Townshend Duties a period of relative peace set in. The tax on tea remained as a reminder of Parliament's claims, but it could be easily avoided by smuggling.

Much goodwill had been lost and colonists remained suspicious of the British government. Many Americans believed the events of the past decade to have been the work of a deliberate conspiracy to take their liberty.

Occasional incidents marred the relative peace. One such incident was the burning, by a seagoing mob of Rhode Islanders disguised as Indians, of the *Gaspee*, a British customs schooner that had run aground offshore. The *Gaspee*'s captain and crew had alienated Rhode Islanders by their extreme zeal for catching smugglers as well as by their theft and vandalism when ashore.

In response to this incident, British authorities appointed a commission to find the guilty parties and bring them to England for trial. Though those responsible for the burning of the *Gaspee* were never found, this action on the part of the British prompted the colonial legislatures to form committees of correspondence to communicate with each other regarding possible threats from the British government.

The Tea Act

The relative peace was brought to an end by the Tea Act of 1773.

In desperate financial condition—partially because the Americans were buying smuggled Dutch tea rather than the taxed British product—the British East India Company sought and obtained from Parliament concessions allowing it to ship tea directly to the colonies rather than only by way of Britain. The result would be that East India Company tea, even with the tax, would be cheaper than smuggled Dutch tea. The colonists would thus, it was hoped, buy the tea, tax and all. The East India Company would be saved and the Americans would be tacitly accepting Parliament's right to tax them.

The Americans, however, proved resistant to this approach; and rather than seem to admit Parliament's right to tax, they vigorously resisted the cheaper tea. Various methods, including tar and feathers, were used to prevent the collection of the tax on tea. In most ports Americans did not allow the tea to be landed.

In Boston, however, pro-British Governor Thomas Hutchinson forced a confrontation by ordering Royal Navy vessels to prevent the tea ships from leaving the harbor. After 20 days this would, by law, result in the cargoes being sold at auction and the tax paid. The night before the time was to expire, December 16, 1773, Bostonians thinly disguised as Indians boarded the ships and threw the tea into the harbor.

Many Americans felt this—the destruction of private property—was going too far, but the reaction of Lord North and Parliament quickly united Americans in support of Boston and opposition to Britain.

The Intolerable Acts

The British responded with four acts collectively titled the Coercive Acts. First, the Boston Port Act closed the port of Boston to all trade until local citizens would agree to pay for the lost tea (they would not).Secondly, the Massachusetts Government Act greatly increased the power of Massachusetts' royal governor at the expense of the legislature. Thirdly, the Administration of Justice Act provided that royal officials accused of crimes in Massachusetts could be tried elsewhere, where chances of acquittal might be greater. Finally, a strengthened Quartering Act allowed the new governor, General Thomas Gage, to quarter his troops anywhere, including unoccupied private homes.

A further act of Parliament also angered and alarmed Americans. This was the Quebec Act, which extended the province of Quebec to the Ohio River, established Roman Catholicism as Quebec's official religion, and set up for Quebec a government without a representative assembly.

For Americans this was a denial of the hopes and expectations of westward expansion for which they had fought the French and Indian War. Also, New Englanders especially saw it as a threat that in their colonies too, Parliament could establish autocratic government and the hated Church of England.

Americans lumped the Quebec Act together with the Coercive Acts and referred to them all as the Intolerable Acts.

In response to the Coercive Acts, the First Continental Congress was called and met in Philadelphia in September 1774. It once again petitioned Parliament for relief but also passed the Suffolk Resolves (so called because they were first passed in Suffolk County, Massachusetts), denouncing the Intolerable Acts and calling for strict nonimportation and rigorous preparation of local militia companies in case the British should resort to military force.

The Congress then narrowly rejected a plan, submitted by Joseph Galloway of Pennsylvania, calling for a union of the colonies within the empire and a rearrangement of relations with Parliament. Most of the delegates felt matters had already gone too far for such a mild measure. Finally, before adjournment, it was agreed that there should be a Second Continental Congress to meet in May of the following year if the colonies' grievances had not been righted by then.

THE WAR FOR INDEPENDENCE

Lexington and Concord

The British government paid little attention to the First Continental Congress, having decided to teach the Americans a military lesson. More troops were sent to Massachusetts, which was officially declared to be in a state of rebellion. Orders were sent to General Gage to arrest the leaders of the resistance or, failing that, to provoke any sort of confrontation that would allow him to turn British military might loose on the Americans.

Gage decided on a reconnaissance-in-force to find and destroy a reported stockpile of colonial arms and ammunition at Concord. Seven hundred British troops set out on this mission on the night of April 18, 1775. Their movement was detected by American surveillance and news was spread throughout the countryside by dispatch riders Paul Revere and William Dawes.

At the little village of Lexington, Captain John Parker and some 70 Minutemen (militiamen trained to respond at a moment's notice) awaited the British on the village green. As the British approached, a British officer shouted at the Minutemen to lay down their arms and disperse. The Minutemen did not lay down their arms but did turn to file off the green. A shot was fired, and then the British opened fire and charged. Eight Americans were killed and several others wounded, most shot in the back.

The British continued to Concord only to find that nearly all of the military supplies they had expected to find had already been moved. Attacked by growing numbers of Minutemen, they began to retreat toward Boston. As the British retreated, Minutemen, swarming from every village for miles around, fired on the column from behind rocks, trees, and stone fences. Only a relief force of additional British troops saved the first column from destruction.

Open warfare had begun, and the myth of British invincibility was destroyed. Militia came in large numbers from all the New England colonies to join the force besieging Gage and his army in Boston.

Bunker Hill

In May 1775, three more British generals, William Howe, Henry Clinton, and John Burgoyne, arrived in Boston urging Gage to further aggressive action. The following month the Americans tightened the noose around Boston by fortifying Breed's Hill (a spur of Bunker Hill), from which they could, if necessary, bombard Boston.

The British determined to remove them by a frontal attack that would demonstrate the awesome power of British arms. Twice the British were thrown back and finally succeeded as the Americans ran out of ammunition. Over a thousand British soldiers were killed or wounded in what turned out to be the bloodiest battle of the war (June 17,1775). Yet the British had gained very little and remained bottled up in Boston.

Meanwhile in May 1775, American forces under Ethan Allen and Benedict Arnold took Fort Ticonderoga on Lake Champlain.

Congress, hoping Canada would join in resistance against Britain, authorized two expeditions into Quebec. One, under General Richard Montgomery took Montreal and then turned toward the city of Quebec. It was met there by the second expedition under Benedict Arnold. The attack on Quebec (December 31, 1775) failed, Montgomery was killed, Arnold wounded, and American hopes for Canada ended.

The Second Continental Congress

While these events were taking place in New England and Canada, the Second Continental Congress met in Philadelphia in May 1775. Congress was divided into two main factions. One was composed mostly of New Englanders and leaned toward declaring independence from Britain. The other drew its strength primarily from the Middle Colonies and was not yet ready to go that far. It was led by John Dickinson of Pennsylvania.

Congress took action to deal with the difficult situation facing the colonies. It adopted the New England army around Boston, calling on the other colonies to send troops and sending George Washington to command it, adopted a "Declaration of the Causes and Necessity for Taking up Arms," and adopted the "Olive Branch Petition" pleading with King George III to intercede with Parliament to restore peace.

This last overture was ignored in Britain, where the king gave his approval to the Prohibitory Act, declaring the colonies in rebellion and no longer under his protection. Preparations were made for full-scale war against America.

Throughout 1775, Americans remained deeply loyal to Britain and King George III despite the king's proclamations declaring them to be in revolt. In Congress moderates still resisted independence.

In January 1776, Thomas Paine published a pamphlet entitled *Common Sense*, calling for immediate independence. Its arguments were extreme and sometimes illogical and its language intemperate, but it sold largely and may have had much influence in favor of independence. Continued evidence of Britain's intention to carry on the war throughout the colonies also weakened the moderates' resistance to independence. The Prohibitory Act, with its virtual declaration of war against America, convinced many that no further moral scruples need stand in the way of such a step.

On June 7, 1776, Richard Henry Lee of Virginia introduced a series of formal resolutions in Congress calling for independence and a national government. Accepting these ideas, Congress named two committees. One, headed by John Dickinson, was to work out a framework for a national government. The other was to draft a statement of the reasons for declaring independence. This statement, the Declaration of Independence, was primarily the work of Thomas Jefferson of Virginia. It was a restatement of political ideas by then commonplace in America, showing why the former colonists felt justified in separating from Great Britain. It was formally adopted by Congress on July 4, 1776.

Washington Takes Command

Britain meanwhile was preparing a massive effort to conquer the United States. Gage was removed as being too timid, and top command went to Howe. To supplement the British army, large numbers of troops were hired from various German principalities. Since many of these Germans came from the state of Hesse-Kassel, Americans referred to all such troops as Hessians.

Although the London authorities desired a quick and smashing campaign, General Howe and his brother, British naval commander Richard, Admiral Lord Howe, intended to move slowly, using their powerful force to cow the Americans into signing loyalty oaths.

In March 1776, Washington placed on Dorchester Heights, overlooking Boston, some of the large cannons that had been captured at Ticonderoga, forcing the British to evacuate the city.

The British shipped their troops to Nova Scotia and then, together with large reinforcements from Britain, landed that summer at New York City.

They hoped to find many loyalists there and make that city the key to their campaign to subdue America.

Washington anticipated the move and was waiting at New York, which Congress had ordered should be defended. However, the under-trained, under-equipped, and badly outnumbered American army was no match for the powerful forces under the Howes. Defeated at the Battle of Long Island (August 27, 1776), Washington narrowly avoided being trapped there (an escape partially due to the Howes' slowness). Defeated again at the Battle of Washington Heights (August 29–30, 1776) on Manhattan, Washington was forced to retreat across New Jersey with the aggressive British General Lord Cornwallis, a subordinate of Howe, in pursuit. By December what was left of Washington's army had made it into Pennsylvania.

With his victory almost complete, Howe decided to wait till spring to finish annihilating Washington's army. Scattering his troops in small detachments so as to hold all of New Jersey, he went into winter quarters.

Washington, with his small army melting away as demoralized soldiers deserted, decided on a bold stroke. On Christmas night 1776, his army crossed the Delaware River and struck the Hessians at Trenton. The Hessians, still groggy from their hard-drinking Christmas party, were easily defeated. A few days later Washington defeated a British force at Princeton (January 3, 1777).

Howe was so shocked by these two unexpected defeats that he pulled his outposts back close to New York. Much of New Jersey was regained. Those who had signed British loyalty oaths in the presence of Howe's army were now at the mercy of their patriot neighbors. And Washington's army was saved from disintegration.

Early in the war France began making covert shipments of arms to the Americans. This it did, not because the French government loved freedom (it did not), but because it hated Britain and saw the war as a way to weaken Britain by depriving it of its colonies. Arms shipments from France were vital for the Americans.

Saratoga and Valley Forge

For the summer of 1777 the British home authorities adopted an elaborate plan of campaign urged on them by General Burgoyne. According to the plan Burgoyne himself would lead an army southward from Canada along the Lake Champlain corridor while another army under Howe moved up the Hudson River to join hands with Burgoyne at Albany. This, it was hoped, would cut off New England and allow the British to subdue that region, which they considered the hotbed of the "rebellion."

Howe had other ideas and shipped his army by sea to Chesapeake Bay, hoping to capture the American capital, Philadelphia, and destroy Washington's army at the same time. At Brandywine Creek (September 1, 1777) Washington tried but failed to stop Howe's advance. Yet the American army, though badly beaten, remained intact. Howe occupied Philadelphia as the Congress fled westward to York, Pennsylvania.

In early October, Washington attempted to drive Howe out of Philadelphia; but his attack at Germantown, though at first successful, failed at least partially due to thick fog and the still imperfect level of training in the American army, both of which contributed to confusion among the troops. Thereafter, Howe settled down to comfortable winter quarters in Philadelphia, and Washington and his army to very uncomfortable ones at nearby Valley Forge, while far to the north, the British strategy that Howe had ignored was going badly awry.

Burgoyne's advance began well but slowed as the Americans placed obstructions on the rough wilderness trails by which his army, including numerous cannons and much bulky baggage, had to advance. A diversionary force of British troops and Iroquois Indians under the command of Colonel Barry St. Leger swung east of Burgoyne's column, but although it defeated and killed American General Nicholas Herkimer at the Battle of Oriskany (August 6, 1777), it was finally forced to withdraw to Canada.

In mid-August, a detachment of Burgoyne's force was defeated by New England militia under General John Stark near Bennington in what is now Vermont. By autumn Burgoyne found his way blocked by an American army: continentals (American regular troops such as those that made up most of Washington's army, paid, in theory at least, by Congress); and New England militia, under General Horatio Gates, at Saratoga, about 30 miles north of Albany. Burgoyne's two attempts to break through (September 19 and October 7,1777) were turned back by the Americans under the brilliant battlefield leadership of Benedict Arnold. On October 17, 1777, Burgoyne surrendered to Gates.

The American victory at Saratoga convinced the French to join openly in the war against England. Eventually, the Spanish (1779) and the Dutch (1780) joined as well, and England was faced with a world war.

The British Move South

The new circumstances brought a change in British strategy. With fewer troops available for service in America, the British would have to depend more on loyalists, and since they imagined that larger numbers of these existed in the South than elsewhere, it was there they turned their attention.

Howe was relieved and replaced by General Henry Clinton, who was ordered to abandon Philadelphia and march to New York. In doing so, he narrowly avoided defeat at the hands of Washington's army—much improved after a winter's drilling at Valley Forge under the direction of Prussian nobleman Baron von Steuben—at the Battle of Monmouth, New Jersey (June 28, 1778).

Clinton was thenceforth to maintain New York as Britain's main base in America while detaching troops to carry out the new Southern strategy. In November 1778 the British easily conquered Georgia. Late the following year Clinton moved on South Carolina with a land and naval force, and in May 1780, U.S. General Benjamin Lincoln surrendered Charleston. Clinton then returned to New York, leaving Cornwallis to continue the Southern campaign.

Congress, alarmed at the British successes, sent General Horatio Gates to lead the forces opposing Cornwallis. Gates blundered to a resounding defeat at the Battle of Camden, in South Carolina (August 16, 1780).

The general outlook seemed bad for America at that point in the war. Washington's officers grumbled about their pay in arrears. The army was understrength and then suffered successive mutinies among the Pennsylvania and New Jersey troops. Benedict Arnold went over to the British. In short, the British seemed to be winning the contest of endurance. This outlook was soon to change.

In the West, George Rogers Clark, acting under the auspices of the state of Virginia, led an expedition down the Ohio River and into the area of present-day Illinois and Indiana, defeating a British force at Vincennes, Indiana, and securing the area north of the Ohio River for the United States.

In the South, Cornwallis began to move northward toward North Carolina, but on October 7, 1780 a detachment of his Loyalist force under Major Patrick Ferguson was defeated by American frontiersman at the Battle of Kings Mountain in northern South Carolina. To further increase the problems facing the British, Cornwallis had unwisely moved north without bothering to secure South Carolina first. The result was that the British would no sooner leave an area than American militia or guerrilla bands, such as that under Francis Marion ("the Swamp Fox"), were once again in control and able to deal with those who had expressed loyalty to Britain in the presence of Cornwallis's army.

To command the continental forces in the South, Washington sent his most able subordinate, military genius Nathaniel Greene. Greene's brilliant strategy led to a crushing victory at Cowpens, South Carolina (January 17, 1781) by troops under Greene's subordinate, General Daniel Morgan of Virginia. It also led to a near victory by Greene's own force at Guilford Court House, North Carolina (March 15, 1781).

Yorktown

The frustrated and impetuous Cornwallis now abandoned the Southern strategy and moved north into Virginia. Clinton, disgusted at this departure from plan, sent instructions for Cornwallis to take up a defensive position and await further orders. Against his better judgment Cornwallis did so, selecting Yorktown, Virginia, on a peninsula that reaches into Chesapeake Bay between the York and James rivers.

Washington now saw and seized the opportunity this presented. With the aid of a French fleet which took control of Chesapeake Bay and a French army that joined him in sealing off the land approaches to Yorktown, Washington succeeded in trapping Cornwallis. After three weeks of siege, Cornwallis surrendered, October 17, 1781.

The War at Sea

Britain had other problems as well. Ships of the small but daring U.S. Navy as well as privateers (privately owned vessels outfitted with guns and authorized by a warring government to capture enemy merchant ships for profit) preyed on the British merchant marine. John Paul Jones, the most famous of American naval leaders, captured ships and carried out audacious raids along the coast of Britain itself. French and Spanish naval forces also struck against various outposts of the British Empire.

The Treaty of Paris of 1783

News of the debacle at Yorktown brought the collapse of Lord North's ministry, and the new cabinet opened peace negotiations. The extremely able American negotiating team was composed of Benjamin Franklin, John Adams, and John Jay. The negotiations continued for some time, delayed by French and Spanish maneuvering. When it became apparent that France and Spain were planning to achieve an agreement unfavorable to the United States, the American envoys negotiated a separate treaty with Britain.

The final agreement became known as the Treaty of Paris of 1783. Its terms stipulated the following: 1) The United States was recognized as an independent nation by the major European powers, including Britain; 2) Its western boundary was set at the Mississippi River; 3) Its southern boundary was set at 31° north latitude (the northern boundary of Florida); 4) Britain retained Canada but had to surrender Florida to Spain; 5) Private British creditors would be free to collect any debts owed by U.S. citizens; and 6) Congress was to recommend that the states restore confiscated loyalist property.

THE CREATION OF NEW GOVERNMENTS

The State Constitutions

After the collapse of British authority in 1775, it became necessary to form new state governments. By the end of 1777 ten new state constitutions had been formed.

Connecticut and Rhode Island kept their colonial charters, which were republican in nature, simply deleting references to British sovereignty. Massachusetts waited until 1780 to complete the adoption of its new constitution. The constitutions ranged from such extremely democratic models as the virtually unworkable Pennsylvania constitution (soon abandoned), in which a unicameral legislature ruled with little check or balance, to more reasonable frameworks such as those of Maryland and Virginia, which included more safeguards against popular excesses.

Massachusetts voters set an important example by insisting that a constitution should be made by a special convention rather than the legislature. This would make the constitution superior to the legislature and, hopefully, assure that the legislature would be subject to the constitution.

Most state constitutions included bills of rights—lists of things the government was not supposed to do to the people.

The Articles of Confederation

In the summer of 1776, Congress appointed a committee to begin devising a framework for national government. When completed, this document was known as the Articles of Confederation. John Dickinson, who had played a leading role in writing the Articles, felt a strong national government was needed; but by the time Congress finished revising them, the Articles went to the opposite extreme of preserving the sovereignty of the states and creating a very weak national government.

The Articles of Confederation provided for a unicameral Congress in which each state would have one vote, as had been the case in the Continental Congress. Executive authority under the Articles would be vested in a committee of 13, one member from each state. In order to amend the Articles, the unanimous consent of all the states was required.

The Articles of Confederation government was empowered to make war, make treaties, determine the amount of troops and money each state should contribute to the war effort, settle disputes between states, admit new states to the Union, and borrow money. More importantly, however, was that it was not empowered to levy taxes, raise troops, or regulate commerce.

Ratification of the Articles of Confederation was delayed by a disagreement over the future status of the lands that lay to the west of the original 13 states. Some states, notably Virginia, held extensive claims to these lands based on their original colonial charters. Maryland, which had no such claim, withheld ratification until in 1781 Virginia agreed to surrender its western claims to the new national government.

Meanwhile, the country was on its way to deep financial trouble. Unable to tax, Congress resorted to printing large amounts of paper money to finance the war; but these inflated "Continentals" were soon worthless. Other financial schemes fell through, and only grants and loans from France and the Netherlands staved off complete financial collapse. A plan to amend the Articles to give Congress power to tax was stopped by the lone opposition of Rhode Island. The army, whose pay was far in arrears, threatened mutiny. Some of those who favored a stronger national government welcomed this development and in what became known as the Newburgh Conspiracy (1783) consulted with army second-in-command Horatio Gates as to the possibility of using the army to force the states to surrender more power to the national government. This movement was stopped by a moving appeal to the officers by Washington himself.

The Trans-Appalachian West and the Northwest Ordinance

For many Americans the enormous trans-Appalachian frontier represented an opportunity to escape the economic hard times that followed the end of the war.

In 1775, Daniel Boone opened the "Wilderness Road" through the Cumberland Gap and on to the "Bluegrass" region of Kentucky. Others scouted down the Ohio River from Pittsburgh. By 1790, over 100,000 had settled in Kentucky and Tennessee, despite the risk of violent death at the hands of Indians. This risk was made worse by the presence of the British in northwestern military posts that should have been evacuated at the end of the war. From these posts they supplied the Indians with guns and encouraged them to use them on Americans. The Spaniards on the Florida frontier behaved in much the same way.

The settlement of Kentucky and Tennessee increased the pressure for the opening of the lands north of the Ohio River. To facilitate this, Congress passed three land ordinances in the years from 1784 to 1787.

The Land Ordinance of 1784 provided for territorial government and an orderly system by which each territory could progress to full statehood (this ordinance is sometimes considered part of the Land Ordinance of 1785).

The Land Ordinance of 1785 provided for the orderly surveying and distribution of land in townships six miles square, each composed of 36 one-square-mile (640 acre) sections, of which one should be set aside for the support of education. (This ordinance is sometimes referred to as the "Northwest Ordinance of 1785.")

The Northwest Ordinance of 1787 provided a bill of rights for settlers and forbade slavery north of the Ohio River. It also provided for the creation of three to five territories which could be admitted as states to the union when they reached sufficient populations.

The Jay-Gardoqui Negotiations

Economic depression followed the end of the war as the United States remained locked into the disadvantageous commercial system of the British Empire but without the trade advantages that system had provided.

One man who thought he saw a way out of the economic quagmire was Congress's secretary of foreign affairs, John Jay. In 1784, Jay began negotiating with Spanish minister Gardoqui a treaty that would have granted lucrative commercial privileges—benefiting large east-coast merchants such as Jay—in exchange for U.S. acceptance of Spain's closure of the Mississippi River as an outlet for the agricultural goods of the rapidly growing settlements in Kentucky and Tennessee. This the Spanish desired because they feared that extensive settlement in what was then the western part of the United States might lead to American hunger for Spanish-held lands.

When Jay reported this to Congress in the summer of 1786, the West and South were outraged. Negotiations were broken off. Some, angered that Jay could show so little concern for the other sections of the country, talked of dissolving the Union; and this helped spur to action those who desired not the dissolution but the strengthening of the Union.

Shays' Rebellion

Nationalists were further stimulated to action by Shays' Rebellion (1786). Economic hard times coupled with high taxes intended to pay off the state's war debt drove western Massachusetts farmers to desperation. Led by war veteran Daniel Shays, they shut down courts to prevent judges from seizing property or condemning people to debtors' prison for failing to pay their taxes.

The unrest created a disproportionate amount of panic in the rest of the state and the nation. The citizens of Boston subscribed money to raise an army to suppress the rebels. The success of this army together with timely tax relief caused the "rebellion" to fizzle out fairly quickly.

Amid the panic caused by the news of the uprising, many came to feel that a stronger government was needed to control such violent public outbursts as those of the western Massachusetts farmers.

3 THE UNITED STATES CONSTITUTION (1787-1789)

DEVELOPMENT AND RATIFICATION

Toward a New Constitution

As time went on the inadequacy of the Articles of Confederation became increasingly apparent. Congress could not compel the states to comply with the terms of the Treaty of Paris of 1783 regarding debts and loyalists' property. The British used this as an excuse for not evacuating their Northwestern posts, hoping to be on hand to make the most of the situation when, as they not unreasonably expected, the new government fell to pieces. In any case, Congress could do nothing to force them out of the posts, nor to solve any of the nation's other increasingly pressing problems.

In these dismal straits, some called for disunion, others for monarchy. Still others felt that republican government could still work if given a better constitution, and they made it their goal to achieve this.

In 1785 a meeting of representatives of Virginia, Maryland, Pennsylvania, and Delaware was held at George Washington's residence, Mt. Vernon, for the purpose of discussing current problems of interstate commerce. At their suggestion the Virginia legislature issued a call for a convention of all the states on the same subject, to meet the following summer in Annapolis, Maryland.

The Annapolis Convention met in September 1786, but only five states were represented. Among those present, however, were such nationalists as Alexander Hamilton, John Dickinson, and James Madison. With so few states represented it was decided instead to call for a convention of all the states to meet the following summer in Philadelphia for the purpose of revising the Articles of Confederation.

The Constitutional Convention

The men who met in Philadelphia in 1787 were remarkably able, highly educated, and exceptionally accomplished. For the most part they were lawyers, merchants, and planters. Though representing individual states, most thought in national terms. Prominent among them were James Madison, Alexander Hamilton, Gouverneur Morris, Robert Morris, John Dickinson, and Benjamin Franklin.

George Washington was unanimously elected to preside, and the enormous respect that he commanded helped hold the convention together through difficult times (as it had the Continental Army) and make the product of the convention's work more attractive to the rest of the nation. The delegates then voted that the convention's discussions should be secret, to avoid the distorting and confusing influence of the press and publicity.

The delegates shared a basic belief in the innate selfishness of man, which must somehow be kept from abusing the power of government. For this purpose, the document that they finally produced contained many checks and balances, designed to prevent the government, or any one branch of the government, from gaining too much power.

Madison, who has been called the "father of the Constitution," devised a plan of national government and persuaded fellow Virginian Edmund Randolph, who was more skilled at public speaking, to introduce it. Known as the "Virginia Plan," it called for an executive branch and two houses of Congress, each based on population.

Smaller states, who would thus have seen their influence decreased, objected and countered with William Paterson's "New Jersey Plan," calling for the continuation of a unicameral legislature with equal representation for the states as well as sharply increased powers for the national government.

A temporary impasse developed that threatened to break up the convention. At this point Benjamin Franklin played an important role in reconciling the often heated delegates, suggesting that the sessions of the convention henceforth begin with prayer (they did) and making various other suggestions that eventually helped the convention arrive at the "Great Compromise." The Great Compromise provided for a presidency, a Senate with all states represented equally (by two Senators each), and a House of Representatives with representation according to population.

Another crisis involved North-South disagreement over the issue of slavery. Here also a compromise was reached. Slavery was neither endorsed nor condemned by the Constitution. Each slave was to count as three-fifths of a person for purposes of apportioning representation and direct taxation on the states (the Three-Fifths Compromise). The federal government was prohibited from stopping the importation of slaves prior to 1808.

The third major area of compromise was the nature of the presidency. This was made easier by the virtual certainty that George Washington would be the first president and the universal trust that he would not abuse the powers of the office or set a bad example for his successors. The result was a strong presidency with control of foreign policy and the power to veto Congress's legislation. Should the president commit an actual crime, Congress would have the power to impeach him. Otherwise the president would serve for a term of four years and be re-electable without limit. As a check to the possible excesses of democracy, the president was to be elected by an Electoral College, in which each state would have the same number of electors as it did Senators and Representatives combined. The person with the second highest total in the Electoral College would be Vice-President. If no one gained a majority in the Electoral College, the President would be chosen by the House of Representatives.

The new Constitution was to take effect when nine states, through special state conventions, had ratified it.

The Struggle for Ratification

As the struggle over ratification got under way, those favoring the Constitution astutely took for themselves the name Federalists (i.e., advocates of centralized power) and labeled their opponents Antifederalists. The Federalists were effective in explaining the convention and the document it had produced. *The Federalist Papers*, written as a series of 85 newspaper articles by Alexander Hamilton, James Madison, and John Jay, brilliantly expounded the Constitution and demonstrated how it was designed to prevent the abuse of power from any direction. These essays are considered to be the best commentary on the Constitution by those who helped write it.

At first, ratification progressed smoothly, with five states approving in quick succession. In Massachusetts, however, a tough fight developed. By skillful maneuvering, Federalists were able to win over to their side such popular opponents of the Constitution as Samuel Adams and John Hancock. Others were won over by the promise that a bill of rights would be added to the Constitution, limiting the federal government just as the state governments were limited by their bills of rights. With such promises, Massachusetts ratified by a narrow margin.

By June 21, 1788, the required nine states had ratified, but the crucial states of New York and Virginia still held out. In Virginia, where George Mason and Patrick Henry opposed the Constitution, the influence of George Washington and the promise of a bill of rights finally prevailed and ratification was achieved there as well. In New York, where Alexander Hamilton led the fight for ratification, *The Federalist Papers*, the promise of a bill of rights, and the news of Virginia's ratification were enough to carry the day.

Only North Carolina and Rhode Island still held out, but they both ratified within the next 15 months.

In March 1789, George Washington was inaugurated as the nation's first president.

OUTLINE OF THE UNITED STATES CONSTITUTION

Articles of the Constitution

Preamble

"We the People of the United States, in order to form a more perfect Union, establish justice, insure domestic tranquility, provide for the common defense, promote the general welfare, and secure the blessings of liberty to ourselves and our posterity, do ordain and establish this Constitution for the United States of America"

Article I—Legislature

The legislature is divided into two parts—the House of Representatives (435 members currently; determined by proportional representation of the population) and the Senate (100 members currently; two from each state).

The House of Representatives may bring impeachment charges. All bills which concern money must originate in the House. Because of the size of the body, debate is limited except in special cases, where all representatives may meet as the Committee of the Whole. The Speaker of the House presides over the proceedings. Elected terms of representatives are two years, re-electable without limit, to persons who are at least 25 years of age.

The Senate, originally elected by state legislatures but now by direct election (Seventeenth Amendment), approves or rejects presidential nominations and treaties, and serves as the court and jury in impeachment proceedings. Debate within the Senate is unlimited. The president pro tempore usually presides, but the vice-president of the United States is the presiding officer, and may vote to break a tie. Senate elected terms are for six years, re-electable without limit, to persons who are at least 30 years of age.

Article II—Executive

The President of the United States is elected for a four-year term, originally electable without limit (the Twenty-second Amendment limits election to two terms), and must be at least 35 years old.

Responsibilities for the president as outlined in the Constitution include acting as the chief of state, the chief executive, commander-in-chief of the armed forces, the chief diplomat, and chief legislator.

Article III—Judiciary

While the Constitution describes the Supreme Court in Article III, the actual construction of the court system was accomplished by the Judiciary Act of 1789. The Supreme Court has jurisdiction for federal courts and appellate cases on appeal from lower courts.

Article IV—Interstate Relations

This article guarantees that court decisions and other legal actions (marriage, incorporation, etc.) valid in one state are valid in another. Extradition of criminals (and, originally, runaway slaves) and the exchange of citizenship benefits are likewise guaranteed. Article IV also provides for the admission of new states and guarantees federal protection against invasion and violence for each state. States admitted maintain the same status as the original states. All states are guaranteed a republican form of government.

Article V—Amendment Process

Amendments are proposed by a two-thirds vote of each house of Congress or by a special convention called by Congress upon the request of two-thirds of the state legislatures. Amendments are ratified by three-fourths of the state legislatures or state conventions.

Article VI—Supremacy Clause

Article VI sets up the hierarchy of laws in the United States. The Constitution is the "supreme law of the land" and supersedes treaties. Treaties supersede federal laws, federal laws (later to include federal regulatory agency directives) supercede state constitutions, state laws, and local laws respectively. All federal and state officials, including judges, must take an oath to support and defend the Constitution.

Article VII—Ratification

This article specified the ratification process necessary for the Constitution to take effect. Nine of the original 13 states had to ratify the Constitution before it became operative.

Amendments to the Constitution

The Amendments to the Constitution guarantee certain individual rights and amend original dictates of the Constitution. The first ten amendments are known as the Bill of Rights.

1. Freedom of religion, speech, press, assembly, and government petition (1791)
2. Right to bear arms in a regulated militia (1791)
3. Troops will not be quartered (housed) in private citizens' homes (1791)
4. Protects against unreasonable search and seizure (need for search warrant) (1791)
5. Protects the rights of the accused, including required indictments, double jeopardy, self-incrimination, due process, and just compensation (1791)
6. Guarantees a speedy and public trial, the confrontation by witnesses, and the right to call one's own witnesses on behalf (1791)
7. Guarantees a jury trial (1791)
8. Protects against excessive bail and cruel and unusual punishment (1791)
9. States that all rights not enumerated are nonetheless retained by the people (1791)
10. States that all powers not specifically delegated to the federal government are retained by the states (1791)
11. States may not be sued by individuals (1798)
12. Dictates that electors will cast separate ballots for president and vice president; in the event of no clear winner, the House will select the president and the senate the vice-president (1804)
13. Abolished slavery (1865)
14. Extended citizenship to all persons; made Confederate debt void and Confederate leaders ineligible for public office; states which denied voting rights to qualified citizens (blacks) would have their represen-

tation in Congress reduced; conferred "dual" citizenship (both of the United States and of a specific state) on all citizens (1868)

15. Extended voting rights to blacks (1870)
16. Legalized the income tax (1913)
17. Provided for the direct election of senators (1913)
18. Prohibited the general manufacture, sale, and use of alcoholic beverages (1919)
19. Extended voting rights to women (1920)
20. Changed inauguration date from March 4 to January 20; eliminated the "lame duck" session of Congress (after the November elections) (1933)
21. Repealed the Eighteenth Amendment (1933)
22. Limited presidents to two terms (1951)
23. Gave presidential electoral votes to the District of Columbia (1961)
24. Prohibited poll taxes (1964)
25. Changed the order of the presidential line of succession and provided guidelines for presidential disability (1967)
26. Extended voting rights to 18-year-olds (1971)
27. Restricted the practice of congressional salary adjustment (1992)

SEPARATION AND LIMITATION OF POWERS

Powers Reserved for the Federal Government Only

- Foreign commerce regulation
- Interstate commerce regulation
- Mint money
- Create and establish post offices
- Regulate naturalization and immigration
- Grant copyrights and patents
- Declare and wage war, declare peace
- Admit new states
- Fix standards for weights and measures

- Raise and maintain an army and navy
- Govern the federal city (Washington, D.C.)
- Conduct relations with foreign powers
- Universalize bankruptcy laws

Powers Reserved for the State Governments Only

- Conduct and monitor elections
- Establish voter qualifications
- Provide for local governments
- Ratify proposed amendments to the Constitution
- Regulate contracts and wills
- Regulate intrastate commerce
- Provide education for its citizens
- Levy direct taxes (the Sixteenth Amendment permits the federal government to levy direct taxes)
- Maintain police power over public health, safety and morals
- Maintain integrity of state borders

Powers Shared by Federal and State Governments

- Taxing, borrowing, and spending money
- Controlling the militia
- Acting directly on individuals

Restrictions on the Federal Government

- No ex post facto laws
- No bills of attainder
- Two-year limit on appropriation for the military
- No suspension of habeus corpus (except in a crisis)
- One port may not be favored over another
- All guarantees as stated in the Bill of Rights

Restrictions on State Governments

- May not enter into treaties, alliances, or confederations
- Letters of marque and reprisal may not be granted
- Contracts may not be impaired
- Money may not be printed or bills of credit emitted
- No import or export taxes
- May not wage war (unless invaded)

Required Percentages of Voting

Actions which require a simple majority include raising taxes, requesting appropriations, declaring war, increasing the national debt, instituting a draft, and introducing impeachment charges (House).

Actions which require a two-thirds majority include overriding a presidential veto, proposing amendments to the Constitution, expelling a member of Congress (in the individual house only), ratifying treaties (Senate), acting as a jury for impeachment (Senate), ratifying presidential appointments (Senate).

The action which requires a three-fourths majority is approving a proposed constitutional amendment (states).

4 THE NEW NATION (1789-1824)

THE FEDERALIST ERA

The results of the first elections held under the new Constitution made it clear that the fledgling government was going to be managed by those who had drawn up the document and by their supporters. Few Antifederalists were elected to Congress, and many of the new legislators had served as delegates to the Philadelphia Convention two years before. This Federalist majority immediately set about to draft legislation which would fill in the gaps left by the convention and to erect the structure of a strong central government.

The New Executive

There had never been any doubt as to who would be the first president. George Washington received virtually all the votes of the presidential electors, and John Adams received the next highest number, thus becoming the vice president. After a triumphal journey from Mount Vernon, Washington was inaugurated in New York City, the temporary seat of government, on April 30, 1789.

Congress Erects the Structure of Government

The new national legislature immediately acted to honor the Federalist pledge of a bill of rights made to those voters who had hesitated to ratify the new Constitution. Twelve amendments were drafted which embodied the guarantees of personal liberties, most of which had been traditionally enjoyed by English citizens. Ten of these were ratified by the states by the end of 1791, and they became the Bill of Rights. The first nine spelled out specific guarantees of personal freedoms, such as religion, speech, press, assembly, petition, and a speedy trial by one's peers, and the Tenth Amendment reserved to the states all those powers not specifically withheld, or granted to the federal government. This last was a concession to those who feared the potential of the central government to usurp the sovereignty of the individual states.

The Establishment of the Federal Court System

The Judiciary Act of 1789 provided for a Supreme Court, with six justices, and invested it with the power to rule on the constitutional validity of state laws. It was to be the interpreter of the "supreme law of the land." A system of district courts was established to serve as courts of original jurisdiction, and three courts of appeal were also provided for.

THE ESTABLISHMENT OF THE EXECUTIVE DEPARTMENTS

The Constitution had not specified the names or number of the departments of the executive branch. Congress established three—state, treasury, and war—and also the offices of attorney general and postmaster-general. President Washington immediately appointed Thomas Jefferson, Alexander Hamilton, and Henry Knox, respectively, to fill the executive posts, and Edmund Randolph became attorney general. These four men were called upon regularly by the president for advice, and they later formed the nucleus of what became known as the Cabinet, although no provision for such was made in the Constitution.

WASHINGTON'S ADMINISTRATION, 1789-1797

Hamilton's Financial Program

Treasury Secretary Alexander Hamilton, in his "Report on the Public Credit," proposed the funding of the national debt at face value, federal assumption of state debts, and the establishment of a national bank. In his "Report on Manufactures," Hamilton proposed an extensive program for federal stimulation of industrial development, through subsidies and tax incentives. The money needed to fund these programs, proposed Hamilton, would come from an excise tax on distillers and from tariffs on imports.

Opposition to Hamilton's Program

Jefferson and others objected to the funding proposal because it obviously would benefit speculators who had bought up state and confederation obligations at depressed prices, and now would profit handsomely by their redemption at face value. The original purchasers, they claimed, should at least share in the windfall. They opposed the tax program because it would fall primarily on the small farmers. They saw Hamilton's entire program as enriching a small elite group at the expense of the more worthy common citizen.

The Appearance of Political Parties

Political parties had been considered a detrimental force by the founding fathers, since they were seen to contribute to the rise of "factions."

Thus no mention of such was made in the Constitution. But differences in philosophy very quickly began to drive the leaders of government into opposing camps—the Federalists and the Republicans.

Alexander Hamilton and the Federalists

Hamilton, as the theorist of the group who favored a strong central government, interpreted the Constitution as having vested extensive powers in the federal government. This "implied powers" stance claimed that the government was given all powers that were not expressly denied to it. This is the "broad" interpretation.

Thomas Jefferson and the Republicans

Jefferson and Madison held the view that any action not specifically permitted in the Constitution was thereby prohibited. This is the "strict" interpretation, and the Republicans opposed the establishment of Hamilton's national bank on this view of government. The Jeffersonian supporters, primarily under the guidance of James Madison, began to organize political groups in opposition to the Federalist program, and called themselves Republicans.

Sources of Partisan Support

The Federalists received their strongest support from the business and financial groups in the commercial centers of the Northeast and in the port cities of the South. The strength of the Republicans lay primarily in the rural and frontier areas of the South and West.

FOREIGN AND FRONTIER AFFAIRS

The French Revolution

When revolutionary France went to war with the European powers in 1792, Washington's response was a Proclamation of Neutrality. Citizen Genet violated that policy by trying to encourage popular support in this country for the French government, and embarrassed the president. American merchants traded with both sides, though the most lucrative business was carried on with the French West Indies. This brought retaliation by the British, who began to seize American merchant ships and force their crews into service with the British navy.

Jay's Treaty with Britain (1794)

John Jay negotiated a treaty with the British which attempted to settle the conflict at sea, as well as to curtail English agitation of their Indian allies on the western borders. The agreement actually settled few of the issues and merely bought time for the new nation in the worsening international conflict. Jay was severely criticized for his efforts, and was even hanged in effigy, but the Senate accepted the treaty as the best possible under the circumstances.

The Treaty with Spain (1795)

Thomas Pinckney was invited to the Spanish court to strengthen what Madrid perceived to be her deteriorating position on the American frontier. The result was the Pinckney Treaty, ratified by the Senate in 1796, in which the Spanish opened the Mississippi River to American traffic, including the right of deposit in the port city of New Orleans, and recognized the 31st parallel as the northern boundary of Florida.

Frontier Problems

Indian tribes on the Northwest and Southwest borders were increasingly resisting the encroachments on their lands by the American settlers. British authorities in Canada were encouraging the Indians in their depredations against frontier settlements.

In 1794, General Anthony Wayne decisively defeated the Indians at the Battle of Fallen Timbers, and the resulting Treaty of Greenville cleared the Ohio territory of Indian tribes.

INTERNAL PROBLEMS

The Whiskey Rebellion (1794)

Western farmers refused to pay the excise tax on whiskey which formed the backbone of Hamilton's revenue program. When a group of Pennsylvania farmers terrorized the tax collectors, President Washington sent out a federalized militia force of some 15,000 men, and the rebellion evaporated, thus strengthening the credibility of the young government.

Land Policy

As the original 13 states ceded their Western land claims to the new federal government, new states were organized and admitted to the Union, thus strengthening the ties of the Western farmers to the central government (Vermont, 1791; Kentucky, 1792; and Tennessee, 1796).

JOHN ADAMS' ADMINISTRATION, 1797-1801

The Election of 1796

John Adams was the Federalist candidate, and Thomas Jefferson ran under the opposition banner of the Republicans. Since Jefferson received the second highest number of electoral votes, he became vice president. Thus, a Federalist president and a Republican vice president served together, an obviously awkward arrangement. Adams was a brilliant lawyer and statesman, but too dogmatic and uncompromising to be an effective politician, and he endured a very frustrating and unproductive term in office.

The XYZ Affair

A three-man delegation was sent to France in 1798 to persuade the French to stop harassing American shipping. When they were solicited for a bribe by three subordinates of the French Minister Talleyrand, they indignantly refused, and their report of this insult produced outrage at home. The cry "millions for defense, but not one cent for tribute" was raised, and public feelings against the French ran high. Since Talleyrand's officials were unnamed in the dispatches, the incident became known as the "XYZ Affair."

Quasi-War, 1798-1799

This uproar moved Adams to suspend all trade with the French, and American ship captains were authorized to attack and capture armed French vessels. Congress created a Department of the Navy, and war seemed imminent. In 1800, the new French government, now under Napoleon, signed a new treaty, and the peace was restored.

REPRESSION AND PROTEST

The Alien and Sedition Acts

The elections in 1798 had increased the Federalist majorities in both houses of Congress, and they used their "mandate" to enact legislation to stifle foreign influences. The Alien Act raised new hurdles in the path of immigrants trying to obtain citizenship, and the Sedition Act widened the powers of the Adams administration to muzzle its newspaper critics. Both bills were aimed at actual or potential Republican opposition, and a number of editors were actually jailed for printing critical editorials.

The Kentucky and Virginia Resolves

Republican leaders were convinced that the Alien and Sedition Acts were unconstitutional but the process of deciding on the constitutionality of federal laws was as yet undefined. Jefferson and Madison decided that the state legislatures should have that power, and they drew up a series of resolutions which were presented to the Kentucky and Virginia legislatures, respectively. They proposed that John Locke's "compact theory" be applied, which would empower the state bodies to "nullify" federal laws within those states. These resolutions were adopted, but only in those two states, and so the issue died, but a principle was put forward which was later to bear fruit in the nullification controversy of the 1830s and finally in the secession crisis of 1860-61.

THE REVOLUTION OF 1800

The Election

Thomas Jefferson and Aaron Burr ran on the Republican ticket, against John Adams and Charles Pinckney for the Federalists. The Republican candidates won handily, but both received the same number of electoral votes, thus throwing the selection of the president into the House of Representatives. After a lengthy deadlock, Alexander Hamilton threw his support to Jefferson, and Burr had to accept the vice presidency, the result obviously intended by the electorate. This increased the ill will between Hamilton and Burr and contributed to their famous duel in 1804.

Packing the Judiciary

The Federalist Congress passed a new Judiciary Act early in 1801 and President Adams filled the newly created vacancies with party supporters, many of them with last-minute commissions. John Marshall was then appointed Chief Justice of the U.S. Supreme Court, thus guaranteeing continuation of Federalist policies from the bench of the high court.

THE JEFFERSONIAN ERA

Thomas Jefferson and his Republican followers envisioned a society in vivid contrast to that of Hamilton and the Federalists. They dreamed of a nation of independent farmers, living under a central government that exercised a minimum of control over their lives and served merely to protect the individual liberties guaranteed by the Constitution. This agrarian paradise would be free from the industrial smoke and urban blight of Europe, and would serve as a beacon light of Enlightenment rationalism to a world searching for direction. That vision was to prove a mirage, and Jefferson was to preside over a nation that was growing more industrialized and urban, and which seemed to need an ever stronger hand at the presidential tiller.

The New Federal City

The city of Washington had been designed by Pierre L'Enfant and was briefly occupied by the Adams administration. When Jefferson moved in, it was still a straggling provincial town, with muddy streets and muggy summers. Most of its inhabitants moved out when Congress was not in session.

Jefferson the President

The new president tried to project an image of democratic simplicity, sometimes appearing so casually dressed as to appear slovenly. But he was a brilliant thinker and a shrewd politician. He appointed men to his cabinet who agreed with his political philosophy: James Madison as Secretary of State and Albert Gallatin to the Treasury.

CONFLICT WITH THE JUDGES

Marbury v. Madison

William Marbury, one of Adams' "midnight appointments," sued Secretary of State Madison to force delivery of his commission as a justice of the peace in the federal district. John Marshall, as Supreme Court justice, refused to rule on the request, claiming that the law which gave the Supreme Court jurisdiction over such matters had exceeded the Constitutional grant of powers and thus was unconstitutional. Marshall thus asserted the power of judicial review over federal legislation, a power which has become the foundation of the Supreme Court's check on the other two branches of government.

The Impeachment Episodes

Jefferson began a campaign to remove Federalist judges by impeachment. One district judge was removed, and proceedings were begun to impeach Supreme Court Justice Samuel Chase. That effort failed, but the threat had encouraged the judiciary to be less blatantly political.

DOMESTIC AFFAIRS

Enforcement of the Alien and Sedition Acts was immediately suspended, and the men convicted under those laws were released.

The federal bureaucracy was reduced and expenses were drastically cut. The size of the army was reduced and the expansion program of the navy was canceled.

The excise taxes were repealed and federal income was limited to land sale proceeds and customs duties. Federal land sale policy was liberalized, smaller parcels were authorized, and less cash was required—policies which benefited small farmers.

The Twelfth Amendment was adopted and ratified in 1804, ensuring that a tie vote between candidates of the same party could not again cause the confusion of the Jefferson-Burr affair.

Following the Constitutional mandate, the importation of slaves was stopped by law in 1808.

The Louisiana Purchase

Napoleon, in an effort to regain some of France's New World empire, had obtained the old French trans-Mississippi territory from Spain by political pressure. Jefferson sent a delegation to Paris to try to buy New Orleans, lest the new French officials close it to American traffic. Napoleon's defeat in Santo Domingo persuaded him that Louisiana could not be exploited, and indeed was now subject to potential American incursions. So he offered to sell the entire territory to the United States for $15 million. The American delegation accepted the offer in April 1803, even though they had no authority to buy more than the city of New Orleans.

The Constitutional Dilemma

Jefferson's stand on the strict interpretation of the Constitution would not permit him to purchase land without Congressional approval. But he accepted his advisors' counsel that his treaty-making powers included the authority to buy the land. Congress concurred, after the fact, and the purchase price was appropriated, thus doubling the territory of the nation overnight.

Exploring the West

Even before Napoleon's offer, Jefferson had authorized an expedition to explore the Western territory to the Pacific. The Lewis and Clark group, with 48 men, left St. Louis in 1804, and returned two years later with a wealth of scientific and anthropological information, and having strengthened the United States' claim to the Oregon territory. At the same time, Zebulon Pike and others had been traversing the middle parts of Louisiana and mapping the land.

The Essex Junto (1804)

Some New England Federalists saw the Western expansion as a threat to their position in the Union, and they tried to organize a secessionist movement. They courted Aaron Burr's support by offering to back him in a bid for the governorship of New York. Hamilton led the opposition to that campaign and when Burr lost the election, he challenged Hamilton to a duel, which resulted in Hamilton's death.

The Burr Conspiracy

Aaron Burr was now a fugitive, without a political future. He became involved in a scheme to take Mexico from Spain and establish a new nation in the West.

In the fall of 1806, he led a group of armed men down the Mississippi River system toward New Orleans. He was arrested in Natchez and tried for treason in Richmond, Virginia. Judge John Marshall's decision for acquittal helped to narrow the legal definition of treason. Jefferson's attempts to influence and prejudice the trial were justified by his claims of "executive privilege," but they were fruitless.

John Randolph and the Yazoo Claims

Jefferson's Republican opponents, under the leadership of his cousin John Randolph of Roanoke, called themselves the "Quids." They accused the president of complicity in the Yazoo Land controversy which had followed Georgia's cession of her western lands to the federal government. This created serious strife within the Republican party and weakened Jefferson's effectiveness in his second term.

INTERNATIONAL INVOLVEMENT

The Barbary War

In 1801 Jefferson sent a naval force to the Mediterranean to break the practice of the North African Muslim rulers of exacting tribute from Western merchant ships. Intermittent undeclared war dragged on until 1805, with no decisive settlement.

The Napoleonic Wars

War continued in Europe between France under Napoleon and the European powers led by Britain. Both sides tried to prevent trade with their enemies by neutral powers, especially the United States. Napoleon's "Continental System" was answered by Britain's "Orders in Council." American ships were seized by both sides and American sailors were "impressed" into the British navy.

The Chesapeake-Leopard Affair (1807)

The British ship H.M.S. *Leopard* stopped the U.S.S. *Chesapeake* off the Chesapeake Bay, and four alleged British deserters were taken off. Public outcry for war followed, and Jefferson was hard pressed to remain neutral.

The Embargo of 1807

Jefferson's response to the cry for war was to draft a law prohibiting American ships from leaving port for any foreign destination, thus avoiding contact with vessels of either belligerent. The result was economic depression, particularly in the heavily commercial Northeast. This proved to be his most unpopular policy of both terms in office.

MADISON'S ADMINISTRATION, 1809–1817

The Election of 1808

Republican James Madison won the election over Federalist Charles Pinckney, but the Federalists gained seats in both houses of the Congress. The embargo-induced depression was obviously a heavy political liability, and Madison was to face growing pressures to deal with the international crisis. He was a brilliant man but with few social or political skills. His greatest asset was probably his wife, the vivacious and energetic Dolly.

The War of 1812

Congress had passed a modified embargo just before Madison's inauguration, known as the Non-Intercourse Act, which opened trade to all nations except France and Britain. When it expired in 1810, it was replaced by Macon's Bill No. 2, which gave the president power to prohibit trade with any nation when they violated our neutrality.

The Indian tribes of the Northwest and the Mississippi Valley were resentful of the government's policy of pressured removal to the West, and the British authorities in Canada were exploiting their discontent by encouraging border raids against the American settlements.

The Shawnee chief Tecumseh set out to unite the Mississippi Valley tribes and reestablish Indian dominance in the Old Northwest. With the help of his brother, the Prophet, and the timely New Madrid earthquake, he persuaded a sizeable force of warriors to join him. On November 11, 1811, General William Henry Harrison destroyed Tecumseh's village on Tippecanoe Creek and dashed his hopes for an Indian confederacy.

Southern frontiersmen coveted Spanish Florida, which included the southern ranges of Alabama, Mississippi, and Louisiana. They resented Spanish support of Indian depredations against the borderlands, and since Spain was Britain's ally, they saw Britain as the background cause of their problems.

The Congress in 1811 contained a strong pro-war group called the War Hawks, led by Henry Clay and John C. Calhoun. They gained control of both houses and began agitating for war with the British. On June 1, 1812, President Madison asked for a declaration of war, and Congress complied.

A three-pronged invasion of Canada met with disaster on all three fronts, and the Americans fell back to their own borders. At sea, American privateers and frigates, including "Old Ironsides," scored early victories over British warships, but were soon driven back into their home ports and blockaded by the powerful British ships-of-the-line.

Admiral Oliver Hazard Perry constructed a fleet of ships on Lake Erie and on September 10, 1813, defeated a British force at Put-In Bay and established control of the lake. His flagship flew the banner, "Don't Give Up the Ship." This victory opened the way for William Henry Harrison to invade Canada in October and defeat a combination British and Indian force at the Battle of the Thames.

The War in the Southwest

Andrew Jackson led a force of frontier militia into Alabama in pursuit of Creek Indians who had massacred the white inhabitants of Fort Mims. On March 27, 1814, he crushed the Indians at Horseshoe Bend, and then seized the Spanish garrison at Pensacola.

British Strategy Changes, 1814

A British force came down Lake Champlain and met defeat at Plattsburgh, New York, in September. A British armada sailed up the Chesapeake Bay and sacked and burned Washington, D.C. They then proceeded up the Bay toward Baltimore, which was guarded by Fort McHenry. That fort held firm through the British bombardment, inspiring Key's "Star Spangled Banner."

The Battle of New Orleans

The most serious British threat came at the port of New Orleans. A powerful invasion force was sent there to close the mouth of the Mississippi River, but Andrew Jackson decisively defeated it with a polyglot army of frontiersmen, blacks, creoles and pirates. The battle was fought on January 8, 1815, two weeks after a peace treaty had been signed at the city of Ghent, in Belgium.

The Treaty of Ghent, Christmas Eve 1814

With the European wars ended, the major causes for the dispute with Britain had ceased to be important, so both sides were eager for peace. The treaty provided for the acceptance of the status quo at the beginning of hostilities and so both sides restored their wartime conquests to the other.

The Hartford Convention, December 1814

The Federalists had become increasingly a minority party. They vehemently opposed the war and Daniel Webster and other New England Congressmen consistently blocked the administration's efforts to prosecute the war effort. On December 15, 1814, delegates from the New England states met in Hartford, Connecticut, and drafted a set of resolutions suggesting nullification—and even secession—if their interests were not protected against the growing influence of the South and the West.

Soon after the convention adjourned, the news of the victory at New Orleans was announced and their actions were discredited. The Federalist party ceased to be a political force from this point.

POST-WAR DEVELOPMENTS

Protective Tariff (1816)

The first protective tariff in the nation's history was passed in 1816 to slow the flood of cheap British manufactures into the country.

Rush-Bagot Treaty (1817)

An agreement was reached in 1817 between Britain and the United States to stop maintaining armed fleets on the Great Lakes. This first "disarmament" agreement is still in effect.

Jackson's Florida Invasion (1817)

Indian troubles in the newly acquired areas of western Florida prompted General Andrew Jackson, acting under dubious authority, to invade Spanish East Florida and to hang two British subjects whom he suspected of selling guns and supplies to the Indians. Then he re-occupied Pensacola and raised the American flag, a clear violation of international law. Only wide public support prevented his arrest and prosecution by the government.

Indian Policy

The government began to systematically pressure all the Indian tribes remaining in the East to cede their lands and accept new homes west of the Mississippi, a policy which met with disappointing results. Most declined the offer.

The Barbary Wars (1815)

In response to continued piracy and extortion in the Mediterranean, Congress declared war on the Muslim state of Algiers in 1815 and dispatched a naval force to the area under Stephen Decatur. He quickly defeated the North African pirates and forced them to pay indemnities for past tribute they had exacted from American ship captains. This action finally gained the United States free access to the Mediterranean basin.

The Adams-Onis Treaty (1819)

Spain had decided to sell the remainder of the Florida territory to the Americans before they took it anyway. Under this agreement, the Spanish surrendered all their claims to the territory and drew the boundary of Mexico all the way to the Pacific. The United States in exchange agreed to assume $5 million in debts owed to American merchants.

The Monroe Doctrine

Around 1810, national revolutions had begun in Latin America, so the colonial populations refused to accept the rule of the new Napoleonic governments in Europe. Leaders like San Martin and Bolivar had declared independence for their countries and, after Napoleon's fall in 1814, were defying the restored Hapsburg and Bourbon rulers of Europe.

British and American leaders feared that the new European governments would try to restore the former New World colonies to their erstwhile royal owners.

In December 1823, President Monroe included in his annual message to Congress a statement that the American hemisphere was "henceforth not to be considered as subjects for future colonization by any European powers." Thus began a 30-year period of freedom from serious foreign involvement for the United States.

INTERNAL DEVELOPMENT, 1820-1830

The years following the War of 1812 were years of rapid economic and social development. Too rapid, in fact, and they were followed by a severe depression in 1819. But this slump was temporary, and it became obvious that the country was moving rapidly from its agrarian origins toward an industrial, urban future. Westward expansion accelerated, and the mood of the people became very positive. In fact, these years were referred to as the "Era of Good Feelings."

The Monroe Presidency, 1817-1823

James Monroe, the last of the "Virginia Dynasty," had been handpicked by the retiring Madison, and he was elected with only one electoral vote opposed: a symbol of national unity.

Post-War Boom

The years following the war were characterized by a high foreign demand for American cotton, grain, and tobacco; commerce flourished. The Second National Bank, through its overly liberal credit policies, proved to be an inflationary influence, and the price level rose rapidly.

The Depression of 1819

Inventories of British manufactured goods had built up during the war, and English merchants began to dump their products on the American market at cut-rate prices. American manufacturers suffered from this influx of imports. The U.S. Bank tried to slow the inflationary spiral by tightening credit, and a sharp business slump resulted.

This depression was most severe in the newly expanding West, partly because of its economic dependency, partly because of heavy speculation in Western lands.

THE MARSHALL COURT

John Marshall delivered the majority opinions in a number of critical decisions in these formative years, all of which served to strengthen the power of the federal government and restrict the powers of state governments.

Marbury v. Madison (1803)

This case established the precedent of the Supreme Court's power to rule on the constitutionality of federal laws.

Fletcher v. Peck (1810)

The Georgia legislature had issued extensive land grants in a shady deal with the Yazoo Land Company. A subsequent legislative session repealed that action because of the corruption that had attended the original grant. The Court decided that the original action by the Georgia Assembly had constituted a valid contract which could not be broken regardless of the corruption which had followed. This was the first time a state law was voided on the grounds that it violated a principle of the U.S. Constitution.

Dartmouth College v. Woodward (1819)

The quarrel between the president and the trustees of the New Hampshire college became a political issue when the Republicans backed the president and the Federalists supported the trustees. The president tried to change Dartmouth from a private to a public institution by having its charter revoked. The Court ruled that the charter, though issued by the king during colonial days, still constituted a contract, and thus could not be arbitrarily changed or revoked without the consent of both parties. The result of this decision was to severely limit the power of state governments to control the corporation, which was the emerging form of business organization.

McCulloch v. Maryland (1819)

The state of Maryland had tried to levy a tax on the Baltimore branch of the Bank of the United States, and so protect the competitive position of its own state banks. Marshall's ruling declared that no state has the right to control an agency of the federal government. Since "the power to tax is the power to destroy," such state action violated Congress' "implied powers" to establish and operate a national bank.

Gibbons v. Ogden (1824)

The State of New York had granted a monopoly to Ogden to operate a steamboat between New York and New Jersey. Gibbons obtained a Congressional permit to operate a steamboat line in the same waters. When Ogden sued to maintain his monopoly, the New York courts ruled in his favor. Gibbons' appeal went to the Supreme Court. John Marshall ruled that commerce included navigation, and that only Congress has the right to regulate commerce among states. Thus, the state-granted monopoly was void.

The Missouri Compromise (1820)

The Missouri Territory, the first to be organized from the Louisiana Purchase, applied for statehood in 1819. Since the Senate membership was evenly divided between slave-holding and free states at that time, the admission of a new state was obviously going to give the voting advantage either to the North or to the South. Slavery was already well-established in the new territory, so the Southern states were confident in their advantage, until Representative Tallmadge of New York proposed an amendment to the bill which would prohibit slavery in Missouri.

The Southern outcry was immediate, and the ensuing debate grew hot. The Senate was deadlocked.

Henry Clay's Compromise Solution

As the debate dragged on, the northern territory of Massachusetts applied for admission as the state of Maine. This offered a way out of the dilemma, and House Speaker Clay formulated a package that both sides could accept. The two admission bills were combined, with Maine coming in free and Missouri as a slave state. To make the package palatable for the House, a provision was added to prohibit slavery in the remainder of the Louisiana Territory, north of the southern boundary of Missouri (latitude 36 degrees 30'). Clay guided this bill through the House and it became law, thus maintaining the balance of power.

The debates in Congress had reminded everyone of the deep division between the sections, and some saw it as evidence of trouble to come. Thomas Jefferson, in retirement at Monticello, remarked that the news from Washington was like a "fire-ball in the night."

THE EXPANDING ECONOMY

The Growing Population

Population continued to double every 25 years. The migration of people to the West increased in volume and by 1840 over one-third of all Americans lived west of the Alleghenies. Immigration from abroad was not significant until 1820; then it began to increase rapidly, mostly from the British Isles.

The Farming Sector

As markets for farm products grew in the expanding cities, coupled with liberal land sale policies by the federal government, the growing of staple agricultural crops became more profitable. More and more land was put into cultivation, and the prevailing system of clearing and planting became more wasteful of timber as well as of the fertility of the land.

The Cotton Kingdom

The new lands in the Southwest, then made up by Alabama, Mississippi, Louisiana, and Texas, proved ideal for the production of short-staple cotton. Eli Whitney's invention of the cotton "gin" solved the problem of separating the seeds from the fibers, and the cotton boom was under way.

The growing market for food and work animals in the cotton South provided the opportunity for the new Western farmers to specialize in those items and further stimulated the westward movement.

Fishing

New England and Chesapeake fishing proved very profitable. Deep-sea whaling became a significant enterprise, particularly from the Massachusetts/Rhode Island ports.

Lumbering

The expanding population created a need for building materials, and timber remained a profitable export item. Shipbuilding thrived in a number of Eastern Seaboard and Gulf Coast ports.

Fur Trade

John Jacob Astor and others opened up business all the way to the Northwest coast. "Mountain men" probed deeper and deeper into the Rocky Mountain ranges in search of beavers.

Trade with the Spanish

The Santa Fe Trail, which ran from New Mexico northeast to Independence, Missouri, became an active trading corridor, opening up the Spanish territories to American migration and influence, and also providing the basis for future territorial claims.

THE TRANSPORTATION REVOLUTION

The first half of the nineteenth century witnessed an extraordinary sequence of inventions and innovations which produced a true revolution in transport and communications.

River Traffic

The steamboats built by Robert Fulton, the *Clermont* in 1807 and the *New Orleans* in 1811, transformed river transport. As shipment times and freight rates both plummeted, regular steam service was established on all the major river systems.

Roadbuilding

By 1818, the National Road, which was built with federal funds, had been completed from Cumberland, Maryland to Wheeling, Virginia, linking the Potomac with the Ohio River. A network of privately-owned toll roads (turnpikes) began to reach out from every sizeable city. They were usually built for only a few miles out, and they never accounted for a significant share of the total freight tonnage moved, but they formed the nucleus for a growing road system in the new nation.

The Canal Era

The Erie Canal, linking the Hudson River at Albany, New York, with Lake Erie, was completed in 1825 and became the first and most successful example. It was followed by a rash of construction until canals linked every major waterway system east of the Mississippi River.

Canals were the first development projects to receive large amounts of public funding. They ran east-west and so tied the new West to the old East, with later implications for sectional divisions.

The Rise of New York City

Its location as a transport hub, coupled with innovations in business practices, boosted New York City into a primary trade center, and America's largest city by 1830. One such innovation was the packet boat, which operated on a guaranteed schedule and helped to rationalize commerce, both internal and international.

New York soon dominated the domestic market for cotton, a situation which progressively reduced the South to the status of an economic colony.

INDUSTRIALIZATION

The Rise of the Factory System

Samuel Slater had migrated from Britain in 1789, having served as an apprentice under inventor Richard Arkwright and then as a mill manager. He used his knowledge to build the first successful cotton-spinning mill in this country. The first cotton manufacturing plant in the world to include all the elements of manufacturing under one roof was built in Boston in 1813.

Eli Whitney's development and application of the principle of interchangeable parts, first used in his firearms factories, helped to speed the growth of mass-production operations.

The expansion of markets in Latin America and the Far East, as well as domestic markets, both resulted from and helped to develop the factory system.

Manufacturers and industrialists found it necessary to organize banks, insurance companies, and real estate firms to meet the needs of their growing business organizations.

The Corporation

The corporate form with its limited liability and its potential for raising and utilizing large amounts of capital, became the typical type of business organization. By the 1830s, most states had enacted general laws for incorporating.

The Labor Supply

In the early days, the "Lowell System" became a popular way to staff the New England factories. Young women were hired from the surrounding countryside, brought to town and housed in dormitories in the mill towns. They were paid low wages for hard work under poor conditions, but they were only working for a short time, to earn a dowry or help out with the family income, so they soon went back home. This "rotating labor supply" was ideal for the owners, since the girls were not motivated to agitate for better wages and conditions.

Labor was always in short supply in this country, so the system depended on technology to increase production. This situation always placed a premium on innovation in machinery and technique.

The Growth of Unions

The factory system separated the owners from the workers and thus depersonalized the workplace. It also made the skilled artisan less important, since the repetitive processes of the mill could be performed by relatively unskilled laborers.

Although the first organized strike took place in 1828, in Paterson, New Jersey, by child workers, periodic economic downturns helped keep workers relatively dependent and passive until the 1850s.

A major goal of early unions was the 10-hour day, and this effort sparked a period of growth in organized labor which was later effectively quenched by the depression of 1837.

EDUCATIONAL DEVELOPMENT

The Growth of Public Schools

Before 1815, there were no public schools to speak of in this country. Some states had endorsed the idea of free schools for the people, but they shrank from the task of financing such a system. Jefferson had outlined such a plan for Virginia, but it came to nothing.

Schools were primarily sponsored by private institutions—corporate academies in the Northeast and religious institutions in the South and mid-Atlantic states. Most were aristocratic in orientation, training the nation's leaders, and few had any interest in schooling the children of the poor.

Women were likewise considered unfit for academic training, and those female schools which existed concentrated on homemaking skills and the fine arts which would make "ornaments" of the young ladies enrolled.

The New York Free School, one of those rare examples of a school for the poor, experimented for a time with the Lancastrian system, in which older students tutored the younger ones, thus stretching the scarce budget dollars.

Higher Education

Although the number of institutions of higher learning increased sharply in the early years of the nineteenth century, none was truly public. All relied upon high tuition rates for survival, so less than one in ten young men, and no women, ever attended a college or university.

The training these schools provided was very limited as well. The only professional training was in theology, and only a scattering of colleges offered brief courses of study in law or medicine. The University of Pennsylvania, for example, offered one year of medical schooling, after which a person could obtain a license to practice the healing arts. Needless to say, medical practice was quite primitive.

The Growth of Cultural Nationalism

Jeffersonian Americans tried to demonstrate their newly won independence by championing a strong sense of cultural nationalism, a feeling that their young republic represented the "final stage" of civilization, the "last great hope of mankind."

Literary Nationalism

Although most Americans had access to one or more newspapers, the market for native authors was quite limited. Publishers preferred to print works from British authors or to import books from Europe. A few Americans who were willing to pay the costs of publishing their own works found a growing number of readers.

Significant American Authors

Washington Irving was by far the best-known native writer in America. He excelled in the telling of folk tales and local color stories, and is best remembered for his portraits of Hudson River characters.

Mercy Otis Warren, the revolutionary pamphleteer, published a multivolume *History of the Revolution* in 1805.

"Parson" Mason Weems wrote the best-seller *Life of Washington* in 1806, which was short on historical accuracy but long on nationalistic hero-worship.

Educational Literature

Early schoolbooks, like Noah Webster's "Blue Backed Speller," as well as his dictionary of the "American" language, reflected the intense desire to promote patriotism and a feeling of national identity.

DEVELOPMENTS IN RELIGIOUS LIFE

The Post-Revolution Years

The Revolutionary War weakened the position of the traditional, established churches. The doctrines of the Enlightenment became very popular, and its religious expression, deism, gained a considerable following among the educated classes. Rationalism, Unitarianism, and Universalism all saw a period of popularity. Thomas Paine's exposition of the rationalist posture, *The Age of Reason*, attacked the traditional Christian values and was read widely.

The Second Great Awakening

The reaction to the trend toward rationalism, the decline in church membership, and the lack of piety was a renewal of personal, heart-felt evangelicalism. It began in 1801 at Cane Ridge, Kentucky, in the first "camp meeting."

As the revival spread, its characteristics became more uniform—an emphasis on personal salvation, an emotional response to God's grace, an individualistic faith. Women took a major part in the movement. Blacks were also heavily involved, and the individualistic emphasis created unrest among their ranks, particularly in the slave-holding South.

The revival produced strong nationalistic overtones, and the Protestant ideas of a "called nation" were to flourish later in some of the Manifest Destiny doctrines of expansionism. The social overtones of this religious renewal were to spark the great reform movements of the 1830s and 1840s.

5 JACKSONIAN DEMOCRACY AND WESTWARD EXPANSION (1824-1850)

THE JACKSONIAN DEMOCRACY, 1829-1841

While the "Age of Jackson" did not bring perfect political, social, or economic equality to all Americans, it did mark a transformation in the political life of the nation that attracted the notice of European travelers and observers. Alexis de Tocqueville observed an "equality of condition" here that existed nowhere else in the world, and an egalitarian spirit among the people that was unique. Certainly the electorate had become broadened so that all white males had access to the polls, even if blacks and women were still outside the system. It was, in that sense, the "age of the common man." As to whether Andrew Jackson and his party were actually working for the good of those common men is another matter.

THE ELECTION OF 1824

The Expansion of the Electorate

Most states had already eliminated the property qualifications for voting before the campaigns for this election began. The new Massachusetts state constitution of 1820 had led the way in this liberalization of the franchise, and most Northern states followed soon after, usually with some conservative opposition, but not violent reactions. In Rhode Island, Thomas Dorr led a bloodless "rebellion" in an effort to expand the franchise in that state, and though he was briefly imprisoned for his efforts, the incident led the conservative legislature to relent and grant the vote to non-property owners. The movement for reform was much slower in the Southern states.

Free blacks were excluded from the polls across the South, and in most of the Northern states. In those areas where they had held the franchise, they were gradually excluded from the social and economic mainstream as well as from the political arena in the early years of this period.

National elections had never attracted much enthusiasm until 1824. Legislative caucuses had made the presidential nominations and kept the ruling cliques in power by excluding the voters from the process. But this year the system failed, and the caucuses were bypassed.

The members of the electoral college were now being almost universally elected by the people, rather than by the state legislatures, as in the early days.

The Candidates

Secretary of the Treasury William H. Crawford of Georgia was the pick of the Congressional caucus. Secretary of State John Quincy Adams held the job which traditionally had been the steppingstone to the executive office. Speaker of the House Henry Clay presented the only coherent program to the voters, the "American System," which provided a high tariff on imports to finance an extensive internal improvement package. Andrew Jackson of Tennessee presented himself as a war hero from the 1812 conflict. All four candidates claimed to be Republicans.

The Election

Jackson won 43 percent of the popular vote, but the four-way split meant that he only received 38 percent of the electoral votes. Under the provisions of the Twelfth Amendment, the top three candidates were voted on by the House of Representatives. This left Henry Clay out of the running, and he threw his support to Adams. The votes had no sooner been counted, when the new president, Adams, appointed Henry Clay as his Secretary of State.

Andrew Jackson and his supporters immediately cried "foul!" and accused Clay of making a deal for his vote. The rallying cry of "corrupt bargain" became the impetus for their immediate initiation of the campaign for the 1828 election.

The Adams Administration

The new president pushed for an active federal government in areas like internal improvements and Indian affairs. These policies proved unpopular in an age of increasing sectional jealousies and conflicts over states' rights.

Adams was frustrated at every turn by his Jacksonian opposition, and his unwillingness, or inability, to compromise further antagonized his political enemies. For example, his refusal to endorse and enforce the Creek Indians' land cession to the state of Georgia was negated by their recession of their lands under pressure from Georgia's Jacksonian government.

John C. Calhoun and Nullification

In 1828, Congress passed a new tariff bill which was originally supported by Southern congressmen in order to embarrass the administration.

The finished bill, however, included higher import duties for many goods which were bought by Southern planters, so they bitterly denounced the law as the "Tariff of Abominations."

John C. Calhoun was serving as Adams' vice president, so to protest the tariff and still protect his position, he anonymously published the "South Carolina Exposition and Protest," which outlined his theory of the "concurrent majority": a federal law which was deemed harmful to the interests of an individual state could be declared null and void within that state by a convention of the people. Thus, a state holding a minority position could ignore a law enacted by the majority which they considered unconstitutional (shades of Thomas Jefferson).

The Election of 1828

Adams' supporters now called themselves the National Republicans, and Jackson's party ran as the Democratic Republicans. Andrew Jackson had aggressively campaigned since his defeat in the House in 1825.

It was a dirty campaign. Adams' people accused Jackson of adultery and of the murder of several militiamen who had been executed for desertion during the War of 1812. Jackson's followers in turn defamed Adams and his programs and accused him of extravagance with public funds.

When the votes were counted, Jackson had won 56 percent of the popular vote and swept 178 of the 261 electoral votes. John Calhoun was elected vice president.

Andrew Jackson as President

Jackson was popular with the common man. He seemed to be the prototype of the self-made Westerner: rough-hewn, violent, vindictive, with few ideas but strong convictions. He ignored his appointed cabinet officers and relied instead on the counsel of his "Kitchen Cabinet," a group of partisan supporters who had the ear and the confidence of the president.

Jackson expressed the conviction that government operations could be performed by untrained, common folk, and he threatened the dismissal of large numbers of government employees, to replace them with his supporters. Actually, he talked more about this "spoils system" than he acted on it.

He exercised his veto power more than any other president before him. A famous example was the Maysville Road, a project in Kentucky which would require a federal subsidy. Jackson opposed it because it would exist only within the boundaries of a single state.

Jacksonian Indian Policy

Jackson supported the removal of all Indian tribes to west of the Mississippi River. The Indian Removal Act in 1830 provided for federal enforcement of that process.

The portion of the Cherokee Nation which occupied northern Georgia claimed to be a sovereign political entity within the boundaries of that state. The Supreme Court supported that claim in its decision in *Worcester v. Georgia* (1832), but President Jackson refused to enforce the court's decision. The result of this policy was the Trail of Tears, the forced march, under U.S. Army escort, of thousands of Cherokees to the West. A quarter or more of the Indians, mostly women and children, perished on the journey.

THE WEBSTER-HAYNE DEBATE (1830)

Federal Land Policy

The method of disposing of government land raised sectional differences. Westerners wanted cheap lands available to the masses. Northeasterners opposed this policy because it would lure away their labor supply and drive up wages. Southerners supported the West, hoping to weaken the ties between East and West.

The Senate Confrontation

Senator Robert Hayne of South Carolina made a speech in support of cheap land and he used Calhoun's anti-tariff arguments to support his position. In his remarks, he referred to the possibility of nullification.

Daniel Webster's famous replies to this argument moved the debate from the issue of land policy to the nature of the Union and states' rights within it. Webster argued for the Union as indissoluble and sovereign over the individual states. His concluding statements have become a part of our rhetorical heritage: "It is, Sir, the people's Constitution, the people's government, made for the people, made by the people, and answerable to the people… Liberty and Union, now and for ever, one and inseparable!"

The Second Nullification Crisis

The final split between Andrew Jackson and his vice president, John C. Calhoun, came over the new Tariff of 1832, and over Mrs. Calhoun's snub of Peggy Eaton, the wife of Secretary of War John Eaton.

Mrs. Eaton was a commoner, and the aristocratic Mrs. Calhoun refused to include her on the guest lists for the Washington parties. Jackson, no doubt remembering the slights to his own dear Rachel, defended his friends Peggy and John, and demanded that they be included in the social life of the capitol.

Jackson was a defender of states' rights, but within the context of a dominant Union. When he supported the higher rates of the new tariff, Calhoun resigned his office in a huff and went home to South Carolina. There he composed an Ordinance of Nullification, which was duly approved by a special convention, and the customs officials were ordered to stop collecting the duties at the port of Charleston.

Jackson's response was immediate and decisive. He obtained a Force Bill from Congress (1833), which empowered him to use federal troops to enforce the collection of the taxes. And he suggested the possibility of hanging Calhoun. At the same time, he offered a gradual reduction in the levels of the duties. Calhoun backed down, both sides claimed victory, and the crisis was averted.

THE WAR ON THE BANK

The Controversy

The Bank of the United States had operated under the direction of Nicholas Biddle since 1823. He was a cautious man, and his conservative economic policy enforced conservatism among the state and private banks—which many bankers resented. Many of the Bank's enemies opposed it simply because it was big and powerful. Many still disputed its constitutionality.

The Election of 1832

Andrew Jackson freely voiced his antagonism toward the Bank and his intention to destroy it. During the campaign for the presidency in 1832, Henry Clay and Daniel Webster promoted a bill to recharter the Bank, even though its charter did not expire until 1836. They feared that Jackson would gain support over time and could kill the Bank as a parting shot as he retired. The Congress passed the recharter bill, but Jackson vetoed it. This left that institution a lame duck agency.

Jackson soundly defeated Henry Clay in the presidential race and he considered his victory a mandate from the people to destroy the Bank. His first move was to remove the federal government's deposits from Biddle's vaults and distribute the funds to various state and local banks, called by his critics the "pet banks." Biddle responded by tightening up on credit and calling in loans, hoping to embarrass the government and force a withdrawal by Jackson. Jackson stood firm and the result was a financial recession.

The Panic of 1837

When Biddle was forced to relent through pressure from business interests, the economy immediately rebounded. With credit policies relaxed, inflation began to pick up. The government contributed to this expansion by offering millions of acres of western land for sale to settlers at low prices.

In 1836, Jackson ordered a distribution of surplus funds and thus helped to further fuel the inflationary rise in prices. Finally, even Jackson recognized the danger, and tried to slow the spiral by issuing the Specie Circular, which required payment for public land in hard money—no more paper or credit. Depression quickly followed this move.

The business recession lasted well into the 1840s. The national economy was by this time so tied in with international business and finance that the downturn affected the entire Atlantic community, and was in turn worsened by the global impact. But most Americans blamed everyone in power, including Jackson. This disillusionment helped to initiate and intensify the reform movement which so occupied this nation in the nineteenth century's second quarter.

The Election of 1836

Jackson had hand-picked his Democratic successor, Martin Van Buren of New York. The Whigs ran three regional candidates in hopes of upsetting the Jacksonians. The Whig party had emerged from the ruins of the National Republicans and other groups who opposed Jackson's policies. The name was taken from the British Whig tradition, which simply refers to the "opposition."

Van Buren's Presidency

Van Buren, known as Old Kinderhook (O.K.), inherited all the problems and resentments generated by his mentor. He spent most of his term in office dealing with the financial chaos left by the death of the Second Bank. The best he could do was to eventually persuade Congress to establish an Independent Treasury to handle government funds. It began functioning in 1840.

THE ELECTION OF 1840

The Candidates

The Whigs nominated William Henry Harrison, "Old Tippecanoe," Western Indian fighter. Their choice for vice president was John Tyler, a former Democrat from Virginia. The Democrats put up Van Buren again, but they could not agree on a vice presidential candidate, so they ran no one.

The Campaign

This election saw the largest voter turnout to date. The campaign was a dramatic one. The Whigs stressed the depression and the opulent lifestyle of the incumbent in contrast to the simple "log cabin" origins of their candidate.

Harrison won a narrow popular victory, but swept 80 percent of the electoral vote. Unfortunately for the Whigs, President Harrison died only a month after the inauguration, having served the shortest term in presidential history.

THE MEANING OF JACKSONIAN POLITICS

The Party System

The Age of Jackson was the beginning of the modern two-party system. Popular politics, based on emotional appeal, became the accepted style. The practice of meeting in mass conventions to nominate national candidates for office was established during these Jackson years.

The Strong Executive

Jackson, more than any president before him, used his office to dominate his party and the government to such an extent that he was called "King Andrew" by his critics.

The Changing Emphasis Towards States' Rights

Andrew Jackson supported the authority of the states against the national government, but he drew the line at the concept of nullification. He advocated a strong union made up of sovereign states, and that created some dissonance in his political thinking.

The Supreme Court reflected this shift in thinking in its decision on the Charles River Bridge case in 1837, delivered by Jackson's new Chief Justice, Roger Taney. He ruled that a state could abrogate a grant of monopoly if that original grant had ceased to be in the best interests of the community. This was clearly a reversal of the Dartmouth College principal of the sanctity of contracts, if the general welfare was involved.

Party Philosophies

The Democrats opposed big government and the requirements of modernization: urbanization and industrialization. Their support came from the working classes, small merchants, and small farmers.

The Whigs promoted government participation in commercial and industrial development, the encouragement of banking and corporations, and a cautious approach to westward expansion. Their support came largely from Northern business and manufacturing interests, and from large Southern planters. Calhoun, Clay, and Webster dominated the Whig party during these early decades of the nineteenth century.

Tocqueville's *Democracy in America*

Alexis de Tocqueville, a French civil servant, traveled to this country in the early 1830s to study the American prison system, which was one of the more innovative systems in the world. His book *Democracy in America,* published in 1835, was the result of his observations, and it reflected a broad interest in the entire spectrum of the American democratic process and the society in which it had developed. His insightful commentary on the American way of life has proven to be almost prophetic in many respects, and provides the modern reader with an outsider's objective view of what this country was like in the Age of Jackson.

ANTEBELLUM CULTURE: AN AGE OF REFORM

The American people in 1840 found themselves living in an era of transition and instability. The society was changing and traditional values were being challenged. The responses to this uncertainty were two-fold: a movement toward reform and a rising desire for order and control.

We have a fairly vivid picture of what Americans were like in this period of time, from accounts by hundreds of foreign visitors who came to this country to observe our society-in-the-making. These observers noted a restless population, always on the move, compulsive joiners of associations, committed to progress, hard-working and hard-playing, driven relentlessly by a desire for wealth. They believed in and talked about equality, but the reality was that the system was increasingly creating a class society. Americans seemed to lean toward violence, and mob incidents were common.

The Reform Impulse: Major Sources of Reform

Romanticism held a belief in the innate goodness of man, thus in his improvability. This movement had its roots in turn-of-the-century Europe, and it emphasized the emotions and feelings over rationality. It appeared as a reaction against the excesses of the Enlightenment which had put strong emphasis on reason, to the exclusion of feelings.

There was also a growing need perceived for stability and control over the social order and the forces which were threatening the traditional values.

Both of these major streams of reform activity were centered in the Northeast, especially in New England.

THE FLOWERING OF LITERATURE

Northern Writers and Themes

James Fenimore Cooper's *Leatherstocking Tales* emphasized the independence of the individual, and also the importance of a stable social order.

Walt Whitman's *Leaves of Grass* likewise celebrated the importance of individualism.

Henry Wadsworth Longfellow's epic poems *Evangeline* and *Hiawatha* spoke of the value of tradition, and the impact of the past on the present.

Herman Melville's classic stories—*Typee, Billy Budd, Moby Dick*—all lashed out at the popular optimism of his day. He believed in the Puritan doctrine of original sin and his characters spoke of the mystery of life.

Historian and nationalist Francis Parkman vividly portrayed the struggle for empire between France and Britain in his *Montcalm and Wolfe*. *The Oregon Trail* described the opening frontier of the Rocky Mountains and beyond.

James Russell Lowell, poet and editor, wrote the *Bigelow Papers* and the *Commemoration Ode*, honoring Civil War casualties of Harvard.

A writer of romances and tales, Nathaniel Hawthorne is best remembered for his criticism of Puritan bigotry in *The Scarlet Letter*.

Southern Writers and Themes

Author of *The Raven, Tamerlane* and many tales of terror and darkness, Edgar Allen Poe explored the world of the spirit and the emotions.

South Carolina poet William Gilmore Simms changed from a staunch nationalist to a defender of the slave system and the uniqueness of the Southern way of life.

A Georgia storyteller, Augustus Longstreet used vulgar, earthy language and themes to paint the common folk of the South.

THE FINE ARTS

Artists and Themes

The Hudson River School was a group of landscape painters who portrayed the awesomeness of nature in America, the new world. George Catlin painted the American Indian, whom he saw as a vanishing race. John James Audubon painted the wide array of American birds and animals.

Music and the Theater

The theater was popular, but generally condemned by the church and conservatives as a "vagabond profession." The only original American contribution was the blackface minstrel show.

THE TRANSCENDENTALISTS

Major Themes

This movement had its origins in Concord, Massachusetts. The basic objective of these thinkers was to transcend the bounds of the intellect and to strive for emotional understanding, to attain unity with God, without the help of the institutional church, which they saw as reactionary and stifling to self-expression.

Major Writers

Ralph Waldo Emerson, essayist and lecturer, authored "Nature" and "Self-Reliance." Henry David Thoreau, best known for his *Walden*, repudiated the repression of society and preached civil disobedience to protest unjust laws.

THE UTOPIANS

Their Purpose

The cooperative community was their attempt to improve the life of the common man in the face of increasing impersonal industrialism.

The Utopian Communities

Brook Farm, in Massachusetts, was the earliest commune in America, and it was short-lived. Nathaniel Hawthorne was a short-term resident, and his *Blithedale Romanc*e was drawn from that experience. This work and *The Scarlet Letter* were both condemnations of the life of social isolation.

New Harmony, Indiana was founded by Robert Owen, of the New Lanark experiment in Wales, but it failed after two years. He attacked religion, marriage, and the institution of private property, so he encountered resistance from neighboring communities.

Nashoba was in the environs of Memphis, Tennessee, established by the free-thinking Englishwoman Frances Wright as a communal haven for freed slaves. Needless to say, her community experiment encountered fierce opposition from her slave-holding neighbors and it survived only briefly.

Oneida Community in New York was based on free love and open marriages.

The Shakers were directed by Mother Ann Lee. The communities were socialistic experiments which practiced celibacy, sexual equality, and social discipline. The name was given them by onlookers at their community dancing sessions.

Amana Community, in Iowa, was another socialist experiment, with a rigidly ordered society.

THE MORMONS

The Origins of the Movement

Joseph Smith received the "sacred" writings in New York state in 1830, and organized the Church of Jesus Christ of Latter Day Saints. They were not popular with their neighbors, primarily because of their practice of polygamy, and so were forced to move about, first to Missouri, then to Nauvoo, Illinois. There Smith was killed by a mob, and the community was led to the Great Salt Lake by their new leader, Brigham Young, in one of the great epic migrations to the West.

The Church

The Mormons were the most successful of the communal experiments. They established a highly organized, centrally controlled system, which provided security and order for the faithful. They held a strong belief in human perfectibility, and so were in the mainstream of romantic utopians.

REMAKING SOCIETY: ORGANIZED REFORM

Sources of Inspiration

Transcendentalism, as a branch of European Romanticism, spawned a great deal of interest in remaking society into more humane forms.

Protestant Revivalism was a powerful force for the improvement of society. Evangelist Charles G. Finney, through his "social gospel," offered salvation to all. A strong sectarian spirit split the Protestant movement into many groups; e.g., the Cumberland Presbyterians. Also evident was a strong anti-Catholic element, which was strengthened by the new waves of immigration from Catholic Ireland and southern Germany after 1830.

Temperance

The American Society for Promotion of Temperance was organized in 1826. It was strongly supported by Protestants, but just as strongly opposed by the new Catholic immigrants.

Public Schools

The motivations for the free school crusade were mixed. Some wanted to provide opportunity for all children to learn the skills for self-fulfillment and success in a republic. Others wanted to use schools as agencies for social control—to Americanize the new immigrant children as well as to Protestantize the Catholics, and to defuse the growing problems of urbanization. The stated purpose of the public schools was to instill social values: thrift, order, discipline, and democracy.

Public apathy and even opposition met the early reformers: Horace Mann, the first secretary of the Massachusetts Board of Education, and Henry Barnard, his counterpart in Connecticut and Rhode Island.

The movement picked up momentum in the 1830s, but was very spotty. Few public schools were available in the West, fewer still for Southern whites, and none at all for Southern blacks.

Higher Education

In 1839, the first state-supported school for women, Troy Female Seminary, was founded in Troy, New York. Oberlin College in Ohio was the nation's first co-educational college. The Perkins School for the Blind in Boston was the first of its kind in the United States.

Asylums for the Mentally Ill

Dorothea Dix led the fight for these institutions, advocating more humane treatment for the mentally incompetent.

Prison Reform

The purpose of the new penitentiaries was not to just punish, but to rehabilitate. The first was built in Auburn, New York, in 1821.

Feminism

The Seneca Falls, New York, meeting in 1848, and its "Declaration of Sentiments and Resolutions," was the beginning of the modern feminist movement. The Grimke sisters, Elizabeth Cady Stanton, and Harriet Beecher Stowe were active in these early days. The movement was linked with that of the abolitionists, but suffered because it was considered to be of secondary importance.

The Abolitionist Movement

The early antislavery movement was benign, advocating only the purchase and colonization of slaves. The American Colonization Society was organized in 1817 and established the colony of Liberia in 1830, but by that time the movement had reached a dead end.

In 1831, William Lloyd Garrison started his paper, *The Liberator*, and began to advocate total and immediate emancipation, thus giving new life to the movement. He founded the New England Anti-slavery Society in 1832 and the American Anti-slavery Society in 1833. Theodore Weld pursued the same goals, but advocated more gradual means.

Frederick Douglass, having escaped from his Maryland owner, became a fiery orator for the movement and published his own newspaper, the *North Star*.

There were frequent outbursts of anti-abolition violence in the 1830s, against the fanaticism of the radicals. Abolitionist editor Elijah Lovejoy was killed by a mob in Illinois.

The movement split into two wings: Garrison's radical followers, and the moderates who favored "moral suasion" and petitions to Congress. In 1840, the Liberty Party, the first national anti-slavery party, fielded a presidential candidate on the platform of "free soil," non-expansion of slavery into the new western territories.

The literary crusade continued with Harriet Beecher Stowe's *Uncle Tom's Cabin* being the most influential among the many books which presented the abolitionist message.

Educating the Public

This was the golden age of oratory. Speechmaking drew huge and patient crowds, and four-hour-long orations were not uncommon, especially at public events like the 4th of July celebrations.

Newspapers and magazines multiplied and were available to everyone.

Women more and more became the market for magazines oriented to their interests. Periodicals like *Godey's Ladies Book* reached mass circulation figures.

Colleges sprang up everywhere, the products of religious sectarianism as well as local pride, which produced "booster colleges" in every new community as population moved west. Many of these were poorly funded and managed; many did not survive longer than a few years.

Informal educational "lyceums" became popular, where the public could gather for cultural enrichment.

DIVERGING SOCIETIES—LIFE IN THE NORTH

Although the United States was a political entity, with all of the institutions of government and society shared among the peoples of the various states, there had always been a wide diversity of cultural and economic goals among the various states of the union. As the nineteenth century progressed, that diversity seemed to grow more pronounced, and the collection of states seemed to polarize more into the two sections we call the North and the South, with the expanding West becoming ever more identified with the North.

Population Growth, 1790-1860

The new West was the fastest growing area of the country, with population tending to move along parallels westward. From four million in 1790, population had reached 32 million in 1860 with one-half living in states and territories which did not even exist in Washington's administration.

Natural Increase

Birth rates began to drop after 1800, more rapidly in the cities than in the rural areas. Families who had averaged six children in 1800 only had five in 1860. Some of the reasons were economic: children were becoming liabilities rather than assets. The new "cult of domesticity" reflected a shift in family responsibilities. Father was out of the home working, and the burden of child-rearing fell more heavily on mother. Primitive birth control methods were used, and abortion was becoming common enough that several states passed laws restricting it. One result of all this was an aging population with the median age rising from 16 to 20 years.

Immigration

The influx of immigrants had slowed during the conflicts with France and England, but the flow increased between 1815 and 1837, when the economic downturn again sharply reduced their numbers. Thus the overall rise in population during these years was due more to incoming foreigners than to natural increase. Most of the newcomers were from Britain, Germany, and southern Ireland. The Germans usually fared best, since they brought more money and more skills. Discrimination was common in the job market, primarily directed against the Catholics. "Irish Need Not Apply" signs were common. However, the persistent labor shortage prevented the natives from totally excluding the foreign elements. These newcomers huddled in ethnic neighborhoods in the cities, or those who could moved west to try their hand at farming.

Growth of the Cities

In 1790 5 percent of the U.S. population lived in cities of 2,500 or more. By 1860, that figure had risen to 25 percent. This rapid urbanization created an array of problems.

Problems of Urbanization

The rapid growth in urban areas was not matched by the growth of services. Clean water, trash removal, housing, and public transportation all lagged behind, and the wealthy got them first. Bad water and poor sanitation produced poor health, and epidemics of typhoid fever, typhus, and cholera were common. Police and fire protection were usually inadequate and the development of professional forces was resisted because of the cost and the potential for political patronage and corruption.

Social Unrest

Rapid growth helped to produce a wave of violence in the cities. In New York City in 1834, the Democrats fought the Whigs with such vigor that the state militia had to be called in. New York and Philadelphia witnessed race riots in the mid-1830s, and a New York mob sacked a Catholic convent in 1834. In the 1830s, 115 major incidents of mob violence were recorded. Street crime was common in all the major cities.

THE ROLE OF MINORITIES

Women

Women were treated as minors before the law. In most states the woman's property became her husband's with marriage. Political activity was limited to the formation of associations in support of various pious causes, such as abolition, and religious and benevolent activity. Professional employment was largely limited to school teaching; that occupation became dominated by women. The women's rights movement focused on social and legal discrimination, and women like Lucretia Mott and Sojourner Truth became well-known figures on the speakers' circuit.

Blacks

By 1850, 200,000 free blacks lived in the North and West. Their lives were restricted everywhere by prejudice, and "Jim Crow" laws separated the races. Black citizens organized separate churches and fraternal orders. The African Methodist Episcopal Church, for example, had been organized in 1794 in Philadelphia, and flourished in the major Northern cities. Black Masonic and Odd Fellows lodges were likewise established. The economic security of the free blacks was constantly threatened by the newly arrived immigrants, who were willing to work at the least desirable jobs for less wages. Racial violence was a daily threat.

The Growth of Industry

By 1850, the value of industrial output had surpassed that of agricultural production. The Northeastern states led the way in this movement. Over one-half of the manufacturing establishments were located there, and most of the larger enterprises. Seventy percent of the workers who were employed in manufacturing lived in New England and the middle states, and the Northeast produced more than two-thirds of the manufactured goods.

Inventions and Technology

The level of technology used in American manufacturing already exceeded that of European industry. Eli Whitney's applications of interchangeable parts were being introduced into a wide variety of manufacturing processes. Coal was replacing water as the major source of industrial power. Machine tools were reaching a high level of sophistication. Much of this progress was due to the contributions of America's inventors. Between 1830 and 1850 the number of patents issued for industrial inventions almost doubled. Charles Goodyear's process of vulcanizing rubber was put to 500 different uses and formed the basis for an entire new industry. Elias Howe's sewing machine was to revolutionize the clothing industry. The mass production of iron, with its new techniques and uses, created a new array of businesses, of which the new railroad industry was the largest consumer. Samuel B. Morse's new electric telegraph was first used in 1840 to transmit business news and information.

The Rise of Unions

The growth of the factory system was accompanied by the growth of the corporate form of business ownership, which in turn further separated the owners from the workers. One result was the organization of worker groups to fight for benefits, an early example of which was the 10-hour day. In 1835, Boston construction craftsmen struck for seven months to win a 10-hour work day, and Paterson, New Jersey, textile workers became the first factory workers to strike for shorter hours. The federal government's introduction of the 10-hour day for federal projects, in 1840, helped to speed the acceptance of this goal. The influx of immigrants who were willing to work for low wages helped to spur the drive for unions, and in turn their numbers helped to weaken the bargaining position of union members.

The Revolution in Agriculture

Farm and industry reinforced each other and developed simultaneously. As more urban workers became dependent on food grown by others, the potential profits of farming increased. Many of the technological developments and inventions were applied to farm machinery, which in turn enabled farmers to produce more food more cheaply for the urban workers. As in industry, specialization and mechanization became the rule in agriculture, particularly on the newly opening western prairies of Illinois, Iowa, and Kansas.

Inventions and Technology

Large-scale farming on the prairies spurred critical inventions. McCormick's mechanical reaper, patented in 1834, enabled a crew of six men to harvest in one day as much wheat as 15 men could using older methods. John Deere's steel plow, patented in 1837, provided a more durable tool to break the heavy prairie sod. Jerome Case's threshing machine multiplied the bushels of grain that could be separated from the stalk in a day's time.

The New Market Economy

These developments not only made large-scale production possible, they also shifted the major emphasis from corn to small grain production, and made farming for the international market feasible, which in turn made the Western farmer dependent on economic forces over which he had no control. This dependence produced the rising demand for government provision of free land and the agricultural colleges which later were provided by the Homestead and Morrill bills during the Civil War.

In the East, the trend was toward truck farming for the nearby burgeoning urban areas, and the production of milk, fruits, and berries. Here, as in the West, there was much interest in innovative practices which could increase production efficiency and profits.

The Revolution in Commerce

Before the coming of the railroad, coastal sailing ships practically monopolized domestic trade. The canal construction boom of the 1830s had taken commercial traffic from the river systems, but by 1840 the railroad had begun to emerge as the carrier of the future. Pennsylvania and New York State contained most of the 3,328 miles of track, but the rail system was rapidly expanding across the northern tier of states, tying the industrializing East to the expanding, agricultural West.

EVERYDAY LIFE IN THE NORTH

Between 1800 and 1860 output of goods and services increased 12-fold and the purchasing power of the average worker doubled. The household labor system was breaking down, and the number of wage-earners exceeded for the first time the number of independent, self-employed Americans. Even so, everyday living was still quite primitive. Most people bathed only infrequently, washed clothes and dishes even less. Housing was primitive for most, consisting of one- or two-room cabins, heated by open fireplaces, with water carried in from springs or public faucets. For the working man, rural or urban, life was hard.

DIVERGING SOCIETIES—LIFE IN THE SOUTH

The Southern states experienced dramatic growth in the second quarter of the nineteenth century. The economy grew more productive and more prosperous, but still the section called the South was basically agrarian, with few important cities and scattered industry. The plantation system, with its cash crop production driven by the use of slave labor, remained the dominant institution. In the words of one historian, "The South grew, but it did not develop." And so the South grew more unlike the North, and it became more defensive of its distinctive way of life.

The Cotton Kingdom

The most important economic phenomenon of the early decades of the nineteenth century was the shift in population and production from the old "upper South" of Virginia and the Carolinas to the "lower South" of the newly opened Gulf states of Alabama, Mississippi, and Louisiana. This shift was the direct result of the increasing importance of cotton. In the older Atlantic states, tobacco retained its importance, but had shifted westward to the Piedmont, and was replaced in the east by food grains. The southern Atlantic coast continued to produce rice and southern Louisiana and east Texas retained their emphasis on sugar cane. But the rich black soil of the new Gulf states proved ideal for the production of short-staple cotton, especially after the invention of the "gin," and cotton became the center of the Southern economy. Nearly three million bales were being produced annually by 1850.

By 1860, cotton was to account for two-thirds of the value of U.S. exports. In the words of a Southern legislator of that era, "Cotton is King!"

Classes in the South

Although the large plantation with its white-columned mansion and its aristocratic owners is frequently seen as typical of Southern life, the truth is quite different.

The Planter Class

Owners of large farms who also owned 50 or more slaves actually formed a small minority of the Southern population. Three-fourths of Southern whites owned no slaves at all, almost half of slave-owning families owned fewer than six, and 12 percent owned 20 or more. But this minority of large slave-owners exercised political and economic power far beyond what their numbers would indicate. They became a class to which all others paid deference, and they dominated the political and social life of their region.

The Yeoman Farmers

The largest group of Southern whites were the independent small farmers who worked their land with their family, sometimes side-by-side with one or two slaves, to produce their own food, with sometimes enough surplus to sell for a little extra cash. These simple folk predominated in the upland South and constituted a sizeable element even in the lower cotton-producing states. Their major crop was corn, and indeed the South's corn crop was more valuable than its cotton, but the corn was used at home for dinner tables and for animal feed, and so ranked behind cotton as an item of export. These people were generally poorer than their Northern counterparts.

The Poor Whites

Perhaps a half-million white Southerners lived on the edge of the agrarian economy, in varying degrees of poverty. These "crackers," or "sandhillers," occupied the barren soils of the red hills or sandy bottoms, and they lived in squalor worse than the slaves. They formed a true underclass.

The Institution of Slavery

As the necessary concomitant of this expanding plantation system, the "Peculiar Institution" of black slavery fastened itself upon the Southern people, even as it isolated them from the rest of the world.

Slavery as a Labor System

The utilization of slave labor varied according to the region and the size of the growing unit. The large plantations growing cotton, sugar, or tobacco used the gang system, in which white overseers directed black drivers, who supervised large groups of workers in the fields, all performing the same operation. In the culture of rice, and on the smaller farms, slaves were assigned specific tasks, and when those tasks were finished, the worker had the remainder of the day to himself.

House servants usually were considered the most favored since they were spared the hardest physical labor and enjoyed the most intimate relationship with the owner's family. This could be considered a drawback, since they were frequently deprived of the social communion of the other slaves, enjoyed less privacy, and were more likely to suffer the direct wrath of a dissatisfied mistress.

Historians still debate whether the Southern plantation slaves fared better or worse then the Northern wage laborers. Certainly their lot was better than their counterparts in South America and the Caribbean.

Urban Slavery in the Southern City

A sizeable number of black slaves worked in the towns, serving as factory hands, domestics, artisans, and construction workers. They lived fairly independent lives and indeed a good number purchased their freedom with their savings, or quietly crossed the color line and disappeared into the general population. As the nineteenth century progressed, these people were increasingly seen as a bad model and a threat to the institution, and so urban slavery practically disappeared.

The Slave Trade

The most significant demographic shift in these decades was the movement of blacks from the Old South to the new Southwest. Traders shipped servants by the thousands to the newly opened cotton lands of the Gulf states. A prime field hand fetched an average price of $800, as high as $1,500 in peak years. Families were frequently split apart by this miserable traffic. Planters freely engaged in this trade, but assigned very low status to the traders who carried it out.

Although the importation of slaves from abroad had been outlawed by Congress since 1808, they continued to be smuggled in until the 1850s. The import ban kept the price up and encouraged the continuation of the internal trade.

Slaves' Reaction to Slavery

Blacks in bondage suffered varying degrees of repression and deprivation. The harsh slave codes were comprehensive in their restrictions on individual freedom, but they were unevenly applied, and so there was considerable variety in the severity of life. The typical slave probably received a rough but adequate diet and enjoyed crude but sufficient housing and clothing.

But the loss of freedom and the injustice of the system produced a variety of responses. Many "soldiered" on the job, and refused to work hard, or they found ways to sabotage the machinery or the crops. There was an underground system of ridicule toward the masters which was nurtured, as reflected in such oral literature as the "Brer Rabbit" tales.

Violent reaction to repression was not uncommon. Gabriel Prosser in Richmond (1800), Denmark Vesey in Charleston (1822), and Nat Turner in coastal Virginia (1831) all plotted or led uprisings of blacks against their white masters. Rumors of such uprisings kept whites in a state of constant apprehension.

The ultimate rebellion was to simply leave, and many tried to run away, some successfully. Especially from the states bordering the North, an ever increasing number of slaves fled to freedom, many with the aid of the "underground railroad" and smugglers such as Harriet Tubman, who led over 300 of her family and friends to freedom after she herself had escaped.

Most of those in bondage, however, were forced to simply adapt, and they did. A rich culture was developed within the confines of the system, and included distinctive patterns of language, music, and religion. Kinship ties were probably strengthened in the face of the onslaughts of sale and separation of family members. In the face of incredible odds, the slaves developed a distinctive network of tradition and interdependence, and they survived.

COMMERCE AND INDUSTRY

The lack of manufacturing and business development has frequently been blamed for the South's losing its bid for independence in 1861-1865. Actually, the South was highly industrialized for its day and compared favorably with most European nations in the development of manufacturing capacity. Obviously, it trailed far behind the North, so much so that when war erupted in 1861, the Northern states owned 81 percent of the factory capacity in the United States.

Manufacturing

The Southern states saw considerable development in the 1820s and 1830s in textiles and iron production and in flour milling. Richmond's Tredegar Iron Works compared favorably with the best in the North. Montgomery Bell's forges in Tennessee produced a good proportion of the ironware used in the upper South. Even so, most of the goods manufactured in these plants were for plantation consumption rather than for export, and they never exceeded two percent of the value of the cotton crop.

Commercial Activity

The businessmen of the South worked primarily with the needs and products of the plantation and the factors of New Orleans and Charleston had to serve as bankers and insurance brokers as well as the agents for the planters. An organized network of commerce never developed in the South, even though the planters themselves must be recognized as businessmen, since they operated large, complex staple-producing units.

Voices for Change

There were those who saw their native South sinking ever more into the position of dependency upon Northern bankers and businessmen, and they cried out for reform. James B.D. DeBow's *Review* advocated commercial development and agricultural diversification, but his cries largely fell on deaf ears.

Why were Southerners so wedded to the plantation system, in the face of much evidence that it was retarding development? Certainly one reason is that cotton was profitable. Over the long run, capital return on plantation agriculture was at least as good as on Northern industrial capital. Even though skilled slaves abounded and could have manned factories, they were more profitable in the field.

Since most of the planter's capital was tied up in land and slaves, there was little left to invest in commerce or manufacturing. Most important, perhaps, was the value system of the Southern people, who put great store in traditional rural ideals: chivalry, leisure, and genteel elegance. Even the yeoman farmer held these values and hoped some day to attain to the position the planters held.

LIFE IN THE SOUTHERN STATES

The Role of Women

The position of the Southern woman was similar in many ways to her Northern counterpart, but also very different. They had fewer opportunities for anything but home life. The middle-class wife was heavily involved in the operation of the farm, and served as supervisor and nurse for the servants as well as manager of the household, while the upper-class women served merely as ornaments. Education was rare and centered on the "domestic arts." High birth and death rates took their toll on childbearing women, and many men outlived several wives. The half-breed slave children were constant reminders of the planters' dalliances and produced constant tension and frustration among plantation wives.

Education

Schooling beyond literacy training was available only to the sons of the well-to-do. Academies and colleges abounded, but not for the working classes. And what public schools there were, were usually inferior and ill-supported. By 1860, one-half of all the illiterates in the United States lived in the South.

Daily Life in the South

The accounts of travelers in the Southern states provide us with vivid pictures of living conditions on the average homestead. Housing was primitive, one- or two-room cabins being the rule. Corn, sweet potatoes, and pork formed the staples of the Southern diet and health problems reflected the resulting vitamin deficiencies. Rickets and pellagra were common ailments.

Although the prevalence of violence has probably been overstated, it certainly existed and the duel remained an accepted avenue for settling differences well into the nineteenth century.

Southern Response to the Antislavery Movement

As the crusade for abolition intensified in the North, the South assumed an ever more defensive position. Biblical texts were used to justify the enslavement of an "inferior race." Scientific arguments were advanced to prove the inherent inferiority of the black African. Southern postal authorities refused to deliver any mail that contained information antagonistic to the slave system. Any kind of dissent was brutally suppressed, and the South became more and more a closed society. Literature and scholarship shriveled, and creative writers like Edgar Allen Poe and William Gilmore Simms became the rare exception.

The last serious Southern debate over the institution of slavery took place in the Virginia legislature in 1832, in the aftermath of Nat Turner's revolt. That discussion squelched any move toward emancipation. In 1836 Southern members of the U.S. House of Representatives pushed through the infamous "gag rule," which forbade any discussion on the question of slavery on the floor of the House. That rule remained in effect until 1844.

The most elaborate product of this ferment was John C. Calhoun's theory of the "concurrent majority," in which a dual presidency would insure a South independent of Northern dominance, and would forever keep majority rule at bay.

Beginning in 1837, regular conventions were held across the South to discuss ways to escape Northern economic and political hegemony.

As the decade of the 1840s opened, the two sections were becoming more and more estranged, and the channels of compromise were becoming more and more poisoned by the emotional responses to black slavery. The development which contributed most to keeping the sore festering was westward expansion.

MANIFEST DESTINY AND WESTWARD EXPANSION

Although the term "Manifest Destiny" was not actually coined until 1844, the belief that the American nation was destined to eventually expand all the way to the Pacific Ocean, and to possibly embrace Canada to the North, and Mexico to the South, had been voiced for years by many who believed that American liberty and ideals should be shared with everyone possible, by force if necessary. The rising sense of nationalism which followed the War of 1812 was fed by the rapidly expanding population, the reform impulse of the 1830s, and the desire to acquire new markets and resources for the burgeoning economy of "Young America."

Louisiana and the Far West Fur Trade

The Lewis and Clark expedition had scarcely filed its reports before a variety of adventurous entrepreneurs began to penetrate the newly acquired territory, and the lands beyond. "Mountain men" like Jim Bridges trapped the Rocky Mountain streams and the headwaters of the Missouri River system for the greatly prized beaver pelts, while explorers like Jedediah Smith mapped the vast territory which stretched from the Rockies to the Sierra Nevada range and on into California. John Jacob Astor established a fur post at the mouth of the Columbia River which he named Astoria, and challenged the British claim to the northwest. Though he was forced to sell out his establishment to the British, he lobbied Congress to pass trade restrictions against British furs, and eventually became the first American millionaire from the profits of the American Fur Company. The growing trade with the Orient in furs and other specialty goods was sharpening the desire of many businessmen for American ports on the Pacific coast.

The Oregon Country

The Adams-Onis Treaty of 1819 had set the northern boundary of Spanish possessions near the present northern border of California. The territory north of that line and west of the vague boundaries of the Louisiana Territory had been claimed over the years by Spain, England, Russia, France, and the United States. By the 1820s, all these claims had been yielded to Britain and the United States. The Hudson's Bay Company had established a fur trading station at Fort Vancouver, and claimed control south to the Columbia. The United States claimed all the way north to the 54°40' parallel. Unable to settle the dispute, they had agreed on a joint occupation of the disputed land.

In the 1830s American missionaries followed the traders and trappers to the Oregon country, and began to publicize the richness and beauty of the land, sending back official reports on their work, which were published in the new inexpensive "penny press" papers. Everyone read these reports, and the result was the "Oregon Fever" of the 1840s, as thousands of settlers trekked across the Great Plains and the Rocky Mountains to settle the new Shangri-La.

The Texas Question: 1836-1845

Texas had been a state in the Republic of Mexico since 1822, following the Mexican revolution against Spanish control. The United States had offered to buy the territory at the time, since it had renounced its claim to the area in the Adams-Onis agreement of 1819. The new Mexican government indignantly refused to sell, but immediately began to invite immigration from the north by offering land grants to Stephen Austin and other Americans. They needed to increase the population of the area and to produce revenue for the infant government. The Americans responded in great numbers, and by 1835 approximately 35,000 "gringos" were homesteading on Texas land.

The Mexican officials saw their power base eroding as the foreigners flooded in, and so they moved to tighten control, through restrictions on new immigration, and through tax increases. The Texans responded in 1836 by proclaiming independence and establishing a new republic. The ensuing war was short-lived. The Mexican dictator, Santa Anna, advanced north and annihilated the Texan garrisons at the Alamo and at Goliad. On April 23, 1836, Sam Houston defeated him at San Jacinto, and the Mexicans were forced to let Texas go its way.

Houston immediately asked the American government for recognition and annexation, but President Andrew Jackson feared the revival of the slavery issue since the new state would come in on the slave-holding side of the political balance, and he also feared war with Mexico, so he did nothing. When Van Buren followed suit, the new republic sought foreign recognition and support, which the European nations eagerly provided, hoping thereby to create a counterbalance to rising American power and influence in the Southwest. France and England both quickly concluded trade agreements with the Texans.

New Mexico and California

The district of New Mexico had, like Texas, encouraged American immigration, and for the same reasons. Soon that state was more American than Mexican. The Santa Fe Trail—from Independence, Missouri, to the town of Santa Fe—created a prosperous trade in mules, gold and silver, and furs which moved north in exchange for manufactured goods which went south. American settlements sprung up all along the route.

Though the Mexican officials in California had not encouraged it, American immigration nevertheless had been substantial. First traders and whaling crews, then merchants, arrived to set up stores and developed a brisk trade. As the decade of the 1830s passed, the number of newcomers increased. Since the Missouri Compromise had established the northern limits for slavery at the 36°30' parallel, most of this Mexican territory lay in the potential slave-holding domain, and many of the settlers had carried their bondsmen with them.

Manifest Destiny and Sectional Stress

The question of expansion was universally discussed. Although the strongest sentiment was found in the North and West, the South had its own ambitions, and they usually involved the extension of their "peculiar institution."

The Democrats generally favored the use of force, if necessary, to extend American borders. The Whigs favored more peaceful means, through diplomacy. Some Whigs, like Henry Clay, feared expansion under any circumstances, because of its potential for aggravating the slavery issue.

Clay was closest to the truth. As the decade of the 1840s opened, the questions of Texas, California, and the New Mexican territory were increasingly prominent, and the sectional tension which they produced was destined to light the fires of civil war.

TYLER, POLK, AND CONTINUED WESTWARD EXPANSION

Tyler and the Whigs

When William Henry Harrison became president, he immediately began to rely on Whig leader Henry Clay for advice and direction, just as Clay had planned and expected he would. He appointed to his cabinet those whom Clay suggested, and at Clay's behest he called a special session of Congress to vote the Whig legislative program into action. To the Whigs' dismay, Harrison died of pneumonia just one month into his term, to be replaced by Vice President John Tyler.

A states' rights Southerner and a strict constitutionalist who had been placed on the Whig ticket to draw Southern votes, Tyler rejected the entire Whig program of a national bank, high protective tariffs, and federally funded internal improvements (roads, canals, etc.). Clay stubbornly determined to push the program through anyway. In the resulting legislative confrontations, Tyler vetoed a number of Whig-sponsored bills.

The Whigs were furious. Every cabinet member but one resigned in protest. Tyler was officially expelled from the party and made the target of the first serious impeachment attempt. (It failed.) In opposition to Tyler over the next few years, the Whigs, under the leadership of Clay, transformed themselves from a loose grouping of diverse factions to a coherent political party with an elaborate organization.

One piece of important legislation that did get passed during Tyler's administration was the Preemption Act (1841), allowing settlers who had squatted on unsurveyed federal lands first chance to buy the land (up to 160 acres at low prices) once it was put on the market.

The Webster-Ashburton Treaty

The member of Tyler's cabinet who did not immediately resign in protest was Secretary of State Daniel Webster. He stayed on to negotiate the Webster-Ashburton Treaty with Great Britain.

There were at this time several causes of tension between the U.S. and Great Britain:

1. The Canada-Maine boundary in the area of the Aroostook Valley was disputed. British efforts to build a military road through the disputed area led to reaction by Maine militia in a bloodless confrontation known as the "Aroostook War" (1838).
2. The Caroline Affair (1837) involved an American ship, the *Caroline*, that had been carrying supplies to Canadian rebels. It was burned by Canadian loyalists who crossed the U.S. border in order to do so.
3. In the Creole Incident, Britain declined to return escaped slaves who had taken over a U.S. merchant ship, the *Creole*, and sailed to the British-owned Bahamas.
4. British naval vessels, patrolling the African coast to suppress slave-smuggling, sometimes stopped and searched American ships.

The Webster-Ashburton Treaty (1842) dealt with these problems in a spirit of mutual concession and forbearance:

1. Conflicting claims along the Canada-Maine boundary were compromised.
2. The British expressed regret for the destruction of the *Caroline*.
3. The British promised to avoid "officious interference" in freeing slaves in cases such as that of the *Creole*.
4. Both countries agreed to cooperate in patrolling the African coast to prevent slave-smuggling.

The Webster-Ashburton Treaty was also important in that it helped create an atmosphere of compromise and forbearance in U.S.-British relations.

After negotiating the treaty, Webster also resigned from Tyler's cabinet.

The Texas Issue

Rejected by the Whigs and without ties to the Democrats, Tyler was a politician without a party but not without ambitions. Hoping to gather a political following of his own, he sought an issue with powerful appeal and believed he had found it in the question of Texas annexation.

The Republic of Texas had gained its independence from Mexico in 1836 and, since most of its settlers had come from the U.S., immediately sought admission as a state. It was rejected because antislavery forces in Congress resented the presence of slavery in Texas and because Mexico threatened war should the U.S. annex Texas.

To excite American jealousy and thus hasten annexation, Texas President Sam Houston made much show of negotiating for closer relations with Great Britain. Southerners feared that Britain, which opposed slavery, might bring about its abolition in Texas and then use Texas as a base from which to undermine slavery in the American South. Other Americans were disturbed at the possibility of a British presence in Texas because of the obstacle it would present to what many Americans were coming to believe—and what New York journalist John L. O'Sullivan would soon express—as America's "manifest destiny to overspread the continent."

Tyler's new secretary of state, John C. Calhoun, negotiated an annexation treaty with Texas. Calhoun's identification with extreme pro-slavery forces and his insertion in the treaty of pro-slavery statements brought the treaty's rejection by the Senate (1844). Nevertheless, the Texas issue had been injected into national politics and could not be made to go away.

The Election of 1844

Democratic front-runner Martin Van Buren and Whig front-runner Henry Clay agreed privately that neither would endorse Texas annexation and that it would not become a campaign issue, but expansionists at the Democratic convention succeeded in dumping Van Buren in favor of James K. Polk. Polk, called "Young Hickory" by his supporters, was a staunch Jacksonian who opposed protective tariffs and a national bank but, most important, favored territorial expansion, including not only annexation of

Texas but also occupation of all the Oregon country (up to latitude 54° 40') hitherto jointly occupied by the U.S. and Britain. The latter claim was expressed in his campaign slogan, "Fifty-four forty or fight."

Tyler, despite his introduction of the issue that was to decide that year's presidential campaign, was unable to build a party of his own and withdrew from the race.

The Whigs nominated Clay, who continued to oppose Texas annexation but, sensing the mood of the country was against him, began to equivocate. His wavering cost him votes among those Northerners who were extremely sensitive to the issue of slavery and believed that the settlement, independence, and proposed annexation of Texas was a gigantic plot to add slave states to the Union. Some of these voters shifted to the Liberty party.

The antislavery Liberty party nominated James G. Birney. Apparently because of Clay's wavering on the Texas issue, Birney was able to take enough votes away from Clay in New York to give that state, and thus the election, to Polk.

Tyler, as a lame-duck president, made one more attempt to achieve Texas annexation before leaving office. By means of a joint resolution, which unlike a treaty required only a simple majority rather than a two-thirds vote, he was successful in getting the measure through Congress. Texas was finally admitted to the Union (1845).

Polk as President

Though a relatively unknown "dark horse" at the time of his nomination for the presidency, Polk had considerable political experience within his home state of Tennessee and was an adept politician. He turned out to be a skilful and effective president.

As a good Jacksonian, Polk favored a low, revenue-only tariff rather than a high, protective tariff. This he obtained in the Walker Tariff (1846). He also opposed a national debt and a national bank and re-established Van Buren's Independent Sub-Treasury system, which then remained in effect until 1920.

The Settlement of Oregon

A major issue in the election campaign of 1844, Oregon at this time comprised all the land bounded on the east by the Rockies, the west by the Pacific, the south by latitude 42°, and the north by the boundary of Russian held Alaska at 54° 40'. Oregon had been visited by Lewis and Clark and in later years by American fur traders and especially missionaries such as Jason Lee and Marcus Whitman. Their reports sparked interest in Oregon's favorable soil and climate. During the first half of the 1840s, some 6,000 Americans had taken the 2,000-mile, six-month journey on the Oregon Trail, from Independence, Missouri, across the plains along the Platte River, through the Rockies at South Pass, and down the Snake River to their new homesteads. Most of them settled in the Willamette Valley, south of the Columbia River.

The area had been under the joint occupation of the U.S. and Great Britain since 1818, but Democrats in the election of 1844 had called for U.S. ownership of all of Oregon. Though this stand had helped him win the election, Polk had little desire to fight the British for land he considered unsuitable for agriculture and unavailable for slavery, which he favored. This was all the more so since trouble seemed to be brewing with Mexico over territory Polk considered far more desirable.

The British, for their part, hoped to obtain the area north of the Columbia River, including the natural harbor of Puget Sound (one of only three on the Pacific coast), with its adjoining Strait of Juan de Fuca.

By the terms of the Oregon Treaty (1846), a compromise solution was reached. The current U.S.-Canada boundary east of the Rockies (49°) was extended westward to the Pacific, thus securing Puget Sound and shared use of the Strait of Juan de Fuca for the U.S. Some northern Democrats were angered and felt betrayed by Polk's failure to insist on all of Oregon, but the Senate readily accepted the treaty.

The Mormon Migration

Aside from the thousands of Americans who streamed west on the Oregon Trail during the early 1840s and the smaller number who migrated to what was then Mexican-held California, another large group of Americans moved west but to a different destination and for different reasons. These were the Mormons.

Members of a unique religion founded by Joseph Smith at Palmyra, New York in the 1820s, Mormons, often in trouble with their neighbors, had been forced to migrate to Kirtland, Ohio; Clay County, Missouri; and finally, Nauvoo, Illinois. There, on the banks of the Mississippi River, they built the largest city in the state, had their own militia, and were a political force to be reckoned with.

In 1844 Mormon dissidents published a newspaper critical of church leader Smith and his newly announced doctrine of polygamy. Smith had their printing press destroyed. Arrested by Illinois authorities, Smith and his brother were confined to a jail in Carthage, Illinois, but later killed by a crowd of hostile non-Mormons who forced their way into the jail.

The Mormons then decided to migrate to the Far West, preferably someplace outside U.S. jurisdiction. Their decision to leave was hastened by pressure from their non-Mormon neighbors, among whom anti-Mormon feeling ran high as a response to polygamy and the Mormons' monolithic social and political structure.

Under the leadership of new church leader Brigham Young some 85,000 Mormons trekked overland in 1846 to settle near the Great Salt Lake in what is now Utah (but was then owned by Mexico). Young founded the Mormon republic of Deseret and openly preached (and practiced) polygamy.

After Deseret's annexation by the U.S. as part of the Mexican Cession, Young was made territorial governor of Utah. Nevertheless, friction developed with the federal government. By 1857 public outrage over polygamy prompted then-President James Buchanan to replace Young with a non-Mormon governor. Threats of Mormon defiance led Buchanan to send 2,500 army troops to compel Mormon obedience to federal law. Young responded by calling out the Mormon militia and blocking the passes through which the army would have to advance. This standoff, known as the "Mormon War," was resolved in 1858, with the Mormons accepting the new governor and Buchanan issuing a general pardon.

The Coming of War with Mexico

For some time American interest had been growing in the far western lands then held by Mexico:

1. Since the 1820s Americans had been trading with Santa Fe and other Mexican settlements along the Rio Grande by means of the Santa Fe Trail. Though not extensive enough to be of economic importance, the trade aroused further American interest in the area.

2. Also, since the 1820s, American "mountain men," trappers who sought beaver pelts in the streams of the Rockies, had explored the mountains of the Far West, opening new trails and discovering fertile lands. They later served as guides for settlers moving west.

3. At the same time whaling ships and other American vessels had carried on a thriving trade with the Mexican settlements on the coast of California.

4. Beginning in 1841, American settlers came overland to California by means of the California Trail, a branch from the Oregon Trail that turned southwest in the Rockies and crossed Nevada along the Humbolt River. By 1846 several hundred Americans lived in California.

The steady flow of American pioneers into Mexican-held areas of the Far West led to conflicting territorial desires and was thus an underlying cause of the Mexican War. Several more immediate causes existed:

1. Mexico's ineffective government was unable to protect the lives and property of American citizens in Mexico during the country's frequent and recurring revolutions and repeatedly declined to pay American claims for damages even when such claims were supported by the findings of mutually agreed upon arbitration.
2. Mexico had not reconciled itself to the loss of Texas and considered its annexation by the U.S. a hostile act.
3. The southern boundary of Texas was disputed. Whereas first the independent Republic of Texas and now the U.S. claimed the Rio Grande as the boundary, Mexico claimed the Nueces River, 130 miles farther north, because it had been the boundary of the province of Texas when it had been part of Mexico.
4. Mexican suspicions had been aroused regarding U.S. designs on California when, in 1842, a U.S. naval force under Commodore Thomas Catsby Jones had seized the province in the mistaken belief that war had broken out between the U.S. and Mexico. When the mistake was discovered, the province was returned and apologies made.
5. Mexican politicians had so inflamed the Mexican people against the U.S. that no Mexican leader could afford to take the risk of appearing to make concessions to the U.S. for fear of being overthrown.

Though Mexico broke diplomatic relations with the U.S. immediately upon Texas' admission to the Union, there still seemed to be some hope of a peaceful settlement. In the fall of 1845 Polk sent John Slidell to Mexico City with a proposal for a peaceful settlement of the differences between the two countries. Slidell was empowered to cancel the damage claims and pay $5,000,000 for the disputed land in southern Texas. He was also authorized to offer $25,000,000 for California and $5,000,000 for other Mexican territory in the Far West. Polk was especially anxious to obtain California because he feared the British would snatch it from Mexico's extremely weak grasp.

Nothing came of these attempts at negotiation. Racked by coup and countercoup, the Mexican government refused even to receive Slidell.

Polk thereupon sent U.S. troops into the disputed territory in southern Texas. A force under General Zachary Taylor (who was nicknamed "Old Rough and Ready") took up a position just north of the Rio Grande. Eight days later, on April 5, 1846, Mexican troops attacked an American patrol. When news of the clash reached Washington, Polk sought and received from Congress a declaration of war against Mexico, on May 13, 1846.

The Mexican War

Americans were sharply divided about the war. Some favored it because they felt Mexico had provoked the war or because they felt it was the destiny of America to spread the blessings of freedom to oppressed peoples. Others opposed the war. Some, primarily Polk's political enemies the Whigs, accused the president of having provoked it. Others, generally Northern abolitionists, saw in the war the work of a vast conspiracy of Southern slaveholders greedy for more slave territory.

In planning military strategy, Polk showed genuine skill. American strategy consisted originally of a three-pronged attack: a land movement westward through New Mexico into California, a sea movement against California, and a land movement southward into Mexico.

The first prong of this three-pronged strategy, the advance through New Mexico and into California, was led by Colonel Stephen W. Kearny. Kearny's force easily secured New Mexico, entering Santa Fe on August 16, 1846, before continuing west to California. There American settlers, aided by an army exploring party under John C. Frémont, had already revolted against Mexico's weak rule in what was called the Bear Flag Revolt.

As part of the second prong of U.S. strategy, naval forces under Commodore John D. Sloat had seized Monterey and declared California to be part of the United States. Forces put ashore by Commodore Robert Stockton joined with Kearny's troops to defeat the Mexicans at the Battle of San Gabriel, January 1847, and complete the conquest of California.

The third prong of the American strategy, an advance southward into Mexico, was itself divided into two parts:

1. Troops under Colonel Alexander W. Doniphan defeated Mexicans at El Brazito (December 25-28, 1846) to take El Paso, and then proceeded southward, winning the Battle of Sacramento (February 28, 1847) to take the city of Chihuahua, capital of the Mexican province of that name.

2. The main southward thrust, however, was made by a much larger Ameri-

can army under General Zachary Taylor. After badly defeating larger Mexican forces at the battles of Palo Alto (May 7, 1846) and Resaca de la Palma (May 8, 1846), Taylor advanced into Mexico and defeated an even larger Mexican force at the Battle of Monterey (September 20-24, 1846). Then, after a substantial number of his troops had been transferred to other sectors of the war—and though badly outnumbered—he successfully withstood an attack by a Mexican force under Antonia Lopez de Santa Anna at the Battle of Buena Vista, on February 22-23, 1847.

Despite the success of all three parts of the American strategy, the Mexicans refused to negotiate. Polk therefore ordered U.S. forces under General Winfield Scott to land on the east coast of Mexico, march inland, and take Mexico City.

Scott landed at Veracruz on March 9, 1847, and by March 27 had captured the city with the loss of only 20 American lives. He advanced from there, being careful to maintain good discipline and avoid atrocities in the countryside. At Cerro Gordo (April 18, 1847), in what has been called "the most important single battle of the war," Scott outflanked and soundly defeated a superior enemy force in a seemingly impregnable position. After beating another Mexican army at Churubusco (August 19-20, 1847), Scott paused outside Mexico City to offer the Mexicans another chance to negotiate. When they declined, U.S. forces stormed the fortress of Chapultepec (September 13, 1847) and the next day entered Mexico City. Still Mexico refused to negotiate a peace and instead carried on guerilla warfare.

Negotiated peace finally came about when the State Department clerk Nicholas Trist, though his authority had been revoked and he had been ordered back to Washington two months earlier, negotiated and signed the Treaty of Guadalupe-Hidalgo (February 2, 1848), ending the Mexican War. Under the terms of the treaty, Mexico ceded to the U.S. the territory Polk had originally sought to buy, this time in exchange for a payment of $15,000,000 and the assumption of $3,250,000 in American citizens' claims against the Mexican government. This territory, the Mexican Cession, included the natural harbors at San Francisco and San Diego, thus giving the U.S. all three of the major west-coast natural harbors.

Many, including Polk, felt the treaty was far too generous. There had been talk of annexing all of Mexico or of forcing Mexico to pay an indemnity for the cost of the war. Still, Polk felt compelled to accept the treaty as it was, and the Senate subsequently ratified it.

On the home front many Americans supported the war enthusiastically and flocked to volunteer. Some criticized the war, among them Henry

David Thoreau, who, to display his protest, went to live at Walden Pond and refused to pay his taxes. Jailed for this, he wrote "Civil Disobedience." Another outspoken critic of the war was Illinois Congressman Abraham Lincoln.

Although the Mexican War increased the nation's territory by one-third, it also brought to the surface serious political issues that threatened to divide the country, particularly the question of slavery in the new territories.

6 SECTIONAL CONFLICT AND THE CAUSES OF THE CIVIL WAR (1850-1860)

THE CRISIS OF 1850 AND AMERICA AT MID-CENTURY

The Wilmot Proviso

The Mexican War had no more than started when, on August 8, 1846, freshman Democratic Congressman David Wilmot of Pennsylvania introduced his Wilmot Proviso as a proposed amendment to a war appropriations bill. It stipulated that "neither slavery nor involuntary servitude shall ever exist" in any territory to be acquired from Mexico. It was passed by the House, and though rejected by the Senate it was reintroduced again and again amid increasingly acrimonious debate.

The Wilmot Proviso aroused intense sectional feelings. Southerners, who had supported the war enthusiastically, felt they were being treated unfairly. Northerners, some of whom had been inclined to see the war as a slaveholders' plot to extend slavery, felt they saw their worst suspicions confirmed by the Southerners' furious opposition to the Wilmot Proviso. There came to be four views regarding the status of slavery in the newly acquired territories.

The Southern position was expressed by John C. Calhoun, now serving as senator from South Carolina. He argued that the territories were the property not of the U.S. federal government, but of all the states together, and therefore Congress had no right to prohibit in any territory any type of "property" (by which he meant slaves) that was legal in any of the states.

Antislavery Northerners, pointing to the Northwest Ordinance of 1787 and the Missouri Compromise of 1820 as precedents, argued that Congress had the right to make what laws it saw fit for the territories, including, if it so chose, laws prohibiting slavery.

A compromise proposal favored by President Polk and many moderate Southerners called for the extension of the 36° 30' line of the Missouri Compromise westward through the Mexican Cession to the Pacific, with territory north of the line to be closed to slavery and territory south of it open to slavery.

Another compromise solution, favored by Northern Democrats such as Lewis Cass of Michigan and Stephen A. Douglas of Illinois, was known as "squatter sovereignty" and later as "popular sovereignty." It held that the residents of each territory should be permitted to decide for themselves whether or not to allow slavery, but it was vague as to when they might exercise that right.

The Election of 1848

Both parties sought to avoid as much as possible the hot issue of slavery in the territories as they prepared for the 1848 election campaign.

The Democrats nominated Lewis Cass, and their platform endorsed his middle-of-the-road popular sovereignty position with regard to slavery in the territories.

The Whigs dodged the issue even more effectively by nominating General Zachary Taylor, whose fame in the Mexican War made him a strong candidate. Taylor knew nothing of politics, had never voted, and liked to think of himself as above politics. He took no position at all with respect to slavery in the territories.

Some antislavery Northern Whigs and Democrats, disgusted with their parties' failure to take a clear stand against the spread of slavery, deserted the party ranks to form another antislavery third party. They were known as "Conscience" Whigs (because they voted their conscience) and "Barnburner" Democrats (because they were willing to burn down the whole Democratic "barn" to get rid of the pro-slavery "rats"). Their party was called the Free Soil party, since it stood for keeping the soil of new western territories free of slavery. Its candidate was Martin Van Buren.

The election excited relatively little public interest. Taylor won a narrow victory, apparently because Van Buren took enough votes from Cass in New York and Pennsylvania to throw those states into Taylor's column.

Gold in California

The question of slavery's status in the Western territories was made more immediate when, on January 24, 1848, gold was discovered at Sutter's Mill, not far from Sacramento, California. The next year gold-seekers from the eastern U.S. and from many foreign countries swelled California's population from 14,000 to 100,000.

Once in the gold fields these "forty-niners" proved to contain some rough characters, and that fact, along with the presence, or at least the expectation, of quick and easy riches, made California a wild and lawless place. No territorial government had been organized since the U.S. had received the land as part of the Mexican Cession, and all that existed was an inadequate military government. In September 1849, having more than the requisite population and being much in need of better government, California petitioned for admission to the Union as a state.

Since few slaveholders had chosen to risk their valuable investments in human property in the turbulent atmosphere of California, the people of the area not surprisingly sought admission as a free state, touching off a serious sectional crisis back east.

The Compromise of 1850

President Zachary Taylor, though himself a Louisiana slaveholder, opposed the further spread of slavery. Hoping to sidestep the dangerously divisive issue of slavery in the territories, he encouraged California as well as the rest of the Mexican Cession to organize and seek admission directly as states, thus completely bypassing the territorial stage.

Southerners were furious. They saw the admission of California as a free state to be a backdoor implementation of the hated Wilmot Proviso they had fought so hard to turn back in Congress. They were also growing increasingly alarmed at what was becoming the minority status of their section within the country. Long outnumbered in the House of Representatives, the South would now find itself, should California be admitted as a free state, also outvoted in the Senate.

Other matters created friction between North and South. A large tract of land was disputed between Texas, a slave state, and the as yet unorganized New Mexico Territory, where slavery's future was at best uncertain. Southerners were angered by the small-scale but much talked of efforts of Northern abolitionists' "underground railroad" to aid escaped slaves in reaching permanent freedom in Canada. Northerners were disgusted by the presence of slave pens and slave markets in the nation's capital. Radical Southerners talked of secession and scheduled an all Southern convention to meet in Nashville in June 1850 to propose ways of protecting Southern interests, inside or outside the Union.

At this point the aged Henry Clay attempted to compromise the various matters of contention between North and South. He proposed an eight-part package deal that he hoped would appeal to both sides.

For the North, the package contained these aspects: California would be admitted as a free state; the land in dispute between Texas and New Mexico would go to New Mexico; New Mexico and Utah Territories (all of the Mexican Cession outside of California) would not be specifically reserved for slavery, but its status there would be decided by popular sovereignty; and, the slave trade would be abolished in the District of Columbia.

For the South, the package offered the following: A tougher Fugitive Slave Law would be enacted; the federal government would pay Texas' $10,000,000 pre-annexation debt; Congress would declare that it did not have jurisdiction over the interstate slave trade; and Congress would promise not to abolish slavery itself in the District of Columbia.

What followed the introduction of Clay's compromise proposal was eight months of heated debate, during which Clay, Calhoun, and Daniel Webster— the three great figures of Congress during the first half of the nineteenth century—made some of their greatest speeches. Clay called for compromise and "mutual forbearance." Calhoun gravely warned that the only way to save the Union was for the North to grant all the South's demands and keep quiet on the issue of slavery. Webster abandoned his previous opposition to the spread of slavery (as well as most of his popularity back in his home state of Massachusetts) to support the Compromise in an eloquent speech.

The opponents of the Compromise were many and powerful and ranged from President Taylor, who demanded admission of California without reference to slavery, to Northern extremists, such as Senator William Seward of New York, who spoke of a "higher law" than the Constitution, forbidding the spread of slavery, to Southern extremists, such as Calhoun or Senator Jefferson Davis of Mississippi. By mid-summer all seemed lost for the Compromise, and Clay left Washington exhausted and discouraged.

Then the situation changed dramatically. President Taylor died (apparently of gastroenteritis) on July 9, 1850, and was succeeded by Vice President Millard Fillmore, a quiet but efficient politician and a strong supporter of compromise. In Congress the fight for the Compromise was taken up by Senator Stephen A. Douglas of Illinois. Called the "Little Giant" for his small stature but large political skills, Douglas broke Clay's proposal into its component parts so that he could use varying coalitions to push each part through Congress. This method proved successful, and the Compromise was adopted.

The Compromise of 1850 was received with joy by most of the nation. Sectional harmony returned, for the most part, and the issue of slavery in the territories seemed to have been permanently settled. That this was an illusion became apparent within a few years.

The Election of 1852

The 1852 Democratic convention deadlocked between Cass and Douglas and so instead settled on dark horse Franklin Pierce of New Hampshire. The Whigs, true to form, chose General Winfield Scott, a war hero of no political background.

The result was an easy victory for Pierce, largely because the Whig party, badly divided along North-South lines as a result of the battle over the Compromise of 1850, was beginning to come apart. The Free Soil party's candidate, John P. Hale of New Hampshire, fared poorly, demonstrating the electorate's weariness with the slavery issue.

Pierce and "Young America"

Americans eagerly turned their attention to railroads, cotton, clipper ships, and commerce. The world seemed to be opening up to American trade and influence.

President Pierce expressed the nation's hope that a new era of sectional peace was beginning. To assure this he sought to distract the nation's attention from the slavery issue to an aggressive program of foreign economic and territorial expansion known as "Young America."

In 1853 Commodore Matthew Perry led a U.S. naval force into Tokyo Bay on a peaceful mission to open Japan—previously closed to the outside world—to American diplomacy and commerce.

By means of the Reciprocity Treaty (1854), Pierce succeeded in opening Canada to greater U.S. trade. He also sought to annex Hawaii, increase U.S. interest in Central America, and acquire territories from Mexico and Spain.

From Mexico he acquired in 1853 the Gadsden Purchase, a strip of land in what is now southern New Mexico and Arizona along the Gila River. The purpose of this purchase was to provide a good route for a trans-continental railroad across the southern part of the country.

Pierce sought to buy Cuba from Spain. When Spain declined, three of Pierce's diplomats, meeting in Ostend, Belgium, sent him the Ostend Manifesto urging military seizure of Cuba should Spain remain intransigent.

Pierce was the first "doughface" president—a northern man with southern principles—and his expansionist goals, situated as they were in the South, aroused suspicion and hostility in antislavery northerners. Pierce's administration appeared to be dominated by southerners, such as Secretary of War Jefferson Davis, and whether in seeking a southern route for a trans-continental railroad or seeking to annex potential slave territory such as Cuba, it seemed to be working for the good of the South.

Economic Growth

The chief factor in the economic transformation of America during the 1840s and 1850s was the dynamic rise of the railroads. In 1840 America had less than 3,000 miles of railroad track. By 1860 that number had risen to over 30,000 miles. Railroads pioneered big-business techniques, and by improving transportation helped create a nationwide market. They also helped link the Midwest to the Northeast rather than the South, as would have been the case had only water transportation been available.

Water transportation during the 1850s saw the heyday of the steamboat on inland rivers and the clipper ship on the high seas. The period also saw rapid and sustained industrial growth. The factory system began in the textile industry, where Elias Howe's invention of the sewing machine (1846) and Isaac Singer's improved model (1851) aided the process of mechanization, and spread to other industries.

Agriculture varied according to region. In the South, large plantations and small farms existed side by side for the most part, and both prospered enormously during the 1850s from the production of cotton. Southern leaders referred to the fiber as "King Cotton," an economic power that no one would dare fight against.

In the North the main centers of agricultural production shifted from the Middle Atlantic states to the more fertile lands of the Midwest. The main unit of agriculture was the family farm, and the main products were grain and livestock. Unlike the South where 3,500,000 slaves provided abundant labor, the North faced incentives to introduce labor-saving machines. Cyrus McCormick's mechanical reaper came into wide use, and by 1860 over 100,000 were in operation on Midwestern farms. Mechanical threshers also came into increasing use.

Decline of the Two-Party System

Meanwhile, ominous developments were taking place in politics. America's second two-party system, which had developed during the 1830s, was in the process of breaking down. The Whig party, whose dismal performance in the election of 1852 had signaled its weakness, was now in the process of complete disintegration. Partially this was the result of the issue of slavery, which tended to divide the party along North-South lines. Partially, though, it may have been the result of the nativist movement.

The nativist movement and its political party, the American, or, as it was called, the Know-Nothing party, grew out of alarm on the part of native-born Americans at the rising tide of German and Irish immigration during the late 1840s and early 1850s. The Know-Nothing party, so called because its members were told to answer "I know nothing" when asked about its secret proceedings, was anti-foreign and, since many of the foreigners were Catholic, also anti-Catholic. It surged briefly to become the country's second largest party by 1855 but faded even more quickly due to the ineptness of its leaders and the growing urgency of the slavery question, which, though ignored by the Know-Nothing party, was rapidly coming to overshadow all other issues. To some extent the Know-Nothing movement may simply have benefited from the already progressing disintegration of the Whig party, but it may also have helped to complete that disintegration.

All of this was ominous because the collapse of a viable nationwide two-party system made it much more difficult for the nation's political process to contain the explosive issue of slavery.

THE RETURN OF SECTIONAL CONFLICT

Continuing Sources of Tension

While Americans hailed the apparent sectional harmony created by the Compromise of 1850 and enjoyed the rapid economic growth of the decade that followed, two items which continued to create tension centered on the issue of slavery.

The Strengthened Fugitive Slave Law

The more important of these was a part of the Compromise itself, the strengthened federal Fugitive Slave Law. The law enraged Northerners, many of whom believed it little better than a legalization of kidnapping. Under its provisions blacks living in the North and claimed by slave catchers were denied trial by jury and many of the other protections of due process. Even more distasteful to antislavery Northerners was the provision that required all U.S. citizens to aid, when called upon, in the capture and return of alleged fugitives. So violent was Northern feeling against the law that several riots erupted as a result of attempts to enforce it. Some Northern states passed personal liberty laws in an attempt to prevent the working of the Fugitive Slave Law.

The effect of all this was to polarize the country even further. Many Northerners who had not previously taken an interest in the slavery issue now became opponents of slavery as a result of having its injustices forcibly brought home to them by the Fugitive Slave Law. Southerners saw in Northern resistance to the law further proof that the North was determined to tamper with the institution of slavery.

Publishing of *Uncle Tom's Cabin*

One Northerner who was outraged by the Fugitive Slave Law was Harriet Beecher Stowe. In response, she wrote *Uncle Tom's Cabin*, a fictional book depicting what she perceived as the evils of slavery. Furiously denounced in the South, the book became an overnight bestseller in the North, where it turned many toward active opposition to slavery. This, too, was a note of harsh discord among the seemingly harmonious sectional relations of the early 1850s.

The Kansas-Nebraska Act

All illusion of sectional peace ended abruptly when in 1854 Senator Stephen A. Douglas of Illinois introduced a bill in Congress to organize the area west of Missouri and Iowa as the territories of Kansas and Nebraska. Douglas, who apparently had no moral convictions on slavery one way or the other, hoped organizing the territories would facilitate the building of a trans-continental railroad on a central route, something that would benefit him and his Illinois constituents.

Though he sought to avoid directly addressing the touchy issue of slavery, Douglas was compelled by pressure from Southern senators such as David Atchison of Missouri to include in the bill an explicit repeal of the Missouri Compromise (which banned slavery in the areas in question) and a provision that the status of slavery in the newly organized territories be decided by popular sovereignty.

The bill was opposed by most Northern Democrats and a majority of the remaining Whigs, but with the support of the Southern-dominated Pierce administration, it was passed and signed into law.

The Republican Party

The Kansas-Nebraska Act aroused a storm of outrage in the North, where the repeal of the Missouri Compromise was seen as the breaking of a solemn agreement. It hastened the disintegration of the Whig party and divided the Democratic Party along North-South lines.

In the North, many Democrats left the party and were joined by former Whigs and Know-Nothings in the newly created Republican party. Springing to life almost overnight as a result of Northern fury at the Kansas-Nebraska Act, the Republican party included diverse elements whose sole unifying principle was the firm belief that slavery should be banned from all the nation's territories, confined to the states where it already existed, and allowed to spread no further.

Though its popularity was confined almost entirely to the North, the Republican party quickly became a major power in national politics.

Bleeding Kansas

With the status of Kansas (Nebraska was never in much doubt) to be decided by the voters there, North and South began competing to see which could send the greatest number. Northerners formed the New England Emigrant Aid Company to promote the settling of antislavery men in Kansas, and Southerners responded in kind. Despite these efforts the majority of Kansas settlers were Midwesterners who were generally opposed to the spread of slavery but were more concerned with finding good farm land than deciding the national debate over slavery in the territories.

Despite this large antislavery majority, large-scale election fraud, especially on the part of heavily armed Missouri "border ruffians" who crossed into Kansas on election day to vote their pro-slavery principles early and often, led to the creation of a virulently pro-slavery territorial government. When the presidentially appointed territorial governor protested this gross fraud, Pierce removed him from office.

Free soil Kansans responded by denouncing the pro-slavery government as illegitimate and forming their own free-soil government in an election which the pro-slavery faction boycotted. Kansas now had two rival governments, each claiming to be the only lawful one.

Both sides began blaming themselves and soon the territory was being referred to in the Northern press as "Bleeding Kansas" as full-scale guerilla war erupted. In May 1856, Missouri border ruffians sacked the free-soil town of Lawrence, killing two and destroying homes, businesses, and printing presses. Two days later a small band of antislavery zealots under the leadership of fanatical abolitionist John Brown retaliated by killing and mutilating five unarmed men and boys at a pro-slavery settlement on Pottawatomie Creek. In all, some 200 died in the months of guerilla fighting that followed.

Meanwhile, violence had spread even to Congress itself. In the same month as the Sack of Lawrence and the Pottawatomie Massacre, Senator Charles Sumner of Massachusetts made a two-day speech entitled "The

Crime Against Kansas," in which he not only denounced slavery but also made degrading personal references to aged South Carolina Senator Andrew Butler. Two days later Butler's nephew, Congressman Preston Brooks, also of South Carolina, entered the Senate chamber and, coming on Sumner from behind, beat him about the head and shoulders with a cane, leaving him bloody and unconscious.

Once again the North was outraged, while in the South, Brooks was hailed as a hero. New canes were sent to him to replace the one he had broken over Sumner's head. Denounced by Northerners, he resigned his seat and was overwhelmingly re-elected. Northerners were further incensed and bought thousands of copies of Sumner's inflammatory speech.

The Election of 1856

The election of 1856 was a three-way contest that pitted Democrats, Know-Nothings, and Republicans against each other.

The Democrats dropped Pierce and passed over Douglas to nominate James Buchanan of Pennsylvania. Though a veteran of 40 years of politics, Buchanan was a weak and vacillating man whose chief qualification for the nomination was that during the slavery squabbles of the past few years he had been out of the country as American minister to Great Britain and therefore had not been forced to take public positions on the controversial issues.

The Know-Nothings, including the remnant of the Whigs, nominated Millard Fillmore. However, choice of a Southerner for the nomination of vice president so alienated Northern Know-Nothings that many shifted their support to the Republican candidate.

The Republicans nominated John C. Frémont of California. A former officer in the army's Corps of Topographical Engineers, Frémont was known as "the Pathfinder" for his explorations in the Rockies and the Far West. The Republican platform called for high tariffs, free Western homesteads (160 acres) for settlers, and, most important, no further spread of slavery. Their slogan was "Free Soil, Free Men, and Frémont." Southerners denounced the Republican party as an abolitionist organization and threatened secession should it win the election.

Against divided opposition Buchanan won with apparent ease. However, his victory was largely based on the support of the South, since Frémont carried most of the Northern states. Had the Republicans won Pennsylvania and either Illinois or Indiana, Frémont would have been elected. In the election the Republicans demonstrated surprising strength for a political party only two years old and made clear that they, and not the Know-Nothings, would replace the moribund Whigs as the other major party along with the Democrats.

The Dred Scott Case

Meanwhile, there had been rising through the court system a case that would give the Supreme Court a chance to state its opinion on the question of slavery in the territories. The case was *Dred Scott v. Sanford* and involved a Missouri slave, Dred Scott, who had been encouraged by abolitionists to sue for his freedom on the basis that his owner, an army doctor, had taken him for a stay of several years in a free state, Illinois, and then in a free territory, Wisconsin. By 1856 the case had made its way to the Supreme Court, and by March of the following year the Court was ready to render its decision.

The justices were at first inclined to rule simply that Scott, as a slave, was not a citizen and could not sue in court. Buchanan, however, shortly before his inauguration urged the justices to go farther and attempt to settle the whole slavery issue once and for all, thus removing it from the realm of politics where it might prove embarrassing to the president.

The Court obliged. Under the domination of aging pro-Southern Chief Justice Roger B. Taney of Maryland, it attempted to read the extreme Southern position on slavery into the Constitution, ruling not only that Scott had no standing to sue in federal court, but also that temporary residence in a free state, even for several years, did not make a slave free, and that the Missouri Compromise (already a dead letter by that time) had been unconstitutional all along because Congress did not have the authority to exclude slavery from any territory whatsoever. Nor did territorial governments, which were considered to receive their power from Congress, have the right to prohibit slavery.

Far from settling the sectional controversy, the Dred Scott case only made it worse. Southerners were encouraged to take an extreme position and refuse compromise, while antislavery Northerners became more convinced than ever that there was a pro-slavery conspiracy controlling all branches of government, and expressed an unwillingness to accept the Court's dictate as final.

Buchanan and Kansas

Later in 1857 the pro-slavery government in Kansas, through largely fraudulent means, arranged for a heavily pro-slavery constitutional convention to meet at the town of Lecompton. The result was a state constitution that allowed slavery. To obtain a pretense of popular approval for this constitution, the convention provided for a referendum in which the voters were to be given a choice only to prohibit the entry of additional slaves into the state.

Disgusted free-soilers boycotted the referendum, and the result was a constitution that put no restrictions at all on slavery. Touting this Lecompton constitution, the pro-slavery territorial government petitioned Congress for admission to the Union as a slave state. Meanwhile the free-soilers drafted a constitution of their own and submitted it to Congress as the legitimate one for the prospective state of Kansas.

Eager to appease the South, which had started talking of secession again, and equally eager to suppress antislavery agitation in the North, Buchanan vigorously backed the Lecompton constitution. Douglas, appalled at this travesty of popular sovereignty, broke with the administration to oppose it. He and Buchanan became bitter political enemies, with the president determined to use all the power of the Democratic organization to crush Douglas politically.

After extremely bitter and acrimonious debate, the Senate approved the Lecompton constitution, but the House insisted that Kansans be given a chance to vote on the entire document. Southern congressmen did succeed in managing to apply pressure to the Kansas voters by adding the stipulation that should the Lecompton constitution be approved, Kansas would receive a generous grant of federal land, but should it be voted down, Kansas would remain a territory.

Nevertheless, Kansas voters, when given a chance to express themselves in a fair election, turned down the Lecompton constitution by an overwhelming margin, choosing to remain a territory rather than become a slave state. Kansas was finally admitted as a free state in 1861.

The Panic of 1857

In 1857 the country was struck by a short but severe depression. There were three basic causes for this "Panic of 1857": several years of overspeculation in railroads and lands, faulty banking practices, and an interruption in the flow of European capital into American investments as a result of the Crimean War. The North blamed the Panic on low tariffs, while the South, which had suffered much less than the industrial North, saw the Panic as proof of the superiority of the Southern economy in general and slavery in particular.

The Lincoln-Douglas Debates

The 1858 Illinois senatorial campaign produced a series of debates that got to the heart of the issues that were threatening to divide the nation. In that race incumbent Democratic Senator and front-runner for the 1860 presidential nomination Stephen A. Douglas was opposed by a Springfield lawyer, little known outside the state, by the name of Abraham Lincoln.

Though Douglas had been hailed in some free-soil circles for his opposition to the Lecompton constitution, Lincoln, in a series of seven debates that the candidates agreed to hold during the course of the campaign, stressed that Douglas's doctrine of popular sovereignty failed to recognize slavery for the moral wrong it was. Again and again Lincoln hammered home the theme that Douglas was a secret defender of slavery because he did not take a moral stand against it.

Douglas, for his part, maintained that his guiding principle was democracy, not any moral standard of right or wrong with respect to slavery. The people could, as far as he was concerned, "vote it up or vote it down." At the same time he strove to depict Lincoln as a radical and an abolitionist who believed in racial equality and race mixing.

At the debate held in Freeport, Illinois, Lincoln pressed Douglas to reconcile the principle of popular sovereignty to the Supreme Court's decision in the Dred Scott Case. How could the people "vote it up or vote it down," if, as the Supreme Court alleged, no territorial government could prohibit slavery? Douglas, in what came to be called his "Freeport Doctrine," replied that the people of any territory could exclude slavery simply by declining to pass any of the special laws that slave jurisdictions usually passed for their protection.

Douglas's answer was good enough to win him re-election to the Senate, although by the narrowest of margins, but hurt him in the coming presidential campaign. The Lecompton fight had already destroyed Douglas's hopes of uniting the Democratic party and defusing the slave issue. It had also damaged his 1860 presidential hopes by alienating the South. Now his Freeport Doctrine hardened the opposition of Southerners already angered by his anti-Lecompton stand.

For Lincoln, despite the failure to win the Senate seat, the debates were a major success, propelling him into the national spotlight and strengthening the backbone of the Republican party to resist compromise on the free-soil issue.

THE COMING OF THE CIVIL WAR

John Brown's Raid

On the night of October 16, 1859, John Brown, the Pottawatomie Creek murderer, led 18 followers in seizing the federal arsenal at Harpers Ferry, Virginia (now West Virginia), taking hostages, and endeavoring to incite a slave uprising. Brown, supported and bankrolled by several prominent Northern abolitionists (later referred to as "the Secret Six"), planned to arm local slaves and then spread his uprising across the South. His scheme was ill-conceived and had little chance of success. Quickly cornered by Virginia militia, he was eventually captured by a force of U.S. Marines under the command of Army Colonel Robert E. Lee. Ten of Brown's 18 men were killed in the fight, and Brown himself was wounded.

Charged under Virginia law with treason and various other crimes, Brown was quickly tried, convicted, sentenced, and, on December 2, 1859, hanged. Throughout his trial and at his execution, he conducted himself with fanatical resolution, making eloquent and grandiose statements that convinced many Northerners that he was a martyr rather than a criminal. His death was marked in the North by signs of public mourning.

Though responsible Northerners such as Lincoln denounced Brown's raid as a criminal act that deserved to be punished by death, many Southerners became convinced that the entire Northern public approved of Brown's action and that the only safety for the South lay in a separate Southern confederacy. This was all the more so because Brown, in threatening to create a slave revolt, had touched on the foremost fear of white Southerners.

Hinton Rowan Helper's Book

The second greatest fear of Southern slaveholders was that Southern whites who did not own slaves, by far the majority of the Southern population, would come to see the continuation of slavery as not being in their best interest. This fear was touched on by a book, *The Impending Crisis in the South*, by a North Carolinian named Hinton Rowan Helper. In it Helper argued that slavery was economically harmful to the South and that it enriched the large planter at the expense of the yeoman farmer.

Southerners were enraged, and more so when the Republicans reissued a condensed version of the book as campaign literature. When the new House of Representatives met in December 1859 for the first time since the 1858 elections, angry Southerners determined that no Republican who had endorsed the book should be elected speaker.

The Republicans were the most numerous party in the House although they did not hold a majority. Their candidate for speaker, John Sherman of Ohio, had endorsed Helper's book. A rancorous two-month battle ensued in which the House was unable even to organize itself, let alone transact any business. Secession was talked of openly by Southerners, and as tensions rose congressmen came to the sessions carrying revolvers and Bowie knives. The matter was finally resolved by the withdrawal of Sherman and the election of a moderate Republican as speaker. Tensions remained fairly high.

The Election of 1860

In this mood the country approached the election of 1860, a campaign that eventually became a four-man contest.

The Democrats met in Charleston, South Carolina. Douglas had a majority of the delegates, but at that time a party rule required a two-thirds vote for the nomination. Douglas, faced with the bitter opposition of the Southerners and the Buchanan faction, could not gain this majority. Finally, the convention split up when Southern "fire-eaters" led by William L. Yancey walked out in protest of the convention's refusal to include in the platform a plank demanding federal protection of slavery in all the territories.

A second Democratic convention several weeks later in Baltimore also failed to reach a consensus, and the sundered halves of the party nominated separate candidates. The Southern wing of the party nominated Buchanan's vice president, John C. Breckinridge of Kentucky, on a platform calling for a federal slave code in all the territories. What was left of the national Democratic party nominated Douglas on a platform of popular sovereignty.

A third presidential candidate was added by the Constitutional Union party, a collection of aging former Whigs and Know-Nothings from the southern and border states as well as a handful of moderate Southern Democrats. It nominated John Bell of Tennessee on a platform that sidestepped the issues and called simply for the Constitution, the Union, and the enforcement of the laws.

The Republicans met in Chicago, confident of victory and determined to do nothing to jeopardize their favorable position. Accordingly, they rejected as too radical front-running New York Senator William H. Seward in favor of Illinois favorite son Abraham Lincoln. The platform was designed to have something for all Northerners, including the provisions of the 1856 Republican platform as well as a call for federal support of a trans-continental railroad. Once again, its centerpiece was a call for the containment of slavery.

Douglas, believing only his victory could reconcile North and South, became the first U.S. presidential candidate to make a vigorous nationwide speaking tour. In his speeches he urged support for the Union and opposition to any extremist candidates that might endanger its survival, by which he meant Lincoln and Breckinridge.

On election day the voting went along strictly sectional lines. Breckinridge carried the Deep South; Bell, the border states; and Lincoln, the North. Douglas, although second in popular votes, carried only a single state and part of another. Lincoln led in popular votes, and though he was short of a majority in that category, he did have the needed majority in electoral votes and was elected.

The Secession Crisis

Lincoln had declared he had no intention of disturbing slavery where it already existed, but many Southerners thought otherwise. They also feared further raids of the sort John Brown had attempted and felt their pride injured by the election of a president for whom Southerners had not voted.

On December 20, 1860, South Carolina, by vote of a special convention made up of delegates elected by the people of the state, declared itself out of the Union. By February 1, 1861, six more states (Alabama, Georgia, Florida, Mississippi, Louisiana, and Texas) had followed suit.

Representatives of the seven seceded states met in Montgomery, Alabama, in February 1861 and declared themselves to be the Confederate States of America. They elected former Secretary of War and U.S. Senator Jefferson Davis of Mississippi as president and Alexander Stephens of Georgia as vice president. They also adopted a constitution for the Confederate States which, while similar to the U.S. Constitution in many ways, contained several important differences:

1. Slavery was specifically recognized, and the right to move slaves from one state to another was guaranteed.
2. Protective tariffs were prohibited.
3. The president was to serve for a single non-renewable six-year term.
4. The president was given the right to veto individual items within an appropriations bill.
5. State sovereignty was specifically recognized.

In the North reaction was mixed. Some, such as prominent Republican Horace Greeley of the *New York Tribune*, counseled, "Let erring sisters go in peace." President Buchanan, now a lame duck, seemed to be of this mind, since he declared secession to be unconstitutional but at the same time stated his belief that it was unconstitutional for the federal government to do anything to stop states from seceding. Taking his own advice, he did nothing.

Others, led by Senator John J. Crittenden of Kentucky, strove for a compromise that would preserve the Union. Throughout the period of several weeks as the Southern states one by one declared their secession, Crittenden worked desperately with a congressional compromise committee in hopes of working out some form of agreement.

The compromise proposals centered on the passage of a constitutional amendment forever prohibiting federal meddling with slavery in the states where it existed as well as the extension of the Missouri Compromise line (36° 30') to the Pacific, with slavery specifically protected in all the territories south of it.

Some Congressional Republicans were inclined to accept this compromise, but President-elect Lincoln urged them to stand firm for no further spread of slavery. Southerners would consider no compromise that did not provide for the spread of slavery, and talks broke down.

7 THE CIVIL WAR AND RECONSTRUCTION (1860-1877)

HOSTILITIES BEGIN

Fort Sumter

Lincoln did his best to avoid angering the slave states that had not yet seceded. In his inaugural address he urged Southerners to reconsider their actions but warned that the Union was perpetual, that states could not secede, and that he would therefore hold the federal forts and installations in the South.

Of these only two remained in federal hands: Fort Pickens, off Pensacola, Florida; and Fort Sumter, in the harbor of Charleston, South Carolina. Lincoln soon received word from Major Robert Anderson, commanding the small garrison at Sumter, that supplies were running low. Desiring to send in the needed supplies, Lincoln informed the governor of South Carolina of his intention but promised that no attempt would be made to send arms, ammunition, or reinforcements unless Southerners initiated hostilities.

Not satisfied, Southerners determined to take the fort. Confederate General P. G. T. Beauregard, acting on orders from President Davis, demanded Anderson's surrender. Anderson said he would if not resupplied. Knowing supplies were on the way, the Confederates opened fire at 4:30 a.m. on April 12, 1861. The next day the fort surrendered.

The day following Sumter's surrender Lincoln declared the existence of an insurrection and called for the states to provide 75,000 volunteers to put it down. In response to this, Virginia, Tennessee, North Carolina, and Arkansas declared their secession.

The remaining slave states, Delaware, Kentucky, Maryland, and Missouri, wavered to varying degrees but stayed with the Union. Delaware, which had few slaves, gave little serious consideration to the idea of secession. Kentucky declared itself neutral and then sided with the North when the South failed to respect this neutrality. Maryland's incipient secession movement was crushed by Lincoln's timely imposition of martial law. Missouri was saved for the Union by the quick and decisive use of federal troops as well as the sizeable population of pro-Union, antislavery German immigrants living in St. Louis.

Relative Strengths at the Outset

An assessment of available assets at the beginning of the war would not have looked favorable for the South.

The North enjoyed at least five major advantages over the South. It had overwhelming preponderance in wealth and thus was better able to finance the enormous expense of the war. The North was also vastly superior in industry and thus capable of producing the needed war materials; while the South, as a primarily agricultural society, often had to improvise or do without.

The North furthermore had an advantage of almost three to one in manpower; and over one-third of the South's population was composed of slaves, whom Southerners would not use as soldiers. Unlike the South, the North received large numbers of immigrants during the war. The North retained control of the U.S. Navy, and thus would command the sea and be able, by blockading, to cut the South off from outside sources of supply.

Finally, the North enjoyed a much superior system of railroads, while the South's relatively sparse railroad network was composed of a number of smaller railroads, often not interconnected and with varying gauges of track, more useful for carrying cotton from the interior to port cities than for moving large amounts of war supplies or troops around the country.

The South did, however, have several advantages of its own. It was vast in size, and this would make it difficult to conquer; it did not need to conquer the North, but only resist being conquered itself. Its troops would also be fighting on their own ground, a fact that would give them the advantage of familiarity with the terrain as well as the added motivation of defending their homes and families. Its armies would often have the opportunity of fighting on the defensive, a major advantage in the warfare of that day.

At the outset of the war the South drew a number of highly qualified senior officers, such as Robert E. Lee, Joseph E. Johnston, and Albert Sidney Johnston, from the U.S. Army. By contrast, the Union command structure was already set when the war began, with the aged Winfield Scott, of Mexican War fame, at the top. It took young and talented officers, such as Ulysses S. Grant and William T. Sherman, time to work up to high rank. Meanwhile, Union armies were often led by inferior commanders as Lincoln experimented in search of good generals.

At first glance, the South might also have seemed to have an advantage in its president. Jefferson Davis had extensive military and political experience and was acquainted with the nation's top military men and, presumably, with their relative abilities. On the other hand, Lincoln had been, up until his election to the presidency, less successful politically and had virtually no military experience. In fact, Lincoln was much superior to Davis as a war leader, showing firmness, flexibility, mental toughness, great political skill, and, eventually, an excellent grasp of strategy.

Opposing Strategies

Both sides were full of enthusiasm for the war. In the North the battle cry was "On to Richmond," the new Confederate capital established after the secession of Virginia. In the South it was "On to Washington." Yielding to popular demand, Lincoln ordered General Irvin McDowell to advance on Richmond with his army. At a creek called Bull Run near the town of Manassas Junction, Virginia, just southwest of Washington, D.C., they met a Confederate force under generals P.G.T. Beauregard and Joseph E. Johnston, July 21, 1861. In the First Battle of Bull Run (called First Manassas in the South) the Union army was forced to retreat in confusion back to Washington.

Bull Run demonstrated the unpreparedness and inexperience of both sides. It also demonstrated that the war would be long and hard, and, particularly in the North, that greater efforts would be required. Lincoln would need an overall strategy. To supply this, Winfield Scott suggested his Anaconda Plan to squeeze the life out of the Confederacy, which included a naval blockade to shut out supplies from Europe, a campaign to take the Mississippi River, splitting the South in two, and the taking of a few strategic points and waiting for pro-Union sentiment in the South to overthrow the secessionists. Lincoln liked the first two points of Scott's strategy but considered the third point unrealistic.

He ordered a naval blockade, an overwhelming task considering the South's long coastline. Yet under Secretary of the Navy Gideon Welles, the Navy was expanded enormously and the blockade, derided in the early days as a "paper blockade," became increasingly effective.

Lincoln also ordered a campaign to take the Mississippi River. A major step in this direction was taken when naval forces under Captain David G. Farragut took New Orleans in April 1862.

Rather than waiting for pro-Unionists in the South to gain control, Lincoln hoped to raise huge armies and apply overwhelming pressure from all sides at once until the Confederacy collapsed. The strategy was good; the problem was finding good generals to carry it out.

THE UNION PRESERVED

Lincoln Tries McClellan

To replace the discredited McDowell, Lincoln chose General George B. McClellan. McClellan was a good trainer and organizer and was loved by the troops, but was unable to use effectively the powerful army (now called the Army of the Potomac) he had built up. Despite much prodding from Lincoln, McClellan hesitated to advance, badly overestimating his enemy's numbers.

Finally, in the spring of 1862, he took the Army of the Potomac by water down Chesapeake Bay to land between the York and James Rivers in Virginia. His plan was to advance up the peninsula formed by these rivers directly to Richmond.

The operations that followed were known as the Peninsula Campaign. McClellan advanced slowly and cautiously toward Richmond, while his equally cautious Confederate opponent, General Joseph E. Johnston, drew back to the outskirts of the city before turning to fight at the Battle of Seven Pines. In this inconclusive battle, Johnston was wounded. To replace him Jefferson Davis appointed his military advisor, General Robert E. Lee.

Lee summoned General Thomas J. "Stonewall" Jackson and his army from the Shenandoah Valley (where Jackson had just finished defeating several superior federal forces, causing consternation in Washington) and with the combined forces attacked McClellan.

After two days of bloody but inconclusive fighting, McClellan lost his nerve and began to retreat. In the remainder of what came to be called the Battle of the Seven Days, Lee continued to attack McClellan, forcing him back to his base, though at great cost in lives. McClellan's army was loaded back onto its ships and taken back to Washington.

Before McClellan's army could reach Washington and be completely deployed in northern Virginia, Lee saw and took an opportunity to thrash Union General John Pope, who was operating in northern Virginia with another Northern army, at the Second Battle of Bull Run.

Union Victories in the West

In the western area of the war's operations, essentially everything west of the Appalachian Mountains, matters were proceeding in a much different fashion. The Northern commanders there, Henry W. Halleck and Don Carlos Buell, were no more enterprising than McClellan, but Halleck's subordinate, Ulysses S. Grant, definitely was.

Seeking and obtaining permission from Halleck, Grant mounted a combined operation—army troops and navy gunboats—against two vital Confederate strong-holds, Forts Henry and Donelson, which guarded the Tennessee and Cumberland Rivers in northern Tennessee, and which were the weak point of the thin-stretched Confederate line under General Albert Sidney Johnston. When Grant captured the forts in February 1862, Johnston was forced to retreat to Corinth in northern Mississippi.

Grant pursued but, ordered by Halleck to wait until all was in readiness before proceeding, Grant halted his troops at Pittsburg Landing on the Tennessee River, 25 miles north of Corinth. On April 6, 1862, Johnston, who had received reinforcements and been joined by General P. G. T. Beauregard, surprised Grant there, but in the two-day battle that followed (Shiloh) failed to defeat him. Johnston himself was among the many killed in what was, up to this point, the bloodiest battle in American history.

Grant was severely criticized in the North for having been taken by surprise. Yet with other Union victories and Farragut's capture of New Orleans, the North had taken all of the Mississippi River except for a 110-mile stretch between the Confederate fortresses of Vicksburg, Mississippi, and Port Hudson, Louisiana.

The Success of Northern Diplomacy

Many Southerners believed Britain and France would rejoice in seeing a divided and weakened America. The two countries would likewise be driven by the need of their factories for cotton and thus intervene on the Confederacy's behalf. So strongly was this view held that during the early days of the war, when the Union blockade was still too weak to be very effective, the Confederate government itself prohibited the export of cotton in order to hasten British and French intervention.

This view proved mistaken for several reasons. Britain already had on hand large stocks of cotton from the bumper crops of the years immediately prior to the war. During the war the British were successful in finding alternative sources of cotton, importing the fiber from India and Egypt. British leaders may also have weighed their country's need to import wheat from the northern United States against its desire for cotton from the Southern states. Finally, British public opinion opposed slavery.

Skillful Northern diplomacy had a great impact. In this, Lincoln had the extremely able assistance of Secretary of State William Seward, who took a hard line in warning Europeans not to interfere, and of Ambassador to Great Britain Charles Francis Adams. Britain therefore remained neutral and other European countries, France in particular, followed its lead.

One incident nevertheless came close to fulfilling Southern hopes for British intervention. In November 1861, Captain Charles Wilkes of the U.S.S. *San Jacinto* stopped the British mail and passenger ship *Trent* and forcibly removed Confederate emissaries James M. Mason and John Slidell. News of Wilkes' action brought great rejoicing in the North but outrage in Great Britain, where it was viewed as a violation of Britain's rights on the high seas. Lincoln and Seward, faced with British threats of war at a time the North could ill afford it, wisely chose to release the envoys and smooth things over with Britain.

The Confederacy was able to obtain some loans and to purchase small amounts of arms, ammunition, and even commerce-raiding ships such as the highly successful C.S.S. *Alabama*. However, Union naval superiority kept such supplies to a minimum.

The War at Sea

The Confederacy's major bid to challenge the Union's naval superiority was based on the employment of a technological innovation, the ironclad ship. The first and most successful of the Confederate ironclads was the C.S.S. *Virginia*. Built on the hull of the abandoned Union frigate *Merrimac*, the *Virginia* was protected from cannon fire by iron plates bolted over her sloping wooden sides. In May 1862 she destroyed two wooden warships of the Union naval force at Hampton Roads, Virginia, and was seriously threatening to destroy the rest of the squadron before being met and fought to a standstill by the Union ironclad U. S. S. *Monitor*.

The Home Front

The war on the home front dealt with the problems of maintaining public morale, supplying the armies of the field, and resolving constitutional questions regarding authority and the ability of the respective governments to deal with crises.

For the general purpose of maintaining public morale but also as items many Republicans had advocated even before the war, Congress in 1862 passed two highly important acts dealing with domestic affairs in the North.

The Homestead Act granted 160 acres of government land free of charge to any person who would farm it for at least five years. Much of the West was eventually settled under the provisions of this act. The Morrill Land Grant Act offered large amounts of the federal government's land to states that would establish "agricultural and mechanical" colleges. Many of the nation's large state universities were founded in later years under the provisions of this act.

Keeping the people relatively satisfied was made more difficult by the necessity, apparent by 1863, of imposing conscription in order to obtain adequate manpower for the huge armies that would be needed to crush the South. Especially hated by many working class Northerners was the provision of the conscription act that allowed a drafted individual to avoid service by hiring a substitute or paying $300. Resistance to the draft led to riots in New York City in which hundreds were killed.

The Confederacy, with its much smaller manpower pool on which to draw, had instituted conscription in 1862. Here, too, it did not always meet with cooperation. Some Southern governors objected to it on doctrinaire states' rights grounds, doing all they could to obstruct its operation. A provision of the Southern conscription act allowing one man to stay home as overseer for every 20 slaves led the non-slaveholding whites who made up most of the Southern population to grumble that it was a "rich man's war and a poor man's fight." Draft-dodging and desertion became epidemic in the South by the latter part of the war.

Scarcity of food and other consumer goods in the South as well as high prices led to further desertion as soldiers left the ranks to care for their starving families. Discontent also manifested itself in the form of a "bread riot" in Richmond.

Supplying the war placed an enormous strain on both societies, but one the North was better able to bear.

To finance the Northern side of the war, high tariffs and an income tax (the nation's first) were resorted to, yet even more money was needed. The Treasury Department, under Secretary of the Treasury Salmon P. Chase, issued "greenbacks," an unbacked fiat currency that nevertheless fared better than the Southern paper money because of greater confidence in Northern victory. To facilitate the financing of the war through credit expansion, the National Banking Act was passed in 1863.

The South, with its scant financial resources, found it all but impossible to cope with the expense of war. Excise and income taxes were levied and some small loans were obtained in Europe, yet the Southern Congress still felt compelled to issue paper money in such quantities that it became virtually worthless. That, and the scarcity of almost everything created by the war and its disruption of the economy, led to skyrocketing prices.

The Confederate government responded to the inflation it created by imposing taxes-in-kind and impressment, the seizing of produce, livestock, etc., by Confederate agents in return for payment according to an artificially set schedule of prices. Since payment was in worthless inflated currency, this amounted to confiscation and soon resulted in goods of all sorts becoming even scarcer than otherwise when a Confederate impressment agent was known to be in the neighborhood.

Questions of constitutional authority to deal with crises plagued both presidents.

To deal with the emergency of secession, Lincoln stretched the presidential powers to the limit, or perhaps beyond the limit, of the Constitution. To quell the threat of secession in Maryland, Lincoln suspended the writ of *habeas corpus* and imprisoned numerous suspected secessionists without charges or trial, ignoring the insistence of pro-Southern Chief Justice Roger B. Taney in *ex Parte Merryman* (1861) that such action was unconstitutional.

"Copperheads," Northerners such as Clement L. Vallandigham of Ohio who opposed the war, denounced Lincoln as a tyrant and would-be dictator but remained a minority. Though occasionally subject to arrest and/or deportation for their activities, they were generally allowed a considerable degree of latitude.

Davis encountered obstructionism from various state governors, the Confederate Congress, and even his own vice president, who denounced him as a tyrant for assuming too much power and failing to respect states' rights. Hampered by such attitudes, the Confederate government proved less effective than it might have been.

The Emancipation Proclamation

By mid-1862, Lincoln, under pressure from radical elements of his own party and hoping to create a favorable impression on foreign public opinion, determined to issue the Emancipation Proclamation, declaring free all slaves in areas still in rebellion as of January 1, 1863. In order that this not appear an act of panic and desperation in view of the string of defeats the North had recently suffered on the battlefields of Virginia, Lincoln, at Seward's recommendation, waited to announce the proclamation until the North should win some sort of victory. This was provided by the Battle of Antietam, September 17, 1863.

Though the Radical Republicans, pre-war abolitionists for the most part, had for some time been urging Lincoln to take such a step, Northern public opinion as a whole was less enthusiastic, as the Republicans suffered major losses in the November 1862 congressional elections.

The Turning Point in the East

After his victory of the Second Battle of Bull Run, Lee moved north and crossed into Maryland, where he hoped to win a decisive victory that would force the North to recognize Southern independence.

He was confronted by the Army of the Potomac, once again under the command of General George B. McClellan. Through a stroke of good fortune early in the campaign, detailed plans for Lee's entire audacious operation fell into McClellan's hands, but the Northern general, by extreme caution and slowness, threw away this incomparable chance to annihilate Lee and win—or at least shorten—the war.

The armies finally met along Antietam Creek, just east of the town of Sharpsburg in western Maryland. In a bloody but inconclusive day-long battle, known as Antietam in the North but as Sharpsburg in the South, McClellan's timidity led him to miss another excellent chance to destroy Lee's cornered and badly outnumbered army. After the battle Lee retreated to Virginia, and Lincoln, besides issuing the Emancipation Proclamation, removed McClellan from command.

To replace him, Lincoln chose General Ambrose E. Burnside, who promptly demonstrated his unfitness for command by blundering into a lopsided defeat at Fredericksburg, Virginia, December 13, 1862.

Lincoln then replaced Burnside with General Joseph "Fighting Joe" Hooker. Handsome and hard-drinking, Hooker had bragged of what he would do to "Bobby Lee" when he got at him; but when he took his army south, "Fighting Joe" quickly lost his nerve. He was out-generaled and soundly beaten at the Battle of Chancellorsville, May 5-6, 1863. At this battle the brilliant Southern general "Stonewall" Jackson was accidentally shot by his own men and died several days later.

Lee, anxious to shift the scene of the fighting out of his beloved Virginia, sought and received permission from President Davis to invade Pennsylvania. He was pursued by the Army of the Potomac, now under the command of General George G. Meade, whom Lincoln had selected to replace the discredited Hooker. They met at Gettysburg; and in a three-day battle (July 1-3, 1863) that was the bloodiest of the entire war, Lee, who sorely missed the services of Jackson and whose cavalry leader, the normally reliable J. E. B. Stuart, failed to provide him with timely reconnaissance, was defeated. However, he was allowed by the victorious Meade to retreat to Virginia with his army intact if battered, much to Lincoln's disgust. Still, Lee would never again have the strength to mount such an invasion.

Lincoln Finds Grant

Meanwhile Grant undertook to take Vicksburg, one of the two last Confederate bastions on the Mississippi River. In a brilliant campaign he bottled up the Confederate forces of General John C. Pemberton inside the city and placed them under siege. After six weeks of siege, the defenders surrendered on July 4, 1863. Five days later Port Hudson surrendered as well, giving the Union complete control of the Mississippi.

After Union forces under General William Rosecrans suffered an embarrassing defeat at the Battle of Chickamauga in northwestern Georgia, September 19-20, 1863, Lincoln named Grant overall commander of Union forces in the West.

Grant went to Chattanooga, Tennessee, where Confederate forces under General Braxton Bragg were virtually besieging Rosecrans, and immediately took control of the situation. Gathering Union forces from other portions of the western theater and combining them with reinforcements from the East, Grant won a resounding victory at the Battle of Chattanooga (November 23-25, 1863), in which federal forces stormed seemingly impregnable Confederate positions on Lookout Mountain and Missionary Ridge. This victory put Union forces in position for a drive into Georgia, which began the following spring.

Early in 1864 Lincoln made Grant commander of all Union armies. Grant devised a coordinated plan for constant pressure on the Confederacy. General William T. Sherman would lead a drive toward Atlanta, Georgia, with the goal of destroying the Confederate army under General Joseph E. Johnston (who had replaced Bragg). Grant himself would accompany Meade and the Army of the Potomac in advancing toward Richmond with the goal of destroying Lee's Confederate army.

In a series of bloody battles (the Wilderness, Spotsylvania, Cold Harbor) in May and June of 1864, Grant drove Lee to the outskirts of Richmond. Still unable to take the city or get Lee at a disadvantage, Grant circled around to try to take both by way of the back door, attacking Petersburg, Virginia, an important railroad junction just south of Richmond and the key to that city's—and Lee's—supply lines. Once again turned back by entrenched Confederate troops Grant settled down to besiege Petersburg and Richmond in a stalemate that lasted some nine months.

Sherman had been advancing simultaneously in Georgia. He maneuvered Johnston back to the outskirts of Atlanta with relatively little fighting. At that point Confederate President Davis lost patience with Johnston and replaced him with the aggressive General John B. Hood. Hood and Sherman fought three fierce but inconclusive battles around Atlanta in late July, then settled down to a siege of their own during the month of August.

The Election of 1864 and Northern Victory

In the North discontentment grew with the long casualty lists and seeming lack of results. Yet the South could stand the grinding war even less. By late 1864 Jefferson Davis had reached the point of calling for the use of blacks in the Confederate armies, though the war ended before black troops could see action for the Confederacy. The South's best hope was that Northern war-weariness would bring the defeat of Lincoln and the victory of a peace candidate in the election of 1864.

Lincoln ran on the ticket of the National Union party, essentially the Republican party with loyal or "War" Democrats. His vice-presidential candidate was Andrew Johnson, a loyal Democrat from Tennessee.

The Democratic party's presidential candidate was General George B. McClellan, who, with some misgivings, ran on a platform labeling the war a failure and calling for a negotiated peace settlement even it that meant Southern independence.

The outlook was bleak for a time, and even Lincoln himself believed that he would be defeated. Then in September 1864 word came that Sherman had taken Atlanta. The capture of this vital Southern rail and manufacturing center brought an enormous boost to northern morale. Along with other Northern victories that summer and fall, it insured a resounding election victory for Lincoln and the continuation of the war to complete victory for the North.

To speed that victory Sherman marched through Georgia from Atlanta to the sea, arriving at Savannah in December 1864 and turning north into the Carolinas, leaving behind a 60-mile-wide swath of destruction. His goal was to impress on Southerners that continuation of the war could only mean ruin for all of them. He and Grant planned that his army should press on through the Carolinas and into Virginia to join Grant in finishing off Lee.

Before Sherman's troops could arrive, Lee abandoned Richmond (April 3,1865) and attempted to escape with what was left of his army. Pursued by Grant, he was cornered and forced to surrender at Appomattox, Virginia, April 9, 1865. Other Confederate armies still holding out in various parts of the South surrendered over the next few weeks.

Lincoln did not live to receive news of the final surrenders. On April 14, 1865, he was shot in the back of the head while watching a play in Ford's Theater in Washington. His assassin, pro-Southern actor John Wilkes Booth, injured his ankle in making his escape. Hunted down by Union cavalry several days later, he died of a gunshot wound, apparently self-inflicted. Several other individuals were tried, convicted, and hanged by a military tribunal for participating with Booth in a conspiracy to assassinate not only Lincoln, but also Vice President Johnson and Secretary of State Seward.

THE ORDEAL OF RECONSTRUCTION

Lincoln's Plan of Reconstruction

Reconstruction began well before fighting of the Civil War came to an end. It brought a time of difficult adjustments in the South.

Among those who faced such adjustments were the recently freed slaves, who flocked into Union lines or followed advancing Union armies or whose plantations were part of the growing area of the South that came under Union military control. Some slaves had left their plantations, and thus their only means of livelihood, in order to obtain freedom within Union lines. Many felt they had to leave their plantations in order to be truly free, and some sought to find relatives separated during the days of slavery. Some former slaves also seemed to misunderstand the meaning of freedom, thinking they need never work again.

To ease the adjustment for these recently freed slaves, Congress in 1865 created the Freedman's Bureau, to provide food, clothing, and education, and generally look after the interests of former slaves.

Even before the need to deal with this problem had forced itself on the Northern government's awareness, steps had been taken to deal with another major adjustment of Reconstruction, the restoration of loyal governments to the seceded states. By 1863 substantial portions of several Southern states had come under Northern military control, and Lincoln had set forth a policy for re-establishing governments in those states.

Lincoln's policy, known as the Ten Percent Plan, stipulated that Southerners, except for high-ranking rebel officials, could take an oath promising future loyalty to the Union and acceptance of the end of slavery. When the number of those who had taken this oath within any one state reached ten percent of the number who had been registered to vote in that state in 1860, a loyal state government could be formed. Only those who had taken the oath could vote or participate in the new government.

Tennessee, Arkansas, and Louisiana met the requirements and formed loyal governments but were refused recognition by Congress, which was dominated by Radical Republicans.

The Radical Republicans, such as Thaddeus Stevens of Pennsylvania, believed Lincoln's plan did not adequately punish the South, restructure Southern society, and boost the political prospects of the Republican party. The loyal southern states were denied representation in Congress and electoral votes in the election of 1864.

Instead the Radicals in Congress drew up the Wade-Davis Bill. Under its stringent terms a majority of the number who had been alive and registered to vote in 1860 would have to swear an "ironclad" oath stating that they were now loyal and had never been disloyal. This was obviously impossible in any former Confederate state unless blacks were given the vote, something Radical Republicans desired but Southerners definitely did not. Unless the requisite number swore the "ironclad" oath, Congress would not allow the state to have a government.

Lincoln killed the Wade-Davis Bill with a "pocket veto," and the Radicals were furious. When Lincoln was assassinated the Radicals rejoiced, believing Vice President Andrew Johnson would be less generous to the South or at least easier to control.

Johnson's Attempt at Reconstruction

To the dismay of the Radicals, Johnson followed Lincoln's policies very closely, making them only slightly more stringent by requiring ratification of the Thirteenth Amendment (officially abolishing slavery), repudiation of Confederate debts, and renunciation of secession. He also recommended the vote be given to blacks.

Southern states proved reluctant to accept these conditions, some declining to repudiate Confederate debts or ratify the Thirteenth Amendment (it nevertheless received the ratification of the necessary number of states and was declared part of the Constitution in December 1865). No Southern state extended the vote to blacks (at this time no Northern state did, either). Instead the Southern states promulgated black codes, imposing various restrictions on the freedom of the former slaves.

Foreign Policy Under Johnson

On coming into office Johnson had inherited a foreign policy problem involving Mexico and France. The French Emperor, Napoleon III, had made Mexico the target of one of his many grandiose foreign adventures. In 1862, while the U.S. was occupied with the Civil War and therefore unable to prevent this violation of the Monroe Doctrine, Napoleon III had Archduke Maximilian of Austria installed as a puppet emperor of Mexico, supported by French troops. The U.S. had protested but for the time could do nothing.

With the war over, Johnson and Secretary of State Seward were able to take more vigorous steps. General Philip Sheridan was sent to the Rio Grande with a military force. At the same time Mexican revolutionary leader Benito Juarez was given the tacit recognition of the U.S. government. Johnson and Seward continued to invoke the Monroe Doctrine and to place quiet pressure on Napoleon III to withdraw his troops. In May 1866, facing difficulties of his own in Europe, the French emperor did so, leaving the unfortunate Maximilian to face a Mexican firing squad.

Johnson's and Seward's course of action in preventing the extension of the French Empire into the Western Hemisphere strengthened America's commitment to and the rest of the world's respect for the Monroe Doctrine.

In 1866 the Russian minister approached Seward with an offer to sell Alaska to the U.S. The Russians desired to sell Alaska because its fur resources had been largely exhausted and because they feared that in a possible war with Great Britain (something that seemed likely at the time) they would lose Alaska anyway.

Seward, who was an ardent expansionist, pushed hard for the purchase of Alaska, known as "Seward's Folly" by its critics, and it was largely through his efforts that it was pushed through Congress. It was urged that purchasing Alaska would reward the Russians for their friendly stance toward the U.S. government during the Civil War at a time when Britain and France had seemed to favor the Confederacy.

In 1867 the sale went through and Alaska was purchased for $7,200,000.

Congressional Reconstruction

Southern intransigence in the face of Johnson's relatively mild plan of Reconstruction was manifested in the refusal of some states to repudiate the Confederate debt and ratify the Thirteenth Amendment. The refusal to give the vote to blacks, the passage of black codes, and the election of many former high-ranking Confederates to Congress and other top positions in the Southern states, played into the hands of the Radicals, who were anxious to impose harsh rule on the South. They could now assert that the South was refusing to accept the verdict of the war.

Once again Congress excluded the representatives of the Southern states. Determined to reconstruct the South as it saw fit, Congress passed a Civil Rights Act and extended the authority of the Freedman's Bureau, giving it both quasi-judicial and quasi-executive powers.

Johnson vetoed both bills, claiming they were unconstitutional; but Congress overrode the vetoes. Fearing that the Supreme Court would agree with Johnson and overturn the laws, Congress approved and sent on to the states for ratification (June 1866) the Fourteenth Amendment, making constitutional the laws Congress had just passed. The Fourteenth Amendment defined citizenship and forbade states to deny various rights to citizens, reduced the representation in Congress of states that did not allow blacks to vote, forbade the paying of the Confederate debt, and made former Confederates ineligible to hold public office. With only one Southern state, Tennessee, ratifying, the amendment failed to receive the necessary approval of three-fourths of the states. But the Radicals in Congress were not finished. Strengthened by victory in the 1866 elections, they passed, over Johnson's veto, the Military Reconstruction Act, dividing the South into five military districts to be ruled by military governors with almost dictatorial powers. Tennessee, having ratified the Fourteenth Amendment, was spared the wrath of the Radicals. The rest of the Southern states were ordered to produce constitutions giving the vote to blacks and to ratify the Fourteenth Amendment before they could be "readmitted." In this manner the Fourteenth Amendment was ratified.

Realizing the unprecedented nature of these actions, Congress moved to prevent any check or balance from the other two branches of government. Steps were taken toward limiting the jurisdiction of the Supreme Court so that it could not review cases pertaining to congressional Reconstruction policies. This proved unnecessary as the Court, now headed by Chief Justice Salmon P. Chase in place of the deceased Taney, readily acquiesced and declined to overturn the Reconstruction acts.

To control the president, Congress passed the Army Act, reducing the president's control over the army. In obtaining the cooperation of the army, the Radicals had the aid of General Grant, who already had his eye on the 1868 Republican presidential nomination. Congress also passed the Tenure of Office Act, forbidding Johnson to dismiss cabinet members without the Senate's permission. In passing the latter act, Congress was especially thinking of Radical Secretary of War Edwin M. Stanton, a Lincoln holdover whom Johnson desired to dismiss.

Johnson obeyed the letter but not the spirit of the Reconstruction acts, and Congress, angry at his refusal to cooperate, sought in vain for grounds to impeach him until in August 1867, Johnson violated the Tenure of Office Act (by dismissing Stanton) in order to test its constitutionality. The matter was not tested in the courts, however, but in Congress, where Johnson was impeached by the House of Representatives and came within one vote of being removed by the Senate. For the remaining months of his term he offered little further resistance to the Radicals.

The Election of 1868 and the Fifteenth Amendment

In 1868 the Republican convention, dominated by the Radicals, drew up a platform endorsing Radical Reconstruction. For president, the Republicans nominated Ulysses S. Grant, who had no political record and whose views—if any—on national issues were unknown. The vice-presidential nominee was Schuyler Colfax.

Though the Democratic nomination was sought by Andrew Johnson, the party knew he could not win and instead nominated former Governor Horatio Seymour of New York for president and Francis P. Blair, Jr. of Missouri for vice president. Both had been Union generals during the war. The Democratic platform mildly criticized the excesses of Radical Reconstruction and called for continued payment of the war debt in greenbacks, although Seymour himself was a hard-money man.

Grant, despite his enormous popularity as a war hero, won by only a narrow margin, drawing only 300,000 more popular votes than Seymour. Some 700,000 blacks had voted in the Southern states under the auspices of Army occupation, and since all of these had almost certainly voted for Grant, it was clear that he had not received a majority of the white vote.

The narrow victory of even such a strong candidate as Grant prompted Republican leaders to decide that it would be politically expedient to give the vote to all blacks, North as well as South. For this purpose the Fifteenth Amendment was drawn up and submitted to the states. Ironically, the idea was so unpopular in the North that it won the necessary three-fourths approval only with its ratification by Southern states required to do so by Congress.

Post-War Life in the South

Reconstruction was a difficult time in the South. During the war approximately one in ten Southern men had been killed. Many more were maimed for life. Those who returned from the war found destruction and poverty. Property of the Confederate government was confiscated by the federal government, and dishonest Treasury agents confiscated private property as well. Capital invested in slaves or in Confederate war bonds was lost. Property values fell to one-tenth of their pre-war level. The economic results of the war stayed with the South for decades.

The political results were less long-lived but more immediately disturbing to Southerners. Southerners complained of widespread corruption in governments sustained by federal troops and composed of "carpetbaggers," "scalawags" (respectively the Southern names for Northerners who came to the South to participate in Reconstruction governments and Southerners who supported the Reconstruction regimes), and recently freed blacks.

Under the Reconstruction governments, social programs were greatly expanded, leading to higher taxes and growing state debts. Some of the financial problems were due to corruption, a problem in both North and South in this era when political machines, such as William Marcy "Boss" Tweed's Tammany Hall machine in New York, dominated many Northern city governments and grew rich.

Southern whites sometimes responded to Reconstruction governments with violence, carried out by groups such as the Ku Klux Klan, aimed at intimidating blacks and white Republicans out of voting. The activities of these organizations were sometimes a response to those of the Union League, an organization used by Southern Republicans to control the black vote. The goal of Southerners not allied with the Reconstruction governments, whether members of the Ku Klux Klan or not, was "redemption" (i.e., the end of the Reconstruction governments).

By 1876 Southern whites had been successful, by legal means or otherwise, in "redeeming" all but three Southern states. The following year the federal government ended its policy of Reconstruction and the troops were withdrawn, leading to a return to power of white Southerners in the remaining states.

Reconstruction ended primarily because the North lost interest. Corruption in government, economic hard times brought on by the Panic of 1873, and general weariness on the part of Northern voters with the effort to remake Southern society all sapped the will to continue. Diehard Radicals such as Thaddeus Stevens and Charles Sumner were dead.

Corruption Under Grant

Having arrived in the presidency with no firm political positions, Grant found that the only principle he had to guide his actions was his instinctive loyalty to his old friends and the politicians who had propelled him into office. This principle did not serve him well as president. Though personally of unquestioned integrity, he naively placed his faith in a number of thoroughly dishonest men. His administration was rocked by one scandalous revelation of government corruption after another. Not every scandal involved members of the executive branch, but together they tended to taint the entire period of Grant's administration as one of unparalleled corruption.

The "Black Friday" Scandal

In the "Black Friday" scandal, two unscrupulous businessmen, Jim Fiske and Jay Gould, schemed to corner the gold market. To further their designs, they got Grant's brother-in-law to convince the president that stopping government gold sales would be good for farmers. Grant naively complied, and many businessmen were ruined as the price of gold was bid up furiously on "Black Friday." By the time Grant realized what was happening, much damage had already been done.

The Credit Mobilier Scandal

In the Credit Mobilier scandal, officials of the Union Pacific Railroad used a dummy construction company called Credit Mobilier to skim off millions of dollars of the subsidies the government was paying the Union Pacific for building a transcontinental railroad. To ensure that Congress would take a benevolent attitude toward all this, the officials bribed many of its members lavishly. Though much of this took place before Grant came into office, its revelation in an 1872 congressional investigation created a general scandal.

The "Salary Grab Act"

In the "Salary Grab Act" of 1873, Congress voted a 100 percent pay raise for the president and a 50 percent increase for itself and made both retroactive two years back. Public outrage led to a Democratic victory in the next congressional election and the law was repealed.

The Sanborn Contract Fraud

In the Sanborn Contract fraud, a politician named Sanborn was given a contract to collect $427,000 in unpaid taxes for a 50 percent commission. The commission found its way into Republican campaign funds.

The Whiskey Ring Fraud

In the Whiskey Ring fraud, distillers and treasury officials conspired to defraud the government of large amounts of money from the excise tax on whiskey. Grant's personal secretary was in on the plot, and Grant himself naively accepted gifts of a questionable nature. When the matter came under investigation, Grant endeavored to shield his secretary.

The Bribing of Belknap

Grant's secretary of war, W. W. Belknap, accepted bribes from corrupt agents involved in his department's administration of Indian affairs. When the matter came out, he resigned to escape impeachment.

The Liberal Republicans

Discontentment within Republican ranks with regard to some of the earlier scandals as well as with the Radicals' vindictive Reconstruction policies led a faction of the party to separate and constitute itself as the Liberal Republicans. Besides opposing corruption and favoring sectional harmony, the Liberal Republicans favored hard money and a laissez-faire approach to economic issues. For the election of 1872 they nominated *New York Tribune* editor Horace Greeley for president. Eccentric, controversial, and ineffective as a campaigner, Greeley proved a poor choice. Though nominated by the Democrats as well as the Liberal Republicans, he was easily defeated by Grant, who was again the nominee of the Radicals.

Economic Issues Under Grant

Many of the economic difficulties the country faced during Grant's administration were caused by the necessary readjustments from a wartime back to a peacetime economy.

The central economic question was deflation versus inflation or, more specifically, whether to retire the unbacked paper money, greenbacks, printed to meet the wartime emergency, or to print more.

Economic conservatives, creditors, and business interests usually favored retirement of the greenbacks and an early return to the gold standard.

Debtors, who had looked forward to paying off their obligations in depreciated paper money worth less than the gold-backed money they had borrowed, favored a continuation of currency inflation through the use of more greenbacks. The deflation that would come through the retirement of existing greenbacks would make debts contracted during or immediately after the war much harder to pay.

Generally, Grant's policy was to let the greenbacks float until they were on par with gold and could then be retired without economic dislocation.

Early in Grant's second term the country was hit by an economic depression known as the Panic of 1873. Brought on by the overexpansive tendencies of railroad builders and businessmen during the immediate postwar boom, the Panic was triggered by economic downturns in Europe and, more immediately, by the failure of Jay Cooke and Company, a major American financial firm.

The financial hardship brought on by the Panic led to renewed clamor for the printing of more greenbacks. In 1874 Congress authorized a small new issue of greenbacks, but it was vetoed by Grant. Pro-inflation forces were further enraged when Congress in 1873 demonetized silver, going to a straight gold standard. Silver was becoming more plentiful due to Western mining and was seen by some as a potential source of inflation. Pro-inflation forces referred to the demonetization of silver as the "Crime of '73."

In 1875 Congress took a further step toward retirement of the greenbacks and return to a working gold standard when, under the leadership of John Sherman, it passed the Specie Resumption Act, calling for the resumption of specie payments (i.e., the redeemability of the nation's paper money in gold) by January 1, 1879.

Disgruntled proponents of inflation formed the Greenback party and nominated Peter Cooper for president in 1876. However, they gained only an insignificant number of votes.

The Disputed Election of 1876

In the election of 1876, the Democrats campaigned against corruption and nominated New York Governor Samuel J. Tilden, who had broken the Tweed political machine of New York City.

The Republicans passed over Grant, who was interested in another term and had the backing of the remaining hard-core Radicals, and turned instead to Governor Rutherford B. Hayes of Ohio. Like Tilden, Hayes was decent, honest, in favor of hard money and civil service reform, and opposed to government regulation of the economy. In their campaigning, the Republicans resorted to a tactic known as "waving the bloody shirt." Successfully used in the last two presidential elections, this meant basically playing on wartime animosities, urging Northerners to vote the way they had shot, and suggested that a Democratic victory and a Confederate victory would be about the same thing.

This time the tactic was less successful. Tilden won the popular vote and led in the electoral vote 184 to 165. However, 185 electoral votes were needed for election, and 20 votes, from the three Southern states still occupied by federal troops and run by Republican governments, were disputed.

Though there had been extensive fraud on both sides, Tilden undoubtedly deserved at least the one vote he needed to win. Congress created a special commission to decide the matter. It was to be composed of five members each from the Senate, the House, and the Supreme Court. Of these, seven were to be Republicans, seven Democrats, and one an independent. The Republicans arranged, however, for the independent justice's state legislature to elect him to the Senate. When the justice resigned to take his Senate seat, it left all the remaining Supreme Court justices Republican. One of them was chosen, and in a series of eight-to-seven votes along straight party lines, the commission voted to give all 20 disputed votes—and the election—to Hayes.

When outraged congressional Democrats threatened to reject these obviously fraudulent results, a compromise was worked out. In the Compromise of 1877, Hayes promised to show consideration for Southern interests, end Reconstruction, and withdraw the remaining federal troops from the South in exchange for Democratic acquiescence in his election.

Reconstruction would probably have ended anyway, since the North had already lost interest in it.

PRACTICE TEST 1

This test is also on CD-ROM in our special interactive CLEP History of the United States I TEST*ware*®. It is highly recommended that you first take this exam on computer. You will then have the additional study features and benefits of enforced timed conditions, individual diagnostic analysis, and instant scoring. See page 2 for guidance on how to get the most out of our CLEP History of the United States I book and software.

CLEP HISTORY OF THE UNITED STATES I
Practice Test 1

(Answer sheets appear in the back of this book.)

TIME: 90 Minutes
120 Questions

DIRECTIONS: Each of the questions or incomplete statements below is followed by five possible answers or completions. Select the best choice in each case and fill in the corresponding oval on the answer sheet.

1. In the impeachment process against the president, the __________ determines the guilt or innocence of the president.

   (A) House of Representatives
   (B) Senate
   (C) Supreme Court
   (D) Cabinet
   (E) American people

2. The right to a speedy trial is guaranteed Americans by

   (A) the Declaration of Independence.
   (B) the First Amendment.
   (C) the Third Amendment.
   (D) the Sixth Amendment.
   (E) Article II of the Constitution.

3. According to Article II of the U.S. Constitution, the sole authority to suspend the writ of *habeas corpus* resides in

   (A) the Supreme Court.
   (B) the president.
   (C) the attorney general.
   (D) the Congress.
   (E) the state governors.

4. In James Madison's "Federalist Paper Number Ten," the most dangerous threat to the U.S. Constitution was presented by

   (A) the president's war powers.

   (B) factions.

   (C) the Supreme Court.

   (D) a standing army.

   (E) freedom of speech.

5. The Dutch colony at New Netherland was categorized by all of the following EXCEPT

   (A) its great reliance upon the fur trade.

   (B) friendly relations with neighboring Amerindians.

   (C) relatively small population.

   (D) ethnic diversity of settlers.

   (E) a desire for its own wealth.

6. North American Indian cultures were characterized by all of the following EXCEPT

   (A) a diversified economy of hunting, fishing, and farming.

   (B) a division of labor by gender.

   (C) a reliance on oral culture.

   (D) an animistic religion that worshipped the spiritual elements of nature.

   (E) the lack of the presence of warfare.

7. Spanish colonization of the New World was characterized by all of the following EXCEPT

   (A) ruthless exploitation of the Indians.

   (B) establishing African slavery in the Americas.

   (C) reliance upon large families as settlers.

   (D) introduction of the horse to America.

   (E) the creation of large agricultural plantations.

8. The Puritans left England to settle in America in order to

   (A) establish religious freedom for all Christians.

   (B) emulate the Spanish conquistadors.

   (C) create a perfect religious utopia.

   (D) avoid serving in the English army.

   (E) protest the persecution of the Pilgrims.

9. Seventeenth-century English settlers of New England differed from those in Virginia by

   (A) living shorter lives because of the harsh climate.

   (B) importing large numbers of slaves.

   (C) settling on isolated farms.

   (D) living in tightly clustered communities.

   (E) having large families.

10. King Philip's War of 1675–1676 was fought to

    (A) remove Spanish Catholics from Florida.

    (B) end Spanish control over the African slave trade.

    (C) establish New England trade with the West Indies.

    (D) stop the French from settling the Ohio River Valley.

    (E) establish English control over the Indians in New England.

11. The only eighteenth century North American British colony with a black population majority was

    (A) North Carolina.

    (B) Virginia.

    (C) Maryland.

    (D) South Carolina.

    (E) Georgia.

12. From 1689 until 1763, England fought a series of wars with France for control of North America. Which of the following wars was not part of this series?

    (A) King William's War
    (B) Queen Anne's War
    (C) The Seven Years' War
    (D) King George's War
    (E) King Philip's War

13. Colonial government in British North America did NOT allow

    (A) universal manhood suffrage.
    (B) bicameral legislatures.
    (C) annual elections.
    (D) for a republican form of government.
    (E) local units of government to exist.

14. James Otis earned fame for his defense of American political freedom in

    (A) his book, *Common Sense*.
    (B) the Writs of Assistance case.
    (C) the Virginia House of Burgesses.
    (D) the Second Continental Congress.
    (E) the Boston Tea Party.

15. The Boston Massacre occurred after which of the following events?

    (A) The Intolerable Acts
    (B) The Townshend Duties
    (C) The First Continental Congress
    (D) The Battle of Lexington and Concord
    (E) The Boston Tea Party

QUESTIONS 16 and 17 refer to the following passage.

I am directly opposed to any purpose of secession. The Constitution was made, not merely for the generation which then existed, but for posterity, undefined, unlimited, permanent, and perpetual . . . and for every subsequent state which might come into the Union, binding themselves by that indissoluble bond.

16. The passage most nearly represents the views of

    I. Henry Clay.

    II. John C. Calhoun.

    III. Daniel Webster.

    (A) I only.

    (B) II only.

    (C) I and II only.

    (D) I and III only.

    (E) I, II, and III.

17. The passage is from the only debate in which William Seward, Henry Clay, John C. Calhoun, Daniel Webster, Stephen A. Douglas, Salmon Chase, and Jefferson Davis all took part. This debate resulted in

    (A) the secession of South Carolina from the Union in 1861.

    (B) the Kansas-Nebraska Acts of 1854.

    (C) the Missouri Compromise of 1820.

    (D) the Compromise of 1850.

    (E) the location of the Mason-Dixon line.

18. The battle of Saratoga in 1777 was best known for

    (A) near total defeat of Washington by Howe.

    (B) securing America an alliance with France.

    (C) the first signs of Benedict Arnold's treason.

    (D) being the first battle in the South.

    (E) the splitting of the American states in half by the Howe brothers.

19. In 1632, England allowed its first proprietary colony as a refuge for Catholics in

    (A) Connecticut.
    (B) Maryland.
    (C) New York.
    (D) New Hampshire.
    (E) Delaware.

20. Prior to 1763, the British policy of mercantilism encouraged the American colonies to

    (A) develop native American manufactures.
    (B) trade with the French West Indies.
    (C) cease importing African slaves.
    (D) supply England with raw materials.
    (E) All of the above.

21. At the Philadelphia Convention of 1788, the author of the Great Compromise to the U.S. Constitution was

    (A) Patrick Henry.
    (B) John Adams.
    (C) Thomas Jefferson.
    (D) Roger Sherman.
    (E) James Madison.

22. During the ratification contest, the Antifederalist critique of the proposed U.S. Constitution contained all of the following arguments EXCEPT

    (A) the lack of a written Bill of Rights.
    (B) the lack of a popular vote for the presidency.
    (C) the location of the new government in Washington, D.C.
    (D) the powers of the Supreme Court.
    (E) the large territory of the United States.

23. Opposition to the Jay Treaty in the U.S. Senate centered around

    (A) the opening of American trade with the West Indies.
    (B) the British refusal to withdraw troops from American soil.

(C) the settlement of American debts to British merchants.

(D) its inability to stop the practice of British impressment.

(E) None of the above.

24. "Millions for defense, not one cent for tribute" became the nation's rallying cry during

(A) the Whiskey Rebellion.
(B) the Jay Treaty.
(C) Hamilton's fiscal policies.
(D) the XYZ Affair.
(E) Fries Rebellion.

25. In the election of 1800, the House of Representatives selected the president because of the deadlocked election between

(A) John Adams and Thomas Jefferson.
(B) Thomas Jefferson and Aaron Burr.
(C) Thomas Jefferson and Charles Pickney.
(D) James Madison and John Adams.
(E) George Washington and John Adams.

26. Women emerged from the American Revolution with the prescribed new responsibility of

(A) enjoying the vote.
(B) serving in local political office.
(C) becoming public school teachers.
(D) raising sons and daughters as good republican citizens.
(E) All of the above.

27. The Lewis and Clark expedition occurred AFTER which event?

(A) War of 1812
(B) Louisiana Purchase
(C) Embargo of 1807
(D) Nullification Controversy
(E) Missouri Compromise

28. The "Burr Conspiracy" refers to

(A) Aaron Burr's attempt to steal the presidency from Thomas Jefferson in 1800.

(B) Burr's scheme to create a new nation from the Southern territory of the United States.

(C) Burr's attempt to assassinate President James Madison.

(D) Burr's attempt to defraud the Bank of the United States of $20 million.

(E) None of the above.

29. During the War of 1812, the battle waged AFTER the signing of the peace treaty at Ghent was the

(A) Invasion of Canada.

(B) Battle of Lake Erie.

(C) burning of Washington, D.C.

(D) Battle of New Orleans.

(E) None of the above.

30. The principle that "American continents [were not]...subjects for future colonizations by any European power" is expressed directly in

(A) George Washington's farewell address.

(B) the Monroe Doctrine.

(C) the Truman Doctrine.

(D) *McCulloch v. Maryland.*

(E) the Bill of Rights.

31. "John Marshall has made his decision; now let him enforce it," refers to which Supreme Court decision scorned by President Andrew Jackson?

(A) *Gibbons v. Ogden*

(B) *McCulloch v. Maryland*

(C) Dred Scott Case

(D) *Cherokee Nation v. Georgia*

(E) *Marbury v. Madison*

32. The rise of the "market economy" in the 1820s refers to the

(A) rise of the New England textile industry.

(B) rise of commercial agriculture.

(C) rise of subsistence agriculture.

(D) rise of American factories.

(E) rise of the Second Bank of the United States.

33. All of the following were major reform movements during the 1830s EXCEPT

(A) Temperence.

(B) Revivalism.

(C) Women's Rights.

(D) Education.

(E) Labor Unions.

34. Andrew Jackson referred to the Election of 1824 as "the corrupt bargain" because of

(A) the Whig election smear campaign against him.

(B) wide-scale fraud in the popular vote.

(C) the selection of Henry Clay as President John Quincy Adams' secretary of state.

(D) the Senate's choice of John Quincy Adams as president.

(E) the lack of a popular vote for the electoral college.

35. Andrew Jackson's impact on the office of the presidency is characterized by a reliance on

(A) the veto as a political weapon.

(B) a "kitchen cabinet."

(C) the spoils system.

(D) public opinion.

(E) All of the above.

36. Jackson's reasons for his veto of the Second Bank of the United States included

(A) the Bank of the United States was a monopoly.

(B) fear of foreign control of the United States through the Bank.

(C) the Bank's political uses of its funding.

(D) the Bank was unconstitutional.

(E) All of the above.

37. The historian most associated with the view of slavery as crushing African-Americans into a "sambo personality" is

(A) Herbert Aptheker.

(B) George Fitzhugh.

(C) Harriet Beecher Stowe.

(D) Eugene Genovese.

(E) Stanley Elkins.

38. The slavery as a "positive good" argument was presented by

(A) Benjamin Lundy.

(B) Henry Clay.

(C) George Fitzhugh.

(D) Stephen Douglas.

(E) William Lloyd Garrison.

39. Although Texas claimed its independence from Mexico in 1837, it was not admitted as an American state until 1845 because

(A) of prolonged treaty negotiations with Mexico.

(B) of the doctrine of Manifest Destiny.

(C) Sam Houston's hatred of President Martin Van Buren.

(D) the North's fear of a growing slave power in the United States.

(E) of strong anti-American sentiment among Texas settlers.

40. Select the statement which BEST represents Abraham Lincoln's public position on slavery in the Election of 1860.

(A) "We must purge this land by blood."

(B) "We consider the slaveholder a relentless tyrant."

(C) "On the issue of slavery I will not retreat a single inch."

(D) "If I can maintain the Union with slavery I shall; if I can maintain the Union without slavery I shall."

(E) "Slavery is the most dreaded disease known to civilized mankind."

41. The Mexican-American War resulted in Mexico ceding all of the following territories to the United States EXCEPT

(A) Texas.

(B) New Mexico.

(C) California.

(D) Nevada.

(E) Washington.

42. Which of the following events occurred last?

(A) Kansas-Nebraska Act

(B) Nat Turner Rebellion

(C) Seneca Falls Convention

(D) Lincoln-Douglas debates

(E) Homestead Act

43. Northern denunciation of the Compromise of 1850 was directed primarily toward

(A) the Fugitive Slave Law.

(B) statehood for California.

(C) the acquisition of New Mexico and Utah as slave territories.

(D) the gag rule in the House of Representatives.

(E) continuation of the African slave trade.

44. The Dred Scott decision in 1857 by Chief Justice Roger Taney declared

(A) African-Americans were citizens.

(B) slaves legally could sue in federal courts.

(C) slaves were not property.

(D) the Missouri Compromise was unconstitutional.

(E) All of the above.

45. In the election of 1860, Abraham Lincoln's total of the popular vote was

    (A) 80 percent.
    (B) 70 percent.
    (C) 60 percent.
    (D) 50 percent.
    (E) 40 percent.

46. The Emancipation Proclamation immediately freed the slaves

    (A) throughout the United States.
    (B) only in the border states.
    (C) throughout the South only.
    (D) in Maryland and Tennessee.
    (E) None of the above.

47. Because of its acceptance of the states' rights doctrine, the Confederacy most closely resembled

    (A) the British Constitution.
    (B) the Articles of Confederation.
    (C) Napoleonic France.
    (D) the United States Constitution.
    (E) None of the above.

48. During the Civil War, President Lincoln gave evidence of his democratic beliefs by

    (A) sponsoring the Homestead Act.
    (B) the recruitment of black soldiers into the Northern Army.
    (C) the Emancipation Proclamation.
    (D) the Fourteenth Amendment.
    (E) his actions during his first four months in office.

49. The vast majority of settlers who traveled to the Far West because of the Homestead Act's grant of a free 160-acre farm

(A) proposed and established democracy in the region.

(B) were supporters of the Democratic party.

(C) returned East after failing as farmers.

(D) were ex-slaves.

(E) were recent immigrants from Eastern Europe.

50. According to most historians, the major failure of Northern Reconstruction was its inability to

(A) educate the ex-slaves.

(B) provide the vote to ex-slaves.

(C) provide economic independence to ex-slaves.

(D) control the Northern desire to punish the South.

(E) establish civil rights for the ex-slaves.

51. The president associated with the Sellout of 1876 was

(A) U.S. Grant.

(B) Ben Tilden.

(C) Andrew Johnson.

(D) Rutherford B. Hayes.

(E) William Howard Taft.

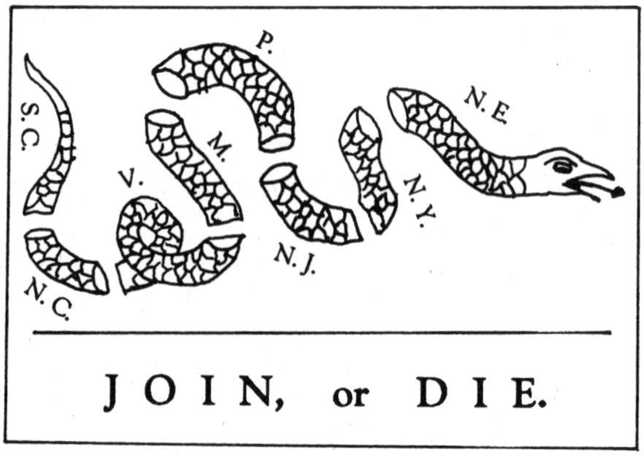

52. The cartoon on the previous page by Benjamin Franklin (1754) offered a warning to the 13 colonies if they

    (A) refused to enter the Seven Years' War.

    (B) continued to follow the British policy of mercantilism.

    (C) did not protest the Stamp Act.

    (D) continued trading with French Canada.

    (E) rejected the Albany Plan.

QUESTIONS 53 and 54 refer to the following passage.

The major problems of this country today are the result of too many immigrants and the corrupt influence of Papists (Roman Catholics). The immigrants are stealing jobs that belong to the native-born American citizens. Their low moral values threaten the very fabric of our society. The Papists serve Rome, not the United States. They would turn governmental power over to the Pope in a second, if given the chance. Therefore we believe that Papists should not be allowed to hold political office in the United States. Immigrants should be required to live in the United States for at least 21 years before being eligible to vote.

53. The passage most closely represents the views of which political party?

    (A) Free Soil party

    (B) Know-Nothing party

    (C) Populist party

    (D) Republican party

    (E) Whig party

54. The political philosophy represented in this passage achieved its peak in popularity around

    (A) 1825.

    (B) 1835.

    (C) 1845.

    (D) 1855.

    (E) 1865.

55. Which of the following led to European discovery and exploration of the Americas?

    (A) Discovery of new land routes to Asia

(B) Breakdown of the Genoese and Venetian monopoly over Mediterranean-European trade

(C) Decline of commercial banking

(D) Development of new navigational instruments

(E) Success of the Crusades in bringing Christian control of the Middle East

56. Roger Williams came into conflict with the Puritan authorities for advocating that

(A) the land belonged by right to the English.

(B) government rested upon the consent of the governed.

(C) political leaders could have no authority over religious matters.

(D) religion should be based on direct intuition of God and his love.

(E) no one had the right to worship according to their individual conscience.

57. Which of the following was NOT one of the Middle Colonies?

(A) New Jersey

(B) Connecticut

(C) New York

(D) Delaware

(E) Pennsylvania

58. Which of the following did NOT characterize French settlement in the New World?

(A) The French controlled access to the Mississippi River and the St. Lawrence River.

(B) The French established trade in furs.

(C) The French developed widespread settlement in the interior of the continent.

(D) The French established a single government for all of New France.

(E) The French generally established good relations with the Indians.

59. The key British victory in the French and Indian War was at

(A) Louisburg.
(B) Fort Frontenac.
(C) Fort Duquesne.
(D) Crown Point.
(E) Ticonderoga.

60. Which of the following prevented the entrance of Texas into the Union after it gained independence in 1836?

(A) Texas wanted to permit slavery
(B) Opposition to Mexicans residing within American territory
(C) Inability to control Indian tribes in the area
(D) The influence of Catholicism on Texas
(E) Disagreement over the southern boundary of Texas

61. The "Middle Passage" refers to

(A) the route traveled by Lewis and Clark through the Rocky Mountains.
(B) the route to the Orient sought by Henry Hudson.
(C) the road established between Cumberland, Maryland, and Vandalia, Illinois.
(D) the route across Panama for those heading to the California gold fields.
(E) the voyage between Africa and the Americas taken by the slave traders.

62. All of the following were advocates of religious toleration EXCEPT

(A) William Penn.
(B) John Winthrop.
(C) Roger Williams.
(D) Lord Baltimore.
(E) Thomas Jefferson.

63. According to British mercantilist policy, the colonies would perform all of the following functions EXCEPT

(A) provide markets for British goods.
(B) produce manufactured goods.
(C) provide raw materials for British manufacturing.
(D) encourage the growth of a strong merchant fleet.
(E) provide bases for the Royal Navy.

64. The Intolerable Acts of 1774 were passed in response to

(A) the Boston Tea Party.
(B) the Boston Massacre.
(C) formation of the Continental Congress.
(D) the Gaspee Affair.
(E) creation of the Committee of Correspondence.

65. Which of the following served as an American commander during the American Revolution?

(A) William Howe
(B) John Burgoyne
(C) Nathaniel Greene
(D) Barry St. Leger
(E) Henry Clinton

66. The Constitutional Convention took place in 1787 in what city?

(A) New York
(B) Philadelphia
(C) Washington, D.C.
(D) Baltimore
(E) Boston

67. Alexander Hamilton's "Report on Public Credit" proposed which of the following?

(A) Repudiate the Confederate debts
(B) Establish a protective tariff
(C) Offer bonuses to encourage manufacturing
(D) Assume the state debts
(E) Establish a national bank

68. Under Thomas Jefferson, the Republicans

(A) reversed Federalist measures for funding the national debt.
(B) renewed the charter of the Bank of the United States.
(C) reduced the federal budget.
(D) enlarged the United States Army.
(E) increased the national debt.

69. The Adams-Onis Treaty (1819) gave the United States

(A) Louisiana.
(B) Oregon.
(C) Texas.
(D) California.
(E) Florida.

70. Which of the following is NOT associated with the "American System"?

(A) A protective tariff to stimulate new industries

(B) Henry Clay

(C) The Second Bank of the United States

(D) Federally funded internal improvements

(E) Bonuses to new industries

71. The Bill of Rights

(A) is the first ten amendments to the Constitution.

(B) limited the powers of the federal government to those specifically named in the Constitution.

(C) gave citizens freedom of religion, assembly, speech and press, and the right of petition.

(D) guaranteed the rights of persons accused of crime.

(E) All of the above.

72. The most important difference between the South and other sections of the United States prior to 1860 was which of the following?

(A) Slavery

(B) Economic diversification

(C) Rural patterns of living

(D) Development of transportation systems

(E) Population growth

73. The Jacksonian era was notable for its

(A) decrease in the number of active voters.

(B) destruction of the spoils system.

(C) opposition to party nominating conventions.

(D) support of Indian rights.

(E) rhetorical egalitarianism.

74. What group of immigrants prior to the Civil War helped stimulate formation of the American, or "Know-Nothing," party?

(A) Italians

(B) Russian Jews

(C) Slavs

(D) Irish

(E) Chinese

75. The term "scalawag" was used during Reconstruction to describe

(A) the freed slaves.

(B) Northerners who came into the South.

(C) members of the Ku Klux Klan.

(D) native-born Southerners who cooperated with the Northerners.

(E) blacks who served in the Southern state legislatures.

76. The "Crime of '73" refers to

(A) the Bland-Allison bill which required the Treasury Department to purchase between $2 million and $4 million worth of silver each month.

(B) the Sherman Silver Purchase Act which required the Treasury Department to purchase 4.5 million ounces of silver each month.

(C) the removal of silver coins from the list of standard coins.

(D) the decision to purchase silver at the ratio of 16 to 1 in relation to gold.

(E) the refusal to coin silver purchased by the Treasury Department.

77. Which of the following acts was NOT passed during the Civil War (1861–1865)?

(A) Morrill Tariff Act
(B) National Banking Act
(C) Homestead Act
(D) Conscription Act
(E) Tenure of Office Act

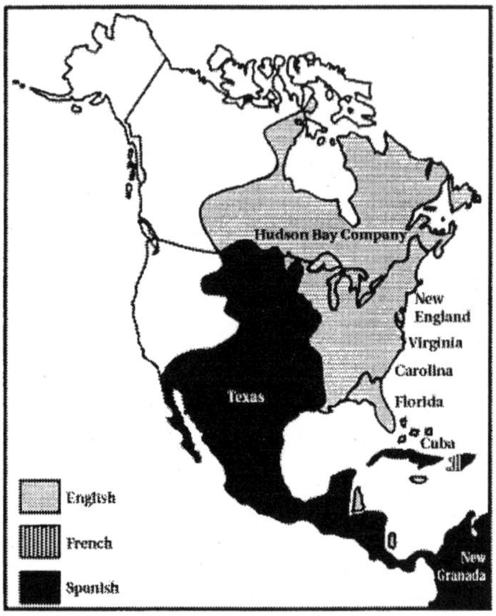

78. This map represents European powers in North America as of

(A) 1600.
(B) 1682.
(C) 1713.
(D) 1763.
(E) 1783.

79. By 1860 approximately how many slaves lived in the South?

(A) 2 million
(B) 3 million
(C) 4 million
(D) 5 million
(E) 6 million

80. Andrew Jackson contributed to the depression of 1837 by doing which of the following?

(A) Placing federal funds in the Bank of the United States
(B) Issuing the Specie Circular

(C) Establishing the Independent Treasury

(D) Opposing the Ordinance of Nullification

(E) Vetoing the renewal of the charter of the Bank of the United States

81. The Twelfth Amendment (1804) to the Constitution

(A) required the electoral college to vote separately for president and vice president.

(B) provided for freedom of religion.

(C) limited the president to two terms.

(D) prohibited the manufacture and sale of alcoholic beverages.

(E) gave the right to bear arms.

82. *The Federalist Papers*

(A) were written anonymously by Alexander Hamilton, John Jay, and James Madison.

(B) argued that under the Constitution the states would relinquish too much sovereignty.

(C) opposed ratification of the Constitution without the addition of a bill of rights.

(D) convinced Patrick Henry to support the Constitution.

(E) stressed that the Constitutional Convention was instructed to revise the Articles of Confederation, not to write a new constitution.

83. The Ostend Manifesto of 1854 concerned which of the following?

(A) Hawaii

(B) Alaska

(C) Puerto Rico

(D) Cuba

(E) Guam

84. The Declaratory Act of 1766

(A) required the colonists to provide barracks and supplies for British troops.

(B) forbade the American colonists to issue paper money.

(C) established a new duty on molasses.

(D) stated that Parliament had the power to make laws binding on the colonies.

(E) established a tax on licenses, legal documents, and newspapers.

85. Which of the following writers was NOT a part of the "American Renaissance" of the mid-nineteenth century?

(A) Henry James
(B) Nathaniel Hawthorne
(C) Walt Whitman
(D) Henry David Thoreau
(E) Herman Melville

86. Secessionist feeling during the War of 1812 was strong in

(A) New England and the West.
(B) New England.
(C) the South.
(D) the South and West.
(E) the West.

87. Which of the following is associated with early English settlement in the New World?

(A) Joint-stock companies
(B) Encomienda
(C) Prince Henry the Navigator
(D) George III
(E) Republicanism

88. After 1840, the Northeast's primary economic concern was

(A) international commerce.
(B) agriculture.
(C) manufacturing of finished products.
(D) production of raw materials.
(E) national commerce.

89. By the middle 1760s the most influential citizens in the New England towns were the

(A) ministers.
(B) artisans.

(C) merchants. (D) farmers.

(E) laborers.

90. Which of the following was NOT a Union strategy in the Civil War?

(A) Fight a defensive war

(B) Blockade the Confederate coastline

(C) Seize control of the Mississippi River

(D) Seize Richmond, Virginia

(E) Control the interior railroad lines of the South

91. Which of the following became president upon the assassination of Abraham Lincoln?

(A) Ulysses S. Grant (D) James A. Garfield

(B) Andrew Johnson (E) Chester A. Arthur

(C) Rutherford B. Hayes

92. The ordinances of 1785 and 1787 established all of the following EXCEPT

(A) division of the Northwestern lands into townships.

(B) reservation of one section in each township for support of public schools.

(C) establishment of territorial government.

(D) protection of slavery.

(E) a procedure for achieving statehood.

93. Which of the following was NOT originally a proprietary colony?

(A) Georgia (D) Virginia

(B) South Carolina (E) Pennsylvania

(C) Maryland

94. Which of the following contributed significantly to the growth of anti-slavery sentiment in the 1850s?

(A) The establishment of the American Anti-Slavery Society

(B) Publication of *Uncle Tom's Cabin*

(C) William Lloyd Garrison's founding of *The Liberator*

(D) Passage of the "gag" rule by the House of Representatives

(E) Creation of the Liberty party

95. The panic of 1857 fundamentally resulted from

(A) the violence in Kansas.

(B) the economic impact of gold from California.

(C) the Dred Scott decision.

(D) excessive investments in railroads.

(E) the secessionist movement in the South.

96. Which of the following was NOT characteristic of Spanish civilization in the New World?

(A) The mission system

(B) Slavery

(C) The viceroy

(D) The search for gold and silver

(E) Republican government

97. All of the following are associated with the Pilgrims EXCEPT

(A) separatism.

(B) Massachusetts Bay Colony.

(C) Mayflower Compact.

(D) Squanto.

(E) Plymouth.

98. Which of the following colonies was established so that debtors freed from English prisons could start a new life?

(A) Georgia

(B) Maryland

(C) North Carolina

(D) New Jersey

(E) Delaware

99. The French and Indian War or Seven Years' War resulted in which of the following after the signing of the Treaty of Paris in 1763?

(A) Spain gained control of Florida.

(B) The British occupied Cuba and the Philippines.

(C) The British gained control of Guadeloupe and Martinique.

(D) The Spanish obtained New Orleans and Louisiana.

(E) The French retained Quebec.

100. Which of the following does NOT correctly describe the Southern colonies?

(A) They were the most English of the colonies.

(B) They were largely urban.

(C) The plantations were on the coastal plains.

(D) Tobacco and rice were the chief cash crops.

(E) Most Southerners lived on small farms.

101. The Treaty of Ghent, which ended the War of 1812, included which of the following?

(A) Settlement of Canadian border problems

(B) Recognition of American neutral rights

(C) Restoration of territory taken during the war

(D) Cessation of the impressment of American seamen

(E) Transfer of Canadian land to the United States

102. The Iroquois Confederation included all of the following Indian tribes EXCEPT

(A) Sioux.

(B) Mohawk.

(C) Seneca.

(D) Oneida.

(E) Cayuga.

103. What was the first college to be established in colonial America?

(A) King's College (Columbia)

(B) College of William and Mary

(C) Harvard College

(D) Queen's College (Rutgers)

(E) College of New Jersey (Princeton)

104. The British government faced all of the following problems in 1763 EXCEPT

(A) war debts.

(B) defense costs.

(C) independence movements in colonial America.

(D) government of Florida and Canada.

(E) ownership of the western lands of colonial America.

105. Which of the following was feared as a mob leader by British colonial authorities?

(A) Thomas Jefferson

(B) Patrick Henry

(C) John Adams

(D) James Otis

(E) Samuel Adams

106. Which of the following does NOT appear in the Declaration of Independence?

(A) A portrayal of the king as an evil ruler

(B) An argument for religious toleration

(C) A statement of the basic principles of democracy

(D) An announcement that a state of war existed with Great Britain

(E) An argument for the right of Americans to revolt

107. The government under the Articles of Confederation had all of the following powers EXCEPT

(A) regulation of weights and measures.

(B) establishment of a post office.

(C) creation of a navy.

(D) coinage of money.

(E) taxation.

108. The Jay Treaty (1794) provided for

(A) the acceptance of American trade with the French West Indies.

(B) free navigation of the Mississippi.

(C) an ending of impressment of American seamen.

(D) the settlement of the Canadian boundary.

(E) evacuation of English troops from their posts along the Great Lakes.

109. The XYZ Affair of 1797–98 resulted in

(A) a new treaty with France.

(B) a quasi-war with France.

(C) an American loan to France.

(D) a declaration of war on France.

(E) an apology to France for remarks that President Adams made to Congress.

Growth of White Population, Massachusetts Bay, 1700-1740

Year	*Total Population*
1700	55,941
1710	62,390
1720	91,008
1730	114,116
1740	151,613

110. Based on the above chart, in what year did the population of Massachusetts Bay grow by the largest percentage?

(A) 1700

(B) 1710

(C) 1720

(D) 1730

(E) 1740

111. Which of the following was resolved by negotiation soon after the Treaty of Ghent (1814)?

(A) Disarmament of the Great Lakes

(B) Impressment of American seamen

(C) Neutral rights

(D) Boundary of the Oregon territory

(E) Elimination of land fortification, armaments, and troops along the Canadian border

112. After 1815, the Southern economy was increasingly tied to what crop?

(A) Wheat

(B) Tobacco

(C) Corn

(D) Rice

(E) Cotton

113. Which of the following states provoked the nullification crisis?

(A) South Carolina

(B) Georgia

(C) Virginia

(D) North Carolina

(E) Alabama

114. Which of the following was NOT involved in American exploration of the West?

(A) Meriwether Lewis

(B) Zebulon Pike

(C) John Charles Frémont

(D) Aaron Burr

(E) William Clark

115. Who served as president of the Second Bank of the United States?

(A) Roger B. Taney

(B) William Morgan

(C) Nicholas Biddle

(D) Daniel Webster

(E) Robert Y. Hayne

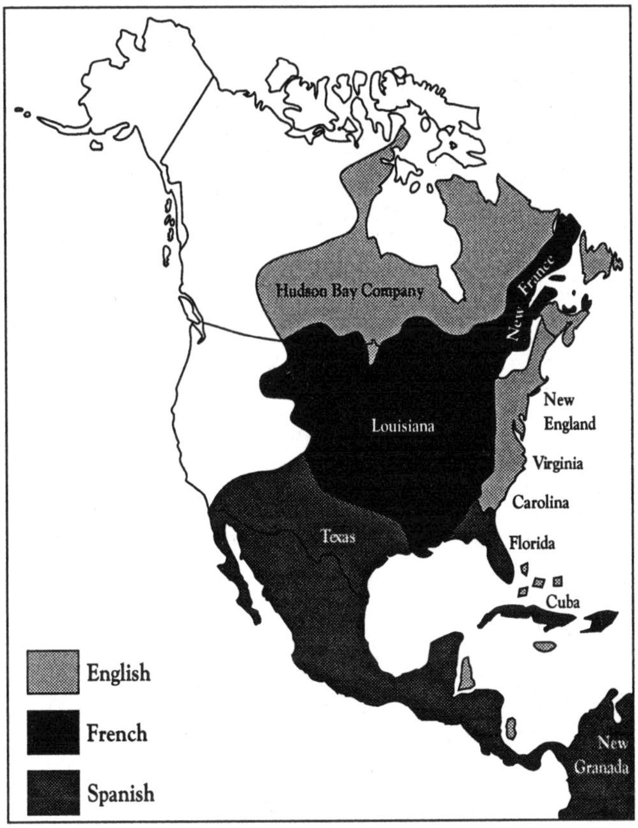

116. The above map represents European powers in North America as of

(A) 1600.
(B) 1682.
(C) 1713.
(D) 1763.
(E) 1783.

117. During the Civil War, the term "Copperhead" referred to

(A) Northerners who opposed the Civil War.
(B) Northerners who called for the abolition of slavery.
(C) Southerners who opposed the Confederacy.
(D) Southerners who called for the abolition of slavery.
(E) Northerners who supported slavery.

118. Which of the following was NOT part of the Radical Republican program for Reconstruction?

(A) Division of the South into military districts

(B) The Fourteenth Amendment

(C) Enlargement of the powers of the Freedmen's Bureau

(D) Division of the plantations and distribution of the land to the freed slaves

(E) Guarantees that the freed slaves could vote and hold office

119. The Treaty of Guadalupe Hidalgo (1848) included all of the following EXCEPT

(A) the United States paid Mexico $15 million.

(B) land south of the Gila River.

(C) the United States took over $3 million in debts owed by the Mexican government to Americans.

(D) the United States gained Texas, New Mexico, and Upper California.

(E) the United States promised to respect the religious preferences and civil and property rights of Mexicans in the newly acquired territory.

120. Which of the following was NOT concerned with either slavery or blacks?

(A) Emancipation Proclamation

(B) Thirteenth Amendment

(C) Sixteenth Amendment

(D) Freedmen's Bureau

(E) Fourteenth Amendment

CLEP HISTORY OF THE UNITED STATES I TEST 1

ANSWER KEY

1.	(B)	31.	(D)	61.	(E)	91.	(B)
2.	(D)	32.	(B)	62.	(B)	92.	(D)
3.	(D)	33.	(E)	63.	(B)	93.	(D)
4.	(B)	34.	(C)	64.	(A)	94.	(B)
5.	(B)	35.	(E)	65.	(C)	95.	(D)
6.	(E)	36.	(E)	66.	(B)	96.	(E)
7.	(C)	37.	(E)	67.	(D)	97.	(B)
8.	(C)	38.	(C)	68.	(C)	98.	(A)
9.	(D)	39.	(D)	69.	(E)	99.	(D)
10.	(E)	40.	(D)	70.	(E)	100.	(B)
11.	(D)	41.	(E)	71.	(E)	101.	(C)
12.	(E)	42.	(E)	72.	(A)	102.	(A)
13.	(A)	43.	(A)	73.	(E)	103.	(C)
14.	(B)	44.	(D)	74.	(D)	104.	(C)
15.	(B)	45.	(E)	75.	(D)	105.	(E)
16.	(D)	46.	(E)	76.	(C)	106.	(B)
17.	(D)	47.	(B)	77.	(E)	107.	(E)
18.	(B)	48.	(A)	78.	(D)	108.	(E)
19.	(B)	49.	(C)	79.	(C)	109.	(B)
20.	(D)	50.	(C)	80.	(B)	110.	(C)
21.	(D)	51.	(D)	81.	(A)	111.	(A)
22.	(C)	52.	(E)	82.	(A)	112.	(E)
23.	(D)	53.	(B)	83.	(D)	113.	(A)
24.	(D)	54.	(D)	84.	(D)	114.	(D)
25.	(B)	55.	(D)	85.	(A)	115.	(C)
26.	(D)	56.	(C)	86.	(B)	116.	(C)
27.	(B)	57.	(B)	87.	(A)	117.	(A)
28.	(B)	58.	(C)	88.	(C)	118.	(C)
29.	(D)	59.	(A)	89.	(C)	119.	(B)
30.	(B)	60.	(A)	90.	(A)	120.	(C)

DETAILED EXPLANATIONS OF ANSWERS

TEST 1

1. **(B)** The impeachment process in American government is actually a two-part process. In Article I, Section 2 (I, 2), the House of Representatives holds the sole right to initiate impeachment against a president. The House acts as a grand jury in this phase and its impeachment of a president only amounts to an announcement to the Senate that the second phase of the process must begin. According to I, 3, the Senate, with the chief justice of the Supreme Court presiding, begins a trial on the guilt or innocence of a president regarding the bill of impeachment. If found guilty, the president is removed from office. Thus, the Senate acts as a petit jury and determines innocence and guilt. Andrew Johnson, the seventeenth president, and Bill Clinton, the forty-second president, have been the only two presidents impeached by the House of Representatives (in 1867 and 1999, respectively). Neither one was removed from office by the Senate. President Richard Nixon was neither impeached nor removed from office by this process.

2. **(D)** It is in the Sixth Amendment that Americans are guaranteed the right to a "speedy trial." The entire amendment deals specifically with the rights of the accused in a criminal procedure. The amendment reflects the fears of the Antifederalists that "justice delayed was justice denied" and that the key to the survival of the Constitution, as with all republics, lay foremost in its capacity to administer justice to its citizens. Although the Declaration of Independence advances principles on the fundamental rights of all people, these rights are stated generally and lack the specific language of the Sixth Amendment. The First Amendment focuses on free speech, assembly, religion, and the right to petition, while the Third Amendment deals with the illegal quartering of soldiers in private homes. Article II focuses on the Congress of the United States and not individual rights.

3. **(D)** Only Congress has the authorization to suspend the writ of *habeas corpus*. The writ is one of our judicial system's basic protections for citizens from arbitrary arrest. The writ demands that arresting officers must present their evidence before a court official within 48 hours after the arrest of a suspect. Thus, the accused is presented with charges and evidence quickly to preserve the principle of innocent until proven guilty. The only American president to suspend the writ without Congressional authorization was Abraham Lincoln, who during the Civil War suspended it in Maryland and Tennessee. This action was later approved by Congress as an emergency wartime action. The attorney general was granted similar emergency powers regarding the writ by Congress in the McCarran Internal Security Act of 1950. This power ceased to function in 1970. Neither the Supreme Court nor the state governors have ever been granted this power temporarily by Congress.

4. **(B)** According to most political scientists, James Madison's *Tenth Federalist* ranks behind only the Declaration of Independence and the U.S. Constitution as a document fundamental to American government. During the ratification contest over the Constitution in New York, Madison, along with Alexander Hamilton and John Jay, authored a series of letters in defense of the Constitution that were signed under the pseudonym "Publius." It was Madison's *Tenth* letter that showed how the Constitution differed from all previous political systems in that it allowed for expansive freedom for its citizens, yet still provided an energetic government. According to Madison, however, the only serious threat to the Constitution would arise from a single interest group, or faction, becoming dominant in our government. Madison believed a large territory and diverse population would prevent that from ever occurring. Madison supported a strong president and Supreme Court, and authored the Bill of Rights in 1790–1791.

5. **(B)** The Dutch had extremely hostile relations with neighboring Amerindians because of the Dutch exploitation of the fur trade. Indeed, one of the bloodiest European-Indian wars occurred in 1643 between the Dutch and the Algonquian Indians which nearly annihilated the tribe. The Dutch came to America to exploit its land and peoples as did the Spanish. They sought wealth primarily through the lucrative fur trade. Because of their small native population, the Dutch were forced to attract settlers from all over Europe to populate their colony. As a result, New Netherland was ethnically diverse and this often led to internal struggling among the diverse colonists. Because of the harsh economic conditions established by the Dutch patroon system of farming, few European settlers were attracted to New Netherland.

6. **(E)** Prior to the arrival of Columbus, North American Indians had a record of warfare no better nor worse than their European counterparts. The primary cause of intra-tribal warfare was the violation by one tribe of another tribe's territories. The Indians did have a diversified economy with the notable exception of the Great Plains Indians who were nomadic hunters only. Generally, Indian males hunted and fished while women practiced communal farming methods. Because of the large number of language groups in North America, Indian culture remained oral and relied upon face-to-face communication. Indian religions stressed that all life was sacred and that all of nature contained a spiritual element. As a result, Indian deities tended to be associated with the forces of nature and nature was seen as animistic.

7. **(C)** The ideal colonial for Spain was an unmarried young male bent on achieving sudden fame and wealth through military exploitation of the Indians. During the sixteenth century about 1,500 conquistadors arrived per year seeking only to gain a rapid fortune and return to Spain. To achieve this end, the conquistadors conquered the Indians through military force and exploited their labor as slaves on large plantations called adelatandos. Only after the Indian population succumbed did the Spanish introduce African slavery to the Americas through the efforts of Charles V and Las Casas. Prior to Columbus' arrival, there were no horses known to the Western Hemisphere.

8. **(C)** As with the Pilgrims, the Puritans sought to create a perfect religious utopia in America. The Puritans believed they were the last hope to establish true Christianity in the world and fled the persecutions of James and Laud to create isolated communities of devoted Puritans. As a result, they feared all outsiders to their ways and punished the practitioners of any other religions in their midst. The Puritans extended their fear of other religious groups to include the Pilgrims and were especially hateful of the Spanish who were much too worldly and Catholic for the Puritans. The Puritans were not pacifists and proved this during the English Civil War, 1641–1660, and the Pequot War in 1675–1676 in New England.

9. **(D)** Contrary to popular views, New Englanders enjoyed a life expectancy of close to 70 years for men and 62 years for women in the seventeenth century. Earlier estimates of life expectancy too often factored a high infant mortality into the equation to conclude with an inaccurate assessment of life expectancies in the 40's for both men and women. Both Virginians and New Englanders had average family sizes of between six and

eight throughout the seventeenth century. Slavery never grew beyond small portions in New England because of the lack of large plantations in the region. Instead, Puritans tended to reside in highly isolated villages or towns. Here each Puritan community huddled together and worked closely to establish their separate religious utopias. The harsh New England climate, rocky soil, and thick forests all worked to support the Puritan pattern of settlement by townships.

10. **(E)** The Puritan Wars of 1675–1676 with the Wampanoag Indians and other New England tribes was a direct result of white settlement encroaching on traditional Indian lands. After the hanging of three Indians in 1675, Metacomet, or King Philip, organized the Wampanoags into a unified force to drive the English from New England. Despite being outnumbered, the Indians destroyed many New England settlements and drove back the Puritans repeatedly. During the winter of 1675–1676, the Puritans counterattacked and defeated the Wampanoags and Philip. Indian losses were close to 40 percent of their population in New England. The war effectively ended Indian resistance to white settlement in New England.

11. **(D)** South Carolina earned its distinct population ratios with a black:white ratio of 20:1. In large part, this was owing to the harsh work in the colony's rice fields, which were little better than marshes and swamps. Because of the fear of diseases such as malaria and the demanding nature of the work on a rice plantation, South Carolina farmers were unable to attract white indentured servants and were compelled to rely on black slaves almost exclusively as a labor force. All the remaining Southern colonies held a black:white ratio where slaves comprised about 12–15 percent of the total population throughout the colonial period.

12. **(E)** King Philip's War in Massachusetts was not part of the four great imperial wars between England and France for control of North America. (See Question 10 on King Philip's War.) Each of the other wars were fought for control of North America. Of the four wars, only the Seven Years' War (1756–1763) began in America and spread to Europe. In this final war, England and France fought for control of the Ohio Territory. The French were finally defeated and ceded all of Canada to England at the peace treaty. Thus, in 1763, England was the master of the entirety of North America for the first time. The other wars for the most part ended without conclusive victors: King William's War (1690–1697); Queen Anne's War (1702–1713); and King George's War (1744–1748).

13. **(A)** Colonial Americans believed that the vote belonged only to those members of society who had a large stake in society's well being. As a result, they allowed only white adult males with sufficient property and in many cases the correct religion to vote. In order to vote in most colonies, one had to be white, male, 21 years or older, a property owner, and a Protestant. These electoral qualifications disenfranchised all blacks, women, non-Protestants, and poor from being politically active through the vote. Annual elections were the rule for the lower legislative houses; local government and county government were very active throughout the colonial period; bicameral legislatures were the norm for the colonies; all 13 colonies claimed to have created a republican form of government to replicate that of England's.

14. **(B)** In 1761, the young Massachusetts lawyer James Otis burst across the political horizon with his assault on the general search warrants issued to British customs officials in the Writs of Assistance case. Since 1760, England had sought a method to curb colonial smuggling and New England trade with France during the Seven Years' War. The issuance of the writs allowed officials to ransack private homes searching for evidence. In arguing against the writs, Otis advanced the view that an act of Parliament was subject to review by the higher law of the English Constitution. Otis lost the case, but advanced a view of higher law and constitutions that most Americans came to accept. Thomas Paine was the author of *Common Sense*. Otis never spoke in Virginia and during the 1770s was to play a minimal political role because of diminishing psychological faculties.

15. **(B)** Taking place in March 1770, the Boston Massacre occurred AFTER the Townshend Duties of 1767. All other events took place after 1770: Boston Tea Party (1773); First Continental Congress (1774); Intolerable Acts (1774); and the Battle of Lexington and Concord (1775). The massacre itself was a relatively small, local incident involving Boston dock workers and British soldiers that resulted in seven Bostonians being shot. However, the radicals used the incident to their advantage and propagandized the event into a major blow against American freedom.

16. **(D)** Both Henry Clay (I) and Daniel Webster (III) were ardent supporters of the Union and believed that once a state had joined the Union that state could never secede. They felt that all grievances must be resolved within the framework of the Constitution, which in their view did not allow states to secede when grievances were not resolved to their liking, or for any other reason. John C. Calhoun (II), however, was a leader in the states' rights movement and believed states could secede

whenever they wanted to. His views were diametrically opposed to those expressed in the passage.

17. **(D)** The passage is from a speech made by Henry Clay during the debate over the Compromise of 1850. The Compromise sought to resolve differences between Northern and Southern states over the issues of slavery and prohibition against its expansion into western territories such as New Mexico and California. This debate was the only one in which all of the people named were present. While Henry Clay was present for the debate of the Missouri Compromise in 1820 (C), younger statesmen such as Stephen A. Douglas, Jefferson Davis, Salmon Chase, and William Seward were not. The Missouri Compromise debate, as well as the decision over the location of the Mason-Dixon line (E), never raised the issue of secession as openly as the debate over the Compromise of 1850, and while impassioned speeches such as the one quoted were given on the issue of slavery, they were not given on the issue of secession. While both the Kansas-Nebraska Acts (B) and the secession of South Carolina (A) sparked impassioned speeches, they both occurred after the deaths of Calhoun and Webster, so they could not have participated in these debates.

18. **(B)** The major victory of the Americans at Saratoga did much to convince the French to join in an alliance with the Americans against England. According to our French ambassador, Benjamin Franklin, the French were hesitant to assist the Americans because they saw little hope for an American military victory over England. However, General Gates' victory over General Burgoyne gave the Americans new hope and the desperately needed French alliance and loan. Now England faced a war on two fronts. Saratoga was the turning point in the military phase of the American Revolution. Neither Washington nor Howe participated at the Battle of Saratoga which took place in New York.

19. **(B)** In 1632, the English Catholic Lord Baltimore purchased the colony of Maryland as a refuge and haven for persecuted English Catholics. As a proprietary colony, Maryland never attracted many Catholics and the settlers constantly were contesting with the Baltimore family for power. New York, New Hampshire, and Delaware were royal colonies directly under the control of the British monarch. Connecticut was a compact/ contract colony that remained largely independent of British rule up to the American Revolution.

20. **(D)** The British policy of mercantilism encouraged the American colonists to serve as a source of raw materials (i.e., fish, fur, lumber, food,

etc.) for the mother country. The policy of mercantilism was an economic policy for the British Empire in North America. It was first proposed in the 1590s by Richard Hakluyt and guided the British Parliament throughout the seventeenth and eighteenth centuries. Under mercantilism, the American colonies were to engage in exclusive trade with England and not any other foreign powers, including the French West Indies. Mercantilism promoted a system of economic specialization between England and America, whereby the colonies would serve as the suppliers of raw materials and the consumers of British manufactured goods (i.e., hats, paints, carriages, clothing). Thus, the policy of mercantilism discouraged the development of American manufacturing as it would prove an unwanted competitor to British industry. The British Parliament never discouraged Americans from the importation of black slave labor.

21. **(D)** Roger Sherman was the author of the Great Compromise at the Philadelphia Convention. The issue at hand was the proposed Virginia Plan versus the New Jersey Plan at the Convention. The delegates were equally divided between support of the Virginia Plan (a legislature based on population and favoring the large/populous states) and the New Jersey Plan (a legislature granting each state an equal vote and favoring the small states). This division resulted in a deadlock and threatened the ability to produce a new government for the nation. The deadlock was broken when Sherman proposed the creation of a two house (bicameral) legislature/congress, with the Senate based on the New Jersey Plan (two senators per state) and the House of Representatives based on the Virginia Plan (one representative per 25,000 inhabitants). With the approval of the compromise, the 55 delegates were able to produce the U.S. Constitution. Patrick Henry, as an Antifederalist, never attended the Convention. Adams and Jefferson also were not in attendance as they were serving overseas as America's ambassadors to England and France, respectively. James Madison, as one of the authors of the Virginia Plan, did not author the Compromise.

22. **(C)** The Antifederalists never voiced concern in 1788–1789 over the location of the government in Washington, D.C. because it was not proposed as the new seat of government until 1790 with the accepted Constitution already in operation. During the newspaper debates over the Constitution, the Antifederalists expressly and vehemently denounced the powers of the Supreme Court as too broad and that the national court would overshadow the state courts under the Constitution. These opponents of the Constitution also feared the indirect election of the president through the electoral college system as one that would encourage plots and conspiracies. Finally, the two gravest defects of the Constitution in the eyes of the

Antifederalists were that it did not guarantee the rights of its citizens in writing (ultimately, this complaint would lead to the Bill of Rights as the first 10 amendments to the Constitution) and that no single republican form of government could effectively rule over such a large territory as the original American states.

23. **(D)** In 1794, George Washington appointed John Jay as special ambassador to negotiate a treaty with Great Britain. Because of his lack of diplomatic leverage, Jay secured a treaty in which England agreed only to the removal of British troops from American soil. England refused to allow the Americans open trade with the West Indies and refused to stop the impressment of American sailors (a practice whereby Americans virtually were kidnapped into serving 10–20 year terms in the British navy). Revolutionary War debts remained open to negotiation by the two parties. Although the Treaty passed the Senate by a single vote, opposition from the Republican party was most intense over the issue of impressment.

24. **(D)** During his first year as president, John Adams faced a crisis with France that threatened the honor and sovereignty of America. In 1796, the French navy began seizing American ships on the Atlantic and confiscating their cargo. Adams was informed by three French agents (X, Y, & Z were their code names) that French minister Talleyrand would accept a bribe of $250,000 and an interest-free loan of $12 million to negotiate this issue. Adams prudently leaked this demand to the American press who rallied the nation around the slogan listed in Question 24. Adams was able to avoid war with France, but did not offer the tribute demanded and saved the honor of the new nation. This was the one event Adams took greatest pride in for the remainder of his life.

25. **(B)** According to the Constitution, the House of Representatives was empowered to select the president from the two top vote getters if no candidate received over 50 percent of the electoral vote. In the election of 1800, John Adams and Charles Pickney were the Federalist party candidates for president and vice president, while Jefferson and Aaron Burr were the nominees of the Democratic-Republican party. However, the ballots cast by the electoral college never indicated who was president and who was vice president. Thus, Jefferson and Burr were tied. Burr sought to steal the presidency from Jefferson and the House cast 37 separate votes before deciding on Jefferson upon the advice of Alexander Hamilton. This election led to the ratification of the Twelfth Amendment to the Constitution in 1804 which ordered all future ballots to designate a candidate's office.

26. **(D)** After the American Revolution, American women were advised by authors and ministers that they could best serve the nation by becoming "republican mothers." This concept encouraged women to retain their domain in the household and seek to enter the public world vicariously through their sons. Mothers were advised to teach their sons the republican virtues of truth, frugality, sense of public service, honor, and wisdom. Women were not granted the right to vote, hold any public office, or teach in public schools. Instead, they were advised to keep the home as their domain and only take a half-step toward public life.

27. **(B)** In 1803, Thomas Jefferson sought to purchase American trade rights to use the Mississippi from France. Because of Napoleon's need for capital to finance his European wars, he offered to sell Jefferson all of the Louisiana Territory instead. After the purchase of this seemingly tractless wilderness, Jefferson witnessed the Lewis and Clark expedition to explore the region embark in 1804. Lewis and Clark crossed the continental United States and reached the Pacific coast in 1806. The Louisiana Purchase was approved by the Senate in 1803. The Nullification Controversy with South Carolina occurred in 1831–1832 and the Missouri Compromise was in 1819–1820.

28. **(B)** In 1805, Aaron Burr entered into one of the boldest schemes in American history. Because he was removed from the vice presidency in 1804 and defeated for governor of New York, Burr desperately planned a plot with Spain to kidnap President Jefferson and accept for ransom a large territory in the southwestern United States as a new independent country under his control. Burr was arrested at the eleventh hour of the conspiracy and placed on trial for treason. Chief Justice John Marshall used the case to embarrass Jefferson in 1807 and actually acquitted Burr of the treason charges on a very liberal reading of the treason law requiring two eyewitnesses to the same overt act. Burr attempted neither to assassinate Madison nor defraud the Bank of the United States.

29. **(D)** The Treaty of Ghent ending the War of 1812 was signed on December 24, 1815. Two weeks later, because news of the treaty had yet to arrive in America, the Battle of New Orleans was fought on January 8, 1815. The Americans under the leadership of Andrew Jackson earned a major victory, killing over 2,000 British soldiers while suffering only 13 casualties. The invasion of Canada, which ended in American defeat, was in 1812. The Battle of Lake Erie took place in 1813 and proved a major American naval victory. The burning of Washington, D.C. by the British took place in 1814.

30. **(B)** In 1823, President James Monroe announced to Congress his three principles for foreign policy that later were labeled the Monroe Doctrine. In addition to pledging that Americans would remain free of European wars and threatening American war for any future European colonization of the Western Hemisphere, Monroe uttered the words quoted in Question 30. This doctrine established the areas of North and South America as an American sphere of influence. England supported the doctrine primarily to prevent a major European war over the crumbling Spanish empire. The issue of American continents and European colonization was not the focus of any of the other choices. Washington's farewell address of 1796 only warned Americans to avoid future European wars; the Truman Doctrine of 1947 was Truman's outline for combatting worldwide Communism; *McCulloch v. Maryland* involved the rights of the national government over the states in 1819. The Bill of Rights does not deal with foreign policy matters directly.

31. **(D)** In 1832, Jackson is said to have uttered these words in reaction to Chief Justice Marshall's decision in the case of the *Cherokee Nation v. Georgia*. Although Marshall rejected the Cherokee nation's argument that they existed as a "nation within a nation," he nonetheless ruled that the Cherokees could not be legally moved from their lands as the state of Georgia desired. The Cherokees were finally removed in 1837–1838 along the Trail of Tears. In this case, Jackson reminded the Court that its power was totally dependent upon the Executive branch's willingness to enforce the law. In *Gibbons* (1824), the Court ruled on commerce; in *McCulloch* (1819), the court ruled on the superior power of the national government over the states; *Dred Scott* (1857) was a decision by Roger Taney on slavery; and *Marbury v. Madison* (1803) established the power of judicial review.

32. **(B)** During the 1820s, American farmers moved away from subsistence farming (growing food for one's own consumption only) to commercial market farming (growing a single cash crop for export). After the War of 1812, high crop prices enticed most American farmers to venture cash crop production. For many of these farmers, commercial affairs and market demands proved far more complex than they had expected. The result of this venture was short-term indebtedness for most farmers and becoming dependent pawns in a trans-Atlantic commercial economy. The symbol of the small, independent yeoman farmer no longer fit the reality of the American economy. The rise of textile industry and factories is generally described under the heading of American industrialization and not the market economy. The Second Bank of the United States under the directorship of Nicholas

Biddle earned fame through its struggles with President Andrew Jackson and not as an innovative economic force in the 1820s.

33. **(E)** During the 1830s, America underwent a series of major reform movements in an effort to create the perfect society. One of the largest movements throughout the decade was the Temperance Movement to rid American society of its reliance upon alcoholic consumption. (Consumption of alcohol averaged one-half pint per male per day throughout the decade.) In addition, the attempt to perfect Americans through the means of religion gave rise to the Second Great Awakening, or revivalism. The Seneca Falls Convention of 1848 announced the drive for women's rights during this time, as well as efforts to reform America's schools and greatly expand the public school system. The only movement that did not enjoy a large following was the activity of labor unions. Generally, unions were depicted as forces opposed to American individualism and a foreign import from Europe that threatened basic American freedoms.

34. **(C)** In 1824, no candidate received a clear majority in the electoral college. Although Jackson had outpolled his nearest rival in the popular vote, 43 percent to 30 percent, the House of Representatives still selected the second candidate, John Quincy Adams, over Jackson. Jackson became outraged when he discovered that Henry Clay, a presidential candidate, swung his support to Adams and was named secretary of state by Adams. Jackson was convinced that a deal had been struck and the popular vote denied. Jackson never discussed fraudulent voting practices and the Whig party was not identified with campaign smears during this election.

35. **(E)** Andrew Jackson had the single greatest impact on the office of the presidency of any president other than Washington during the nineteenth century. Jackson completely transformed the office from a pawn of political parties to a strong and independent force in American government and politics. He established his power through the use of the veto (i.e., the Maysville Veto, the veto of the Second Bank of the United States, etc.) as an offensive rather than defensive political weapon. In addition, he was able to bypass both congressional and party control of his Cabinet by appointing an unofficial inner circle of top advisors called "the kitchen cabinet." Jackson also used his power to appoint civil servants for the federal government with a vengeance and replaced earlier office holders with officials who were personally loyal to him, creating the "spoils system." Finally, Jackson skillfully used public opinion to back his policies whenever he felt it was required, as in his struggles with Nicholas Biddle over the Second Bank of the United States.

36. **(E)** President Jackson led an assault on the Second Bank under the directorship of Nicholas Biddle in 1832. Known as Jackson's Bank War, the president was outraged by the Bank's pro-Eastern and pro-business policies under Biddle. In 1832, Jackson refused to recharter the Bank on the grounds that the Bank was an illegal monopoly and had no constitutional authority to exist. In addition, Jackson publicly rallied the American people around his crusade by stating fears that the Bank's foreign creditors could use the Bank to control American foreign policy and that the Bank catered to the needs and interests of a wealthy elite at the cost of high taxes and no benefits to the American farmer and workingman.

37. **(E)** In 1961, Stanley Elkins published his controversial work *Slavery*. In this study, Elkins likened the conditions of blacks under slavery to Jewish inmates of Nazi concentration camps during World War II. According to Elkins, the American system of slavery relied upon physical and psychological torture of African-Americans to such a degree that it crushed them psychologically and produced the "Sambo personality"—infantile-like adults who lacked strong self-esteem and initiative and who often adopted the views of white racism as their own internal values of self-hate. Herbert Aptheker was a Marxist scholar who advanced the view of slaves as heroic rebels. George Fitzhugh was the Southern champion of slavery as a positive good in the 1850s and viewed all black people as innately inferior to whites and as a result they advanced under slavery. Stowe's depiction of slaves in *Uncle Tom's Cabin* displayed blacks as human beings with a full range of virtues and courage. Eugene Genovese is a contemporary historian whose classic *Roll Jordan Roll* examines African-American slave culture and depicts a strong culture grounded by strong and stable people and not "Sambo" personalities.

38. **(C)** In the 1850s, the most ardent defender of Southern slavery was George Fitzhugh. In works such as *Cannibals All*, Fitzhugh pointed out that all great empires and civilizations of the past had relied upon slavery and that slave owners actually were civilizing "savage" Africans as much as could be expected under slavery. Fitzhugh also pointed out that unlike the treatment of "wage slaves" up north (factory workers), slaves were cared for while aged and infirm by the slave owner. It was Fitzhugh's view that because of the community of interest under slavery, slavery actually proved more human toward its workers (slaves) than Northern capitalism did toward its workers. Benjamin Lundy sought to end slavery through the American Colonization Society, as did William Lloyd Garrison through the Abolitionists or American Anti-Slavery Society. Both Henry Clay and

Stephen Douglas sought compromise solutions to the political crisis of slavery that adopted a strong stance on neither side of the slavery issue.

39. **(D)** The delay in admitting Texas to the Union was largely owing to Northern fears that the great size of the Texas territory would produce at least 10 new slave states and thus shift the balance of power established under the Missouri Compromise of 1819 to the slave states. Texas settlers since gaining their independence from Mexico in 1837 had been clamoring for entry into the United States and appealed to the American belief that it was the nation's destiny to reach the Pacific under Manifest Destiny doctrines. Treaty negotiations with Mexico over the extent of Texas' border did not take place until 1845–1846 and led directly to the Mexican-American War. Sam Houston's views toward Van Buren had little impact on the Texas as a state issue.

40. **(D)** During the election of 1860, Lincoln sought to reduce the issue of slavery to a secondary status before the primary concern of keeping the nation united. As a result, Lincoln varied widely in his public views on slavery, but never waivered from his belief that the primary issue in the election was keeping the union together. John Brown in 1859 uttered the words of needing to purge America by blood of the sin of slavery. The quotes from (B), (C), and (E) were all representative of the extreme abolitionist position adopted by William Lloyd Garrison and his followers who desired to end slavery immediately even at the cost of losing the South to secession. Lincoln never advocated the Abolitionist position.

41. **(E)** At the close of the Mexican-American War in 1847, Mexico ceded to the United States portions of present-day Texas, Nevada, New Mexico, California, Utah, Arizona, and Wyoming for $15 million. The state of Washington was part of the Louisiana Purchase of 1803.

42. **(E)** The Nat Turner Rebellion occurred in 1831 as the bloodiest slave uprising in American history when 55 whites were killed by about 15 slaves in Virginia. The Kansas-Nebraska Act was passed in 1854 and sought to establish the principle of popular sovereignty in the two territories on the issue of slavery to promote the presidential ambitions of Senator Stephen Douglas of Illinois. The Seneca Falls Convention convened in 1848 as a militant expression of women's rights led by Lucretia Mott and Elizabeth Cady Stanton. The Lincoln-Douglas debates took place in 1858 as both candidates vied for the Senate seat in Illinois. The Homestead Act was passed by Congress in 1862 and granted a free 160-acre farm in the Far

West (Great Plains region) to any American citizen 21 years of age or older who would work the land for five years.

43. **(A)** Northerners were outraged by the measure of the Compromise of 1850 known as the Fugitive Slave Law. Although the North had gained victories in the Compromise in California's admission as a free state and the end of slave auctions in Washington, D.C., they felt the price of victory was too high with the Fugitive Slave Law. Under this law, all Americans legally were required to assist in the return of all runaway or "fugitive" slaves to their masters. Abolitionists like Garrison denounced the act as an attempt to force every Northerner to become part of the dreaded slave system. The importation of African slaves legally had ended in 1808 and the Gag Rule on tabling abolition petitions in Congress without discussion was enacted in 1837. Northern concern over Utah and New Mexico had been voiced during debates over the Wilmot Proviso at the end of the Mexican-American War.

44. **(D)** In 1857, the Supreme Court under Roger Taney sought to offer a final solution to the crisis over slavery in the Dred Scott Case. Here a black slave sued for his freedom on the grounds he was in Northern territory which had outlawed slavery. Taney ruled that Scott could not sue in the Court because blacks were not and could never become citizens of the United States. In addition, Taney ruled the Missouri Compromise of 1819 and all other laws prohibiting slavery unconstitutional as violations of the "due process clause" of the Fifth Amendment regarding property.

45. **(E)** In the election of 1860, the strength of sectionalism in the country was apparent with the nomination of four sectional candidates for president. As the Republican party's candidate, Lincoln mustered only 40 percent of the popular vote but carried a majority of electoral college votes to win the election. John Breckinridge for the Southern Democrats earned 18 percent of the popular vote, while Stephen Douglas and the Northern Democrats earned 30 percent. John Bell of the Constitutional Union party was able to gather only 13 percent of the vote. Thus, Lincoln was seen as a minority president lacking a national mandate and representing only the interests of the North.

46. **(E)** Lincoln's issuance of the Emancipation Proclamation in January 1863 was greeted with joyous celebration in the North. However, a strict legal reading of the document indicates that it effectively did not free a slave. Lincoln's proclamation freed only those slaves in territories in rebellion against the United States, an area which by definition Lincoln had no

authority. The proclamation was silent on those slaves who were held in Maryland and Tennessee, two areas under Lincoln's control. Slavery finally was ended by an act of Congress in 1865 through the Thirteenth Amendment to the Constitution.

47. **(B)** The Confederate government's adoption of a states' rights system of government most closely represents the Articles of Confederation from 1784–1788. Both systems of government rely on the friendly cooperation of its member states, have no coercive power over the states, and cannot act directly on its citizens but must go through the states. The British Constitution, U.S. Constitution, and Napoleonic France all established strong central/national governments with local government units that are subordinate to the national government. Another term for the Confederacy and the Articles used by political scientists is state-centered federalism.

48. **(A)** Lincoln's faith in democracy is best reflected in his sponsorship of the Homestead Act, which granted a free 160-acre farm in the Great Plains to any American citizen willing to work the land for five years. This Act gave rise to the great westward migration of up to four million Americans from 1865 to 1900. Lincoln was extremely reluctant to enlist black volunteers during the Civil War and was forced to this action only in 1863 with the creation of the 54th Massachusetts regiment. Black troops, about 185,000, were kept in segregated units under white officers. Lincoln's passage of the Emancipation Proclamation was more an act of political subterfuge than an effort in democracy as the Proclamation never really freed a slave. The Fourteenth Amendment was ratified in 1867 after Lincoln's death. During his first four months in office, Lincoln ran the Civil War as a virtual dictator, usurping Congressional powers of raising and supporting an army while Congress was on leave.

49. **(C)** Despite their great exodus westward under the Homestead Act, the vast majority of the four million homesteaders from 1865 to 1900 failed. The main problem they faced was that a 160-acre farm was too small to support profitable agriculture in this region because of water shortages and soil conditions. The Great Plains required large farming methods that were beyond the means of most homesteaders. Most ex-slaves remained in the South as sharecroppers after the War, although a sizeable minority did serve as cowboys on the Santa Fe cattle drives. Most recent immigrants from Eastern Europe at this time congregated in America's Northern and Eastern cities as factory workers. The homesteaders retained their allegiance to the Republican party for it had sponsored the Act.

50. **(C)** At the close of the Civil War, the Radical Republicans pledged to the ex-slaves that they would establish the freed black's economic independence in the South. The Radicals planned to do this by confiscating all Southern plantations of more than 200 acres and subdividing these farms into 40-acre farms to be given to the ex-slaves along with a free mule. This "40 acres and a mule" program was never established and most ex-slaves were forced to work for their former masters under sharecropping, a system of exploitation that reduced most Southern blacks to abject poverty. The Radicals did establish the Freedman's Bureau which established free public schools in the South for ex-slaves, provided the vote to the ex-slaves, and protected the black voter before the attacks of white terrorist groups such as the Ku Klux Klan and the White Camelia, and satisfied most Northerners that the South was paying for secession and Civil War.

51. **(D)** The Republican President Hayes was responsible for the Sellout of 1876. In the election of 1876, the Republican Hayes and Democrat Tilden ended in an electoral tie for the presidency. Amidst claims of fraudulent election returns, Hayes met with Southern members of the House of Representatives in New Orleans. In return for their votes, Hayes promised to withdraw Union soldiers from the South and end Reconstruction, effectively granting the white South a free hand in dealing with blacks. Hayes won the election in the South and made good on his bargain. Neither Taft, Johnson, nor Grant were involved in the election of 1876.

52. **(E)** Franklin's famous engraving was intended to muster support for his plan for colonial unity in 1754 known as the Albany Plan. The other delegates to the 1754 Congress rejected Franklin's plan. The 13 colonies would not be united under a single plan of government until the American Revolution through the Continental Congress and later the Articles of Confederation. The Seven Years' War did not begin until 1756, while the Stamp Act was in 1765. The colonies never sought to break from the system of mercantilism and traded with Canada even during the Seven Years' War.

53. **(B)** The passage represents the philosophy and major tenets of the "Know-Nothing" party, which developed in the late 1840s as the culmination of the anti-Catholic and anti-immigrant sentiments which were widespread in the United States at that time. People feared that immigrants were destroying social values, adding to unemployment problems, and disrupting the political process. Many of these immigrants were Catholic, and they were particularly targeted because of their supposed subservience to a foreign leader, the pope. The Know-Nothings promised to end this perceived threat by limiting the rights of Catholics and immigrants to vote

and to hold elective office. Free Soilers (A) focused on stopping the expansion of slavery into the western territories. The fledgling Republican party (D) focused on the abolition of slavery. The Whig party (E) was a mainstream party that refused to take radical positions on the issues of Catholicism and immigrants, and was destroyed by the development of the more radical parties. The Populist party (C) was formed in the 1890s by farmers seeking to redress economic concerns ignored by the major political parties. The Populists never blamed their problems on immigrants and Catholics and never included restrictive policies against them in their platform.

54. **(D)** The Know-Nothing party evolved out of a secret society known as the "Order of the Star Spangled Banner." It rapidly gained support, especially in coastal cities where the number of immigrants and Catholics were high. The party became the second largest political party in the country by 1855. However, its narrow focus and its lack of nationally recognized, competent, and experienced leaders left it unable to accomplish its stated goals. People quickly grew disillusioned and flocked to other parties focusing on other issues ignored by the Know-Nothings, such as slavery and states' rights, which were rapidly becoming the major issues. By 1860, the Know-Nothings were no longer a major political force.

55. **(D)** Under Prince Henry of Portugal new navigational instruments, such as the compass and astrolabe, were developed which, along with improvements in sailing ships, made long-distance ocean voyages possible. The Crusades, although not bringing Christian control to the Middle East, helped stimulate the Renaissance, which in turn developed interest in the larger world. The Genoese and Venetian monopoly created interest in finding new routes to the East while the development of banking put together capital for financing the search for new trade routes.

56. **(C)** Roger Williams came into conflict with the Puritan authorities because he argued that political leaders could have no authority over religious matters, that the English settlers must buy the land from the Indians, and that individuals had the right to worship according to their individual conscience. After establishing the colony of Rhode Island, Williams included the principle that government rested upon the consent of the governed in the 1644 charter. Anne Hutchinson was exiled from the Massachusetts Bay Colony for advocating that religion should be based on direct intuition of God and his love rather than religious authorities.

57. **(B)** Connecticut was part of New England. Pennsylvania, Delaware, New Jersey, and New York comprised the Middle Colonies.

58. **(C)** French settlement was largely confined to the area north of Montreal to the mouth of the St. Lawrence River. In addition to controlling the St. Lawrence River, the French also controlled access to the Mississippi at New Orleans. Unlike the 13 British colonies, New France had one central government. And also unlike the British, the French, who emphasized the fur trade, tended not to establish permanent settlements in the interior and therefore did not threaten the forests and game necessary to Indian life. The Six Nations, however, never allied with the French.

59. **(A)** The fall of Louisburg in 1758 gave the British a base from which they could cut off French reinforcements and supplies to America. The British conquered Fort Frontenac and Fort Duquesne in 1758 and Crown Point and Fort Ticonderoga in 1759.

60. **(A)** The principal reason for opposition to Texas' entrance into the Union was that it wanted to permit slavery. There was also concern over possible war with Mexico, because it did not recognize Texan independence. Texas entered the Union in 1845.

61. **(E)** The "Middle Passage" refers to the slave traders' route between Africa and the Americas during which 13 to 33 percent of the slaves died. Lewis and Clark crossed the Rocky Mountains at the Bozeman Pass on their 1804–06 expedition. Henry Hudson sought the Northwest Passage in 1609. The National Road was built between 1806 and 1852, connecting Maryland and Illinois. Gold seekers crossed the Isthmus of Panama in 1849.

62. **(B)** John Winthrop, Governor of Massachusetts Bay Colony, opposed religious toleration, supporting the banishment of Roger Williams and Anne Hutchinson. William Penn established toleration in Pennsylvania, Roger Williams in Rhode Island, and Lord Baltimore in Maryland. Later, Thomas Jefferson wrote the Virginia Statute for Religious Freedom (1786).

63. **(B)** Through laws such as the Wool Act (1699), colonial manufacturing was severely restricted.

64. **(A)** The Intolerable Acts, which included the closing of the Port of Boston, were passed in response to the Boston Tea Party of 1773. The Boston Massacre (1770), Continental Congress (1774), Gaspee Affair (1772), and the Committee of Correspondence (1772) were other elements in the growing tension between Great Britain and its American colonies.

65. **(C)** Nathaniel Greene served as commander of the American troops in the South. The other individuals were all British commanders during the American Revolution.

66. **(B)** The Constitutional Convention met in Philadelphia from May 14 to September 17, 1787. Washington, D.C., did not yet exist.

67. **(D)** Hamilton's "Report on Public Credit" (1790) proposed to assume both the state debts and the debts of the Confederation. In other proposals he sought the establishment of a national bank, a protective tariff, and bounties to encourage manufacturing.

68. **(C)** Largely by reducing the size of the army and navy, Jefferson was able to reduce the federal budget. Although he opposed the Bank of the United States and assumption of state debts, he did not change Federalist policies. Secretary of the Treasury Albert Gallatin tried to pay off the national debt as rapidly as possible.

69. **(E)** The Adams-Onis Treaty (1819) with Spain gave the United States both East and West Florida in return for U.S. payment of up to $5 million in claims by American citizens against the Spanish. Louisiana was purchased in 1803 from France. Texas obtained its independence from Mexico in 1836 and entered the Union in 1845. The 49th parallel was accepted as the border between Canada and Oregon by the U.S. and Great Britain in 1846. And California became an American possession through the Treaty of Guadalupe Hidalgo in 1848.

70. **(E)** Bonuses to new industries were part of Alexander Hamilton's "Report on Manufactures" (1791). Henry Clay's American System included the protective tariff, the Second Bank of the United States, and federally funded internal improvement.

71. **(E)** The Bill of Rights, the first ten amendments to the Constitution, was proposed by Congress (1789) and ratified by the states (1791). The first nine limited Congress by forbidding it to encroach upon certain basic rights—freedom of religion, speech, and press, immunity from arbitrary arrest, and trial by jury. The Tenth Amendment reserved to the states all powers except those specifically withheld from them or delegated to the federal government.

72. **(A)** Although there may be some disagreement among historians, most see slavery as the key element underlying other differences such as the lack of industrialization, rural patterns of living, and slow development of a transportation system, particularly railroads. The existence of slavery also made the South less attractive to immigrants.

73. **(E)** The Jacksonian era was notable for its rhetorical egalitarianism, hence the term "Jacksonian democracy," but recent research indicates that the period did not experience any significant increase in social mobility. The Jacksonian Democrats supported the spoils system and opposed Indian rights. Both the Democrats and the Whigs used the nominating convention. And the number of active voters increased in response to the new campaign tactics.

74. **(D)** Beginning in the 1830s, the Irish came to America in large numbers, stirring up resentment because of their Catholicism, clannishness, dress, and accents. The other groups all came to America in significant numbers after the Civil War.

75. **(D)** "Scalawag" referred to native-born Southerners who cooperated, for whatever reasons, with the Northern authorities during Reconstruction.

76. **(C)** In 1873 Congress passed a law taking silver coins off the list of standard coins. The Bland-Allison Act was passed in 1878 and the Sherman Silver Purchase Act in 1890. In 1834 the government had offered to buy silver at a ratio of 16 to 1 in relation to gold. Despite the Sherman Silver Purchase Act, the Treasury Department refused to coin the silver that it purchased.

77. **(E)** The Tenure of Office Act was passed in 1867 in order to reduce the power of President Andrew Johnson. Congress passed the Morrill Tariff Act in 1861, the Conscription Act in 1863, the Homestead Act in 1862, and the National Banking Act in 1863.

78. **(D)** This map represents European powers in North America after the French and Indian War (or Seven Years' War), 1754–63, transferred Canada from France to Great Britain.

79. **(C)** By 1860 the South had nearly 4 million slaves.

80. **(B)** The issuing of the Specie Circular of 1836, which required that only gold or silver or bank notes backed by gold and silver could be used to pay for public land, helped spark the panic of 1837. His withdrawal of federal funds from the Bank of the United States after his 1832 veto of the renewal of the charter also contributed to the expansion in the circulation of bank notes which led to his Specie Circular.

81. **(A)** Because of the tie between Jefferson and Burr in the electoral college vote of 1800, the Twelfth Amendment required that the college vote separately for president and vice president. The First Amendment provided for freedom of religion; the Twenty-second Amendment limited the president to two terms; the Eighteenth Amendment prohibited the manufacture and sale of alcoholic beverages; and the Second Amendment gave the right to bear arms.

82. **(A)** *The Federalist Papers*, a collection of 85 essays, were written anonymously by Alexander Hamilton, John Jay, and James Madison. Seventy-seven of the essays originally appeared in New York newspapers under the pseudonym "Publius." These essays argued for the ratification of the Constitution by stressing the inadequacies of the Articles of Confederation.

83. **(D)** In 1854 the American ministers to Great Britain, France, and Spain met in Ostend, Belgium and issued a statement that became known as the Ostend Manifesto. It said that if Spain would not sell Cuba to the United States, the U.S. had the right to seize the island by force.

84. **(D)** The Declaratory Act of 1766, passed after Parliament rescinded the Stamp Act (1765), asserted that Parliament had the power to make laws that were binding on the American colonists. The other acts referred to are (A) the Quartering Act (1765), (B) the Currency Act (1764), (C) the Sugar Act (1764), and (E) the Stamp Act (1765).

85. **(A)** Henry James wrote his major novels in the nineteenth and early twentieth centuries. Nathaniel Hawthorne published *The Scarlet Let-*

ter in 1850 and *The House of the Seven Gables* in 1851. Walt Whitman published *Leaves of Grass* in 1855. Henry David Thoreau wrote *Walden* in 1854, and Herman Melville produced *Moby-Dick* in 1851.

86. **(B)** Secessionist feeling was strongest among the New England Federalists who spoke up strongly for separation from the United States at the Hartford Convention of 1814–15. The Convention, however, only recommended constitutional amendments to weaken Southern power and the Democratic party.

87. **(A)** The joint-stock company was the form of business organization that established Jamestown and Massachusetts, among others. The encomienda was a grant to Indians who lived on a specific piece of land in the Spanish colonies. Prince Henry financed the development of new navigation techniques in the fifteenth century. George III was king of England during the American Revolution, 1776–1783, a period during which republicanism became the dominant political ideology.

88. **(C)** Although after 1840 the Northeast's involvement in both national and international commerce increased, manufacturing became its primary concern. Agriculture and the production of raw materials were of declining importance.

89. **(C)** The merchants, together with lawyers and members of the families of the royal governors, were the most influential citizens in the New England towns. Ministers no longer carried the influence they once had.

90. **(A)** In contrast to the Confederacy, the North was not fighting a defensive war. Rather, it sought to strangle the Confederacy with a blockade; split the Confederacy by controlling the Mississippi and interior railroad lines; and seize Richmond, Virginia, the Confederacy's capital.

91. **(B)** Andrew Johnson became president upon Lincoln's death, serving until 1869. Grant was president between 1869 and 1877, Hayes from 1877 to 1881, Garfield in 1881, and Arthur from 1881 to 1885.

92. **(D)** The Northwest Ordinance of 1787 barred slavery from the territories.

93. **(D)** Virginia was founded as a joint-stock company in 1607. It became a Royal Colony in 1624.

94. **(B)** Harriet Beecher Stowe's *Uncle Tom's Cabin* was published in 1851–52. The American Anti-Slavery Society was established in 1833. Garrison founded *The Liberator* in 1831. The "gag" rule was passed in 1836, and the Liberty party first appeared in 1840.

95. **(D)** The panic of 1857 resulted primarily from over-speculation in railroad stocks. Many banks failed across the nation, although the North suffered the most and the South the least. By 1858 the economy began picking up, bolstered by European demand for foodstuffs and cotton.

96. **(E)** All authority was centered on the Spanish king, who was represented in the New World by two viceroys, who ruled in his name. The Indians were enslaved until the 1540s and after that were placed under the *repartimiento*, another system of forced labor. The mission system evangelized the Indians for the Roman Catholic church. Until the gold and silver ran out, the Spanish used its American colonies to a large extent as a source of these precious metals.

97. **(B)** The Massachusetts Bay Colony was founded in 1630 by the Puritans, who wanted to purify rather than separate from the Anglican church. The Pilgrims were Separatists who established Plymouth in 1620. The Mayflower Compact was an agreement, signed before landing at Plymouth, to obey all the laws that the group adopted. Squanto was an Indian who helped the Pilgrims survive during their first year by teaching them how to use the plants and other natural resources of the new land.

98. **(A)** James Oglethorpe founded Georgia in 1732 for the purpose of aiding debtors released from British prisons. Sir George Calvert established Maryland in 1632 as a haven for Catholics. North Carolina, then combined with South Carolina, was created in 1663 and unsuccessfully sought to establish a government based on a plan by John Locke. New Jersey was originally part of New Netherlands but after the English takeover was ceded to Lord John Berkeley and Sir George Carteret in 1664. Delaware was founded by Swedes but was taken over by the British in 1664 and given to William Penn in 1682, after which it was part of Pennsylvania.

99. **(D)** In the Treaty of Paris of 1763 France gave up its claims in America except for four islands, including Guadeloupe and Martinique. The Spanish gave up Florida to Great Britain but obtained New Orleans and Louisiana from the French. Although the British occupied Cuba and the Philippines during the war, they returned them to Spain.

100. **(B)** The Southern colonies were largely rural with only two relatively large cities, Charleston and Baltimore. They were closely tied with England. Tobacco was the main cash crop in Maryland, Virginia, and North Carolina while rice was grown in Georgia and the Carolinas. The population lived largely on the coastal plains (or tidewater area) where plantations dominated the economy but most of the population lived on small farms.

101. **(C)** The Treaty of Ghent (1814) included only the cessation of hostilities and restoration of territory taken during the War of 1812.

102. **(A)** The Iroquois Confederation, formed in the 1500s, included the Seneca, Cayuga, Onondaga, Oneida, and Mowhawk tribes, all of which were Eastern woodland groups. In the 1700s the Tuscaroras joined the Confederation. The Sioux lived on the Great Plains.

103. **(C)** Harvard was founded in 1636. The colonial colleges included the College of New Jersey (Princeton) (1746), Rhode Island College (Brown) (1764), Queen's College (Rutgers) (1766), King's College (Columbia) (1754), College and Academy of Philadelphia (Pennsylvania) (1755), Dartmouth (1761), College of William and Mary (1693), and Yale College (1716).

104. **(C)** The independence movement did not begin until after the British began passing new taxes and duties beginning in 1765. In 1763 the British government had a huge debt resulting from the French and Indian War, the need to defend the new territory, and the need to establish British governments for Canada and Florida. It also had to deal with the conflicting claims to land west of the Appalachians by the American colonies.

105. **(E)** Samuel Adams was active in both the Massachusetts legislature and on the streets of Boston in arousing opposition to British policies. Patrick Henry and Thomas Jefferson were leaders in the Virginia legislature while John Adams served in the Continental Congress. James Otis wrote a number of pamphlets defending American rights.

106. **(B)** There is nothing about religious toleration in the Declaration. The first portion of the Declaration presented the reasons for separation, the second portion outlined a theory of government, and the third section — the final paragraph — announced the existence of a state of war with Great Britain.

107. **(E)** Under the Articles of Confederation, the government could only ask the states for money; it could not directly tax the people. Consequently, the government was crippled even in carrying out the powers assigned to it.

108. **(E)** The Jay Treaty settled the long-standing problem of British troops in American territory, but it did not address adequately such maritime issues as impressment of American sailors by the British and trade in the British West Indies. It did move toward settlement of Canadian boundary problems by establishing a commission to study the matter. Navigation of the Mississippi was settled by the Pinckney Treaty (1795) with Spain.

109. **(B)** Although war was not formally declared, the demand for a bribe before treaty negotiations could begin led to a quasi-war with France in 1797–1798. In addition to the bribe, France had demanded an American loan and an apology for President Adams's remarks regarding France made to the American Congress.

110. **(C)** Between 1710 and 1720 the population of Massachusetts Bay grew by 4.6 percent; between 1700 and 1710 it grew 1.2 percent; between 1720 and 1730 it grew 2.6 percent; and between 1730 and 1740 it grew 3.3 percent.

111. **(A)** In the Rush-Bagot Treaty (1818), Great Britain and the United States agreed to take military ships from the Great Lakes. The other issues either simply faded away or were settled much later.

112. **(E)** With the invention of the cotton gin in 1793 and expansion into the Deep South after 1815, cotton became the dominant cash crop of the Southern economy.

113. **(A)** South Carolina provoked the crisis in 1832 by voting to nullify, or not allowing to go into effect within its borders, the tariffs of 1828 and 1832. The crisis was ended by the 1833 compromise tariff, although Andrew Jackson obtained the power to enforce the revenue laws militarily.

114. **(D)** Aaron Burr served as vice president of the United States between 1801 and 1804. He later was involved in an apparent conspiracy to separate the western states from the Union. Meriwether Lewis and William Clark led an expedition to the West in 1804–06. Zebulon Pike led a

military expedition to Colorado in 1806. John Charles Frémont was involved in several western expeditions in the 1830s and 1840s.

115. **(C)** Nicholas Biddle served as president of the Second Bank of the United States. William Morgan was a former Mason who vanished about 1826 just before he was to publish an exposé about the secret organization. Roger B. Taney served as chief justice of the Supreme Court between 1836 and 1864. Daniel Webster was a leader in the Senate, representing Massachusetts from 1827 to 1850. Robert Y. Hayne represented South Carolina in the Senate between 1822 and 1832, during which he engaged Webster in a famous debate over states' rights.

116. **(C)** This map represents European powers in North America in 1713 after the Treaty of Utrecht transferred Acadia and a portion of Newfoundland from France to Great Britain.

117. **(A)** Northerners who opposed the Union's war effort were called "Copperheads," after the poisonous snake common in the South. Clement L. Vallandigham, a congressman from Ohio, was the most prominent "Copperhead."

118. **(C)** The Radical Republicans did not favor the distribution of plantation land to the freed slaves. The Reconstruction Act of 1867 temporarily divided the South into military districts and guaranteed that freed slaves could vote and hold office. The Radicals also enlarged the powers of the Freedmen's Bureau over the veto of Andrew Johnson and supported the Fourteenth Amendment, which gave the freed slaves certain civil rights.

119. **(B)** Through the Gadsden Purchase in 1853 the land south of the Gila River was purchased from Mexico for a possible transcontinental railroad route. Although Texas had entered the Union in 1845, the Treaty of Guadalupe Hidalgo established Mexican recognition of the acquisition and the southern boundary at the Rio Grande River.

120. **(C)** The Sixteenth Amendment, passed in 1913, provided for a national income tax. The Emancipation Proclamation (1862) freed slaves in Confederate territory. The Freedmen's Bureau (1865) was created to help the freed blacks. The Thirteenth Amendment (1865) abolished slavery, while the Fourteenth Amendment made the freed slaves citizens of the United States.

PRACTICE TEST 2

This test is also on CD-ROM in our special interactive CLEP History of the United States I TEST*ware*®. It is highly recommended that you first take this exam on computer. You will then have the additional study features and benefits of enforced timed conditions, individual diagnostic analysis, and instant scoring. See page 2 for guidance on how to get the most out of our CLEP History of the United States I book and software.

CLEP HISTORY OF THE UNITED STATES I
Practice Test 2

(Answer sheets appear in the back of this book.)

TIME: 90 Minutes
120 Questions

> **DIRECTIONS**: Each of the questions or incomplete statements below is followed by five possible answers or completions. Select the best choice in each case and fill in the corresponding oval on the answer sheet.

1. All of the following were early explorers of North America EXCEPT

   (A) Francisco Coronado.
   (B) Robert La Salle.
   (C) Samuel de Champlain.
   (D) Francisco Pizarro.
   (E) Jacques Marquette.

2. Which of the following best characterizes Southern society before the Civil War?

   (A) Half of the slaveowners owned five or fewer slaves.
   (B) Most white families owned slaves.
   (C) Most slaveowners owned several hundred slaves.
   (D) The percentage of slaveowners was consistent throughout the South.
   (E) Most slaveowners lived in urban areas.

3. Between 1806 and 1809 nonimportation, nonintercourse, and embargo sought to

   (A) bring peace between France and Great Britain.
   (B) encourage domestic American manufacturing.
   (C) force Great Britain to recognize American rights.

(D) balance Southern and Northern economic power.

(E) help Britain in the Napoleonic wars.

4. Which of the following was the first important means of transportation in the United States after independence?

(A) Canals
(B) Turnpikes
(C) Steamboats
(D) Railroads
(E) Clipper ships

5. The Missouri Compromise of 1820 did all of the following EXCEPT

(A) bring in Maine as a free state.

(B) bring in Missouri as a slave state.

(C) prohibit slavery north of latitude 36°30'.

(D) maintain the balance of slave and free states.

(E) establish the principle of popular sovereignty south of 36°30'.

QUESTIONS 6 and 7 refer to the following passage.

During the contest of opinion through which we have passed the animation of discussions and of exertions has sometimes worn an aspect which might impose on strangers unused to think freely and to speak and to write what they think; but this being now decided by the voice of the nation, announced according to the rules of the Constitution, all will, of course, arrange themselves under the will of the law, and unite in common efforts for the common good. . . . Let us, then, fellow-citizens, unite with one heart and one mind. . . . We have called by different names brethren of the same principle.

6. The above passage is most likely to be found in which of the following?

(A) Washington's farewell address

(B) Lincoln's first inaugural address

(C) Jackson's first inaugural address

(D) Jefferson's first inaugural address

(E) Declaration of Independence

7. The author wants primarily to convince his audience that

(A) political parties are harmful.

(B) political strife is foreign to the American character.

(C) party strife is indicative of fundamental philosophical differences.

(D) party strife should be forgotten once the will of the people has been expressed in an election.

(E) only the members of his party are acting in accordance with the rules of the Constitution.

8. The Declaration of Independence stated that

(A) men are created unequal.

(B) governments derive their powers from God.

(C) it was not right that a small island should rule a large continent.

(D) people have the right to abolish governments destructive of their rights.

(E) there shall be no taxation without representation.

9. According to the Treaty of Paris of 1783, the boundaries of the United States were

(A) Canada, the Gulf of Mexico, and the Mississippi River.

(B) Canada, Florida, and the Mississippi River.

(C) Canada, Florida, and the Missouri River.

(D) Canada, Florida, and the Appalachian Mountains.

(E) Canada, the Gulf of Mexico, and the Missouri River.

10. In 1858 at Freeport, Illinois, Stephen Douglas argued that

(A) Congress should bar slavery from the territories.

(B) slavery should be abolished in Washington, D.C.

(C) slavery could be kept out of the territories if people in the territories failed to pass laws to protect it.

(D) the slave trade should be declared illegal.

(E) slavery should be allowed in all the territories.

11. "God has not been preparing the English-speaking and Teutonic peoples for a thousand years for nothing but vain, idle self-admiration. No! He has not made us the master organizers of the world to establish a system where chaos reigns. He has given us the spirit of progress to overwhelm the forces of reaction throughout the earth. He has made us adept in government that we may administer government among savage and senile peoples."

    The passage most nearly represents the philosophy of

    I. Manifest Destiny.

    II. American exceptionalism.

    III. Social Darwinism.

    (A) I only.

    (B) III only.

    (C) I and III only.

    (D) II and III only.

    (E) I, II, and III.

12. Which of the following was NOT involved in the "triangular trade" of the colonial period?

    (A) Rum

    (B) Molasses

    (C) Cotton

    (D) Slaves

    (E) Tobacco

13. Those who supported ratification of the Constitution were called

    (A) Federalists.

    (B) Democrats.

    (C) Whigs.

    (D) Antifederalists.

    (E) Republicans.

14. Robert E. Lee surrendered to Ulysses Grant at

    (A) Spotsylvania.

    (B) Appomattox.

    (C) Cold Harbor.

    (D) Raleigh.

    (E) Richmond.

15. The French and Indian War took place during

    (A) 1740–1748.
    (B) 1754–1763.
    (C) 1689–1699.
    (D) 1702–1713.
    (E) 1776–1783.

16. Colonial law generally defined slaves as chattel. This meant that slaves were considered as

    (A) human beings with limited rights.
    (B) servants who served for a limited period of time.
    (C) slaves who received freedom upon the death of their masters.
    (D) pieces of property with no rights.
    (E) employees who received pay for their work.

17. The Kentucky and Virginia Resolutions of 1798 introduced which of the following ideas?

    (A) Federal laws take precedent over state wishes.
    (B) The years of residence required for naturalization should be increased from five to 14.
    (C) It is illegal to make "false, scandalous, malicious" statements against the federal government.
    (D) Individual states could nullify or set aside federal laws with which they disagreed.
    (E) A protective tariff was harmful to the economic interests of the South.

18. The Judiciary Act of 1789 established

    (A) a nine-judge Supreme Court.
    (B) 13 circuit courts.
    (C) three district courts.
    (D) the office of attorney general.
    (E) the power of the Supreme Court to review the constitutionality of federal laws.

19. Alexander Hamilton's legislative program for the new republic included all of the following EXCEPT

(A) the Bank of the United States.

(B) organization of the federal judiciary.

(C) assumption of Confederation and state debts.

(D) promotion of domestic manufacturing.

(E) a system of excise taxes.

20. "If slavery is not wrong, nothing is wrong! Slavery is a moral evil that cannot be allowed to expand into the western territories although we should not forcefully attempt to eliminate it in states that already allow it. Black Americans are the equal of every living man in their right to life, liberty and the fruit of their own labor. But they are not yet educated enough nor qualified for the full legal rights of citizenship."

This passage most nearly represents the views of

(A) Stephen A. Douglas.

(B) John Brown.

(C) John C. Breckinridge.

(D) Abraham Lincoln.

(E) Dred Scott.

21. The leading scientist in colonial America was

(A) John Peter Zenger.

(B) Jonathan Edwards.

(C) William Byrd.

(D) Benjamin Franklin.

(E) George Whitefield.

22. Which of the following correctly describes women's rights in mid-nineteenth century America?

(A) A married woman controlled her own property.

(B) Husbands were forbidden to beat their wives.

(C) Women could freely enter professions such as medicine and law.

(D) Women could not claim money they had earned.

(E) Women had the right to vote in federal elections.

23. Under Lincoln's plan of Reconstruction, Southern states could resume their part in the Union after

    (A) 50 percent of the voters as of 1860 took an oath of allegiance.

    (B) 10 percent of the voters as of 1860 took an oath of allegiance.

    (C) allowing blacks to vote.

    (D) adopting the Thirteenth Amendment which abolished slavery.

    (E) repudiating debts accumulated under the Confederacy.

RE-CONSTRUCTION,
OR "A WHITE MAN'S GOVERNMENT".

24. Which of the following best expresses the point of view of the cartoon?

    (A) Southern whites and blacks can never be reconciled.

    (B) Southern whites would willingly be reconciled with blacks.

    (C) Blacks have no interest in reconciliation with Southern whites.

    (D) The president must take a forceful role in reconciling Southern whites and blacks.

    (E) Reconciliation of Southern whites and blacks is simply a matter of recognizing the new realities.

25. Which of the following was NOT characteristic of pre-Civil War American cities?

(A) Rapidly rising death rates

(B) Increase of crime

(C) Extensive sewer systems

(D) Growth of slums

(E) Increase of population

26. The first armed conflict in 1775 between the Americans and British soldiers took place at

(A) Fort Ticonderoga.

(B) Bunker Hill.

(C) Lexington-Concord.

(D) Boston.

(E) Yorktown.

27. By opening territory north of 36°30′ to slavery, the Kansas-Nebraska Act repealed the

(A) Dred Scott decision.

(B) Compromise of 1850.

(C) Wilmot Proviso.

(D) Missouri Compromise.

(E) Northwest Ordinance.

28. By February 1, 1861 which group of states had seceded from the Union?

(A) Mississippi, Florida, Alabama, Georgia, Louisiana, Texas, South Carolina

(B) Mississippi, Arkansas, Missouri, Alabama, Georgia, Florida

(C) Arkansas, Tennessee, North Carolina, Virginia

(D) Texas, Louisiana, Arkansas, Mississippi, Alabama

(E) Kentucky, Mississippi, Arkansas, Missouri, Alabama, Georgia

29. In 1819 the United States obtained Florida from

(A) Great Britain.

(B) Spain.

(C) France.

(D) Mexico.

(E) Portugal.

30. Which of the following does NOT describe the Louisiana Purchase of 1803?

    (A) The United States purchased Louisiana from France for $15 million.

    (B) Jefferson expanded the powers of the presidency.

    (C) French power expanded in the Western Hemisphere.

    (D) The United States doubled in size.

    (E) The treaty of cession left some of the boundaries vague.

31. What territory gained independence in 1836?

    (A) California
    (B) Oregon
    (C) Texas
    (D) Kansas-Nebraska
    (E) Missouri

32. The Whiskey Rebellion of 1794 protested

    (A) prohibition.

    (B) a 25 percent tax on whiskey.

    (C) government regulation of whiskey production.

    (D) the lifting of import duties on whiskey.

    (E) a 30 percent drop in whiskey prices.

33. Which of the following best describes the First Bank of the United States?

    (A) It was solely a private business enterprise.

    (B) It was solely a federal government enterprise.

    (C) It was a joint private-public enterprise.

    (D) It was a joint state-federal government enterprise.

    (E) It was a joint state-private enterprise.

34. Which of the following correctly describes the Puritans?

    (A) Their primary goal was to find gold.

    (B) They established the Virginia colony.

(C) They established an economy based on tobacco.

(D) They wanted to build a society based upon biblical teachings.

(E) They established religious toleration.

35. The Federal Constitution

(A) abolished slavery.

(B) did not count slaves for purposes of representation.

(C) counted 3/5 of slaves for purposes of representation.

(D) explicitly legalized slavery.

(E) counted all slaves for purposes of representation.

36. Historians believe the British trade regulations during the colonial period

(A) were bad for all the American colonies.

(B) favored the Southern colonies over the Northern colonies.

(C) provided both advantages and disadvantages for the American colonies.

(D) encouraged the development of colonial industry.

(E) favored the Northern colonies over the Southern colonies.

37. The Northwest Ordinance of 1787 established what precedent for new territories?

(A) Support for public education

(B) Equality of new states with old

(C) Fair treatment of Indians

(D) Prohibition of slavery

(E) Popular sovereignty

38. The American Revolutionaries gained help from which of the following?

(A) France

(B) Mexico

(C) Canada

(D) Italy

(E) Germany

39. In the controversy over the lands belonging by treaty to the "Five Civilized Tribes," the Jackson administration

(A) destroyed the tribes militarily.

(B) forced Georgia to restore the lands to the Indians.

(C) forced the Indians to be removed to the West.

(D) called upon the Supreme Court to decide the issue.

(E) divided the lands between Georgia and the Indians.

40. Which of the following statements best describes the ethnic makeup of colonial America?

(A) French Huguenots settled heavily in New England.

(B) Germans concentrated in Pennsylvania.

(C) The Scotch-Irish moved into the southern tidewater area.

(D) Maryland was largely a Dutch-dominated colony.

(E) Spanish and Portuguese Jews settled in the Appalachian backcountry.

41. After which of the following dates was there little criticism of slavery within the South?

(A) 1776

(B) 1789

(C) 1815

(D) 1832

(E) 1850

42. Which of the following was a response to the Stamp Act?

(A) The Boston Tea Party

(B) The Battle of Lexington

(C) The Paxton Boys' march on Philadelphia

(D) Nonimportation of British goods

(E) The Boston Massacre

43. The American public protested the Jay Treaty of 1794 because it
    (A) failed to get British soldiers out of the Northwest posts.
    (B) arranged compensation for slaves freed by the British during the Revolution.
    (C) allowed extensive trade with the West Indies.
    (D) did nothing about British seizure of American vessels in the French West Indies.
    (E) settled Canadian boundary questions.

44. Which of the following served as a Union general?
    (A) Joseph Johnston
    (B) Thomas Jackson
    (C) William T. Sherman
    (D) Robert E. Lee
    (E) J.E.B. Stuart

45. The central compromise of the Constitutional Convention involved the issue of
    (A) balance of powers within the federal government.
    (B) relationship of state and federal powers.
    (C) abandonment of the Articles of Confederation.
    (D) representation of large and small states.
    (E) the powers of the presidency.

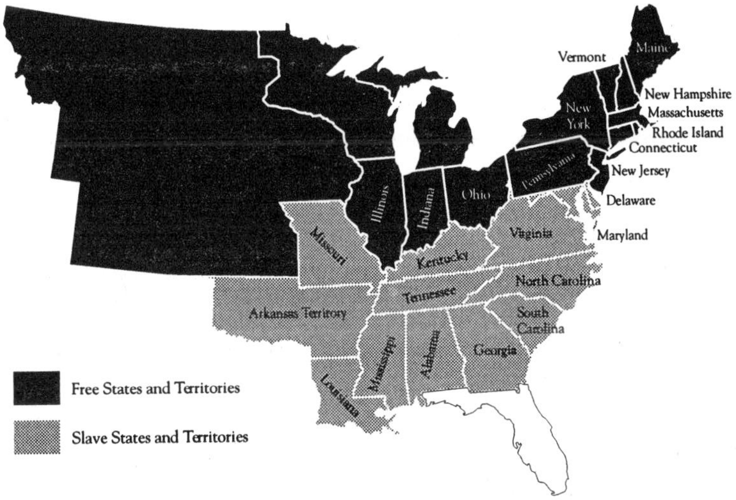

46. The map on the previous page represents the U.S. in what year?

(A) 1804
(B) 1821
(C) 1845
(D) 1848
(E) 1853

47. Which of the following was NOT a cause of the Panic of 1837?

(A) The building up of surpluses in the nation's factories
(B) Destruction of the Second Bank of the United States
(C) Overextension of bank credit
(D) A poor wheat crop
(E) The Specie Circular of 1836

48. "There is a twofold liberty, natural (I mean as our nature is now corrupt) and civil or federal. The first is common to man with beasts and other creatures. By this, man, as he stands in relation to man simply, hath liberty to do what he lists; it is a liberty to evil as well as to good.... The other kind of liberty I call civil or federal, it may also be termed moral, in reference to the covenant between God and man, in the moral law, and the politic covenants and constitutions, amongst men themselves. This liberty is the proper end and object of authority, and cannot subsist without it; and it is a liberty to that only which is good, just, and honest." (John Winthrop, 1630)

In this passage, liberty is understood

(A) primarily in communal terms.
(B) as the most important value.
(C) as something incompatible with Puritan society.
(D) primarily in individual terms.
(E) as something to be achieved only in the future, not in the present.

49. Which Supreme Court chief justice oversaw the development of the Court's power to judge the constitutionality of acts of Congress?

(A) John Marshall
(B) John Jay
(C) Roger Taney
(D) Alexander Hamilton
(E) Oliver Wendell Holmes, Jr.

50. Which of the following opposed rechartering the Second Bank of the United States?

(A) Nicholas Biddle
(B) Henry Clay
(C) Daniel Webster
(D) Andrew Jackson
(E) John Marshall

51. Under the Articles of Confederation, the Congress lacked the power to

(A) control foreign affairs.
(B) coin money.
(C) settle disputes among the states.
(D) tax.
(E) borrow money.

52. In the election of 1860, Abraham Lincoln won

(A) a majority of the popular vote.
(B) the electoral votes of Kentucky and Maryland.
(C) less than half of the electoral vote.
(D) the Northern and Midwestern states.
(E) the electoral votes of Virginia and Tennessee.

53. Which of the following groups tended to support the Federalists?

(A) Small farmers
(B) Small businessmen
(C) Wealthy merchants
(D) Baptist and Methodist ministers
(E) Skilled craftsmen

54. Prior to 1763 the British policy of "salutary neglect"

(A) did not enforce the Navigation Acts.
(B) allowed royal colonies to elect their own governors.
(C) took the Royal Navy off the high seas.
(D) encouraged colonists to establish their own parliament.
(E) withdrew British soldiers from North America.

55. What do Gabriel Prosser, Denmark Vesey, and Nat Turner have in common?

(A) They were active in the Second Great Awakening.

(B) They were early railroad tycoons.

(C) They organized slave rebellions.

(D) They helped form the Whig party.

(E) They were leading New England abolitionists.

56. The *Marbury v. Madison* decision of 1803 established the principle that

(A) the federal government had the power to regulate commerce.

(B) the Supreme Court had the power to declare acts of Congress unconstitutional.

(C) the federal government had the power under the contract clause to protect property rights.

(D) a state lacked the power to block the operation of a federal agency.

(E) that states had the power to determine whether acts of Congress applied within their borders.

57. The Pinckney Treaty with Spain in 1795 gave Americans the "right of deposit" at New Orleans. This meant that

(A) Americans could land goods at New Orleans and ship them out again without paying taxes.

(B) America had full trading rights with the Spanish.

(C) Americans could ship their goods in Spanish vessels.

(D) New Orleans became an American possession.

(E) American banks could be established in New Orleans.

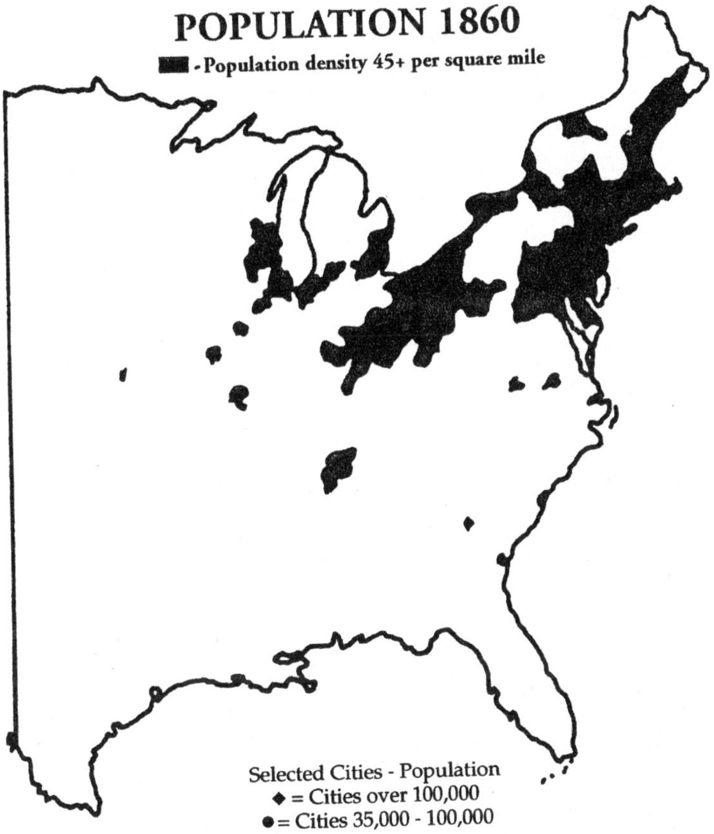

● Albany, NY
◆ Baltimore, MD
◆ Boston, MA
◆ Brooklyn, NY
● Buffalo, NY
● Charleston, SC
◆ Chicago, IL
◆ Cincinnati, OH
● Cleveland, OH
● Detroit, MI
● Lowell, MA
● Louisville, KY
● Montgomery, AL
● New Haven, CT
◆ New Orleans, LA
◆ New York, NY
● Newark, NJ
◆ Philadelphia, PA
● Pittsburgh, PA
● Providence, RI
● Richmond, VA
◆ St. Louis, MO
● Troy, NY
● Washington, DC

58. According to this map, which state had the greatest degree of urbanization in 1860?

(A) New York
(B) Pennsylvania
(C) Illinois
(D) Massachusetts
(E) Virginia

"The Upright Bench," Which Is Above Criticism.

59. This 1871 cartoon by Thomas Nast suggests that

(A) justice prevails in New York.

(B) political influence is sold for cash.

(C) the wealthy control New York politics.

(D) New York government is inefficient.

(E) the people are being well-served by New York government.

60. American factory workers of the pre-Civil War period

    (A) formed powerful unions.

    (B) worked long hours.

    (C) had excellent working conditions.

    (D) included few children.

    (E) were attracted to socialism.

61. Which of the following books was likely to be found in the home of a colonial New Englander?

    (A) *The Scarlet Letter*

    (B) *Walden*

    (C) *Pilgrim's Progress*

    (D) *The Holy Bible,* Douay version

    (E) *Moby-Dick*

62. The Emancipation Proclamation of 1863

    (A) freed all slaves.

    (B) freed slaves in the "border states."

    (C) freed slaves in areas controlled by the Union army.

    (D) freed slaves in areas still in rebellion.

    (E) freed slaves in Washington, D.C.

63. The Proclamation of 1763

(A) ordered that settlement be stopped west of the peaks of the Appalachians.

(B) stated that those who broke the trade laws were to be tried in the admiralty courts.

(C) ended the French and Indian War.

(D) forbade trade with the French, Dutch, and Spanish West Indies.

(E) established new taxes on trade.

64. The Nullification Controversy of 1828 to 1833 arose in response to congressional support for

(A) restrictions on slavery.

(B) protective tariffs.

(C) internal improvements.

(D) the Second Bank of the United States.

(E) popular sovereignty.

65. Debate over ratification of the Constitution in New York resulted in the publication of

(A) *The American Commonwealth.*

(B) *The Federalist Papers.*

(C) *Common Sense.*

(D) *The Age of Reason.*

(E) *Defense of the Constitutions of Government of the United States of America.*

66. Who helped guide the Lewis and Clark expedition and aided in dealing with Indians?

(A) Sacajawea
(B) Zebulon Pike
(C) Sitting Bull
(D) James Wilkinson
(E) Tecumseh

67. Which of the following was part of the Compromise of 1850?

(A) Abolition of the slave trade
(B) A new fugitive slave law
(C) California's entry into the Union on the basis of popular sovereignty
(D) Utah and New Mexico territories to be free
(E) A new eastern border for Texas

68. *Common Sense* was written by

(A) Thomas Paine.
(B) Patrick Henry.
(C) John Locke.
(D) Thomas Jefferson.
(E) John Adams.

69. An indentured servant differed from a slave in that he or she

(A) received wages for their work.

(B) worked for a limited period of time, usually seven years, to repay their passage to America.

(C) was used only for agricultural work.

(D) was held in servitude for life.

(E) was ineligible for the 50 acres of land given under Virginia's headright system.

70. Alexander Hamilton believed that the United States should

(A) repudiate the debts of the Confederation but assume those of the states.

(B) assume the debts of the Confederation but not those of the states.

(C) assume the debts of both the Confederation and the states.

(D) repudiate the debts of both the Confederation and the states.

(E) assume the debts of the Confederation, the states, and local governments.

71. The Bill of Rights guarantees all of the following EXCEPT

(A) the freedom of religion.

(B) the right to a fair trial.

(C) powers not delegated to the federal government by the Constitution are reserved to the states.

(D) the right to bear arms.

(E) the right of women to vote.

72. The followers of Andrew Jackson established what political party?

(A) Whig
(B) Republican
(C) Democratic
(D) Federalist
(E) Populist

73. Beginning in the 1830s, William Lloyd Garrison called for

(A) colonization of slaves.
(B) immediate emancipation of the slaves.
(C) free soil.
(D) step-by-step emancipation of the slaves.
(E) popular sovereignty.

74. The Great Awakening of the 1740s resulted in

(A) the establishment of the Church of England.
(B) a split between religious traditionalists and religious radicals.
(C) an outbreak of witch hunting, resulting in the Salem witchcraft trials.
(D) the hanging of Quakers in Boston.
(E) a revival of denominationalism.

75. George Washington's army faced which of the following problems during the American Revolution?

(A) The British public unanimously supported the policy of its government.
(B) Two-thirds of the colonists opposed the war.
(C) The army was dependent on poorly trained militia.
(D) The army used conventional military tactics.
(E) The British government was able to give its full attention to the war.

76. Regarding interpretation of the Constitution, Alexander Hamilton wrote:

"It leaves, therefore, a criterion of what is constitutional, and of what is not so. This criterion is the *end*, to which the measure relates as a *means*. If the *end* be clearly comprehended within any of the specified powers, and if the measure have an obvious relation to that *end*, and is not forbidden by any particular provision of the Constitution, it may safely be deemed to come within the compass of the national authority."

In this passage Hamilton is arguing that

(A) the Constitution delegates implied powers to the federal government.

(B) the Constitution must specifically state that the federal government has the power to take a particular action.

(C) constitutional questions are to be settled by the Supreme Court.

(D) all implied powers are reserved to the states.

(E) the Constitution states both the ends and means of government action.

77. Which of the following was NOT a major writer of the pre-Civil War period?

(A) Ralph Waldo Emerson

(B) William Dean Howells

(C) Nathaniel Hawthorne

(D) Herman Melville

(E) Washington Irving

78. According to the Dred Scott decision,

(A) only people living within a territory could forbid slavery there.

(B) slaves were citizens of the United States.

(C) Congress had no power over slavery in the territories.

(D) the Missouri Compromise was constitutional.

(E) slaves taken temporarily into a free state were free.

79. Which of the following was NOT a Northern advantage in the Civil War?

(A) It was fighting a defensive war.

(B) It had greater manufacturing capacity.

(C) It owned greater railroad trackage.

(D) It had a larger population.

(E) The mountain chains ran north and south.

80. Which of the following does NOT apply to the Monroe Doctrine?

(A) It forbade Spain from attempting to restore control over its former colonies in the Western Hemisphere.

(B) It was based upon the assumption that the British navy would defend the principles of the Doctrine.

(C) It allowed the United States to take action in European affairs.

(D) It blocked a possible move by Russia to possess the Pacific Coast.

(E) It allowed European nations to use force of arms in order to collect debts from Latin American nations.

81. A revolution in what country made American neutrality an issue in the 1790s?

(A) Great Britain

(B) Spain

(C) Netherlands

(D) France

(E) Germany

82. The Confederacy raised money for their war effort by all of the following means EXCEPT

(A) borrowing money from abroad.

(B) raising taxes.

(C) printing money.

(D) establishing an income tax.

(E) borrowing money from its citizens.

83. The Constitutional Convention took place in

(A) 1776.
(B) 1789.
(C) 1787.
(D) 1781.
(E) 1800.

84. The colonial South was divided into all of the following EXCEPT

(A) the Piedmont.
(B) the Great Plains.
(C) the backcountry.
(D) the Tidewater.
(E) the Fall Line.

85. Andrew Jackson's Specie Circular sought to

(A) pay off the government debts.
(B) slow down speculation in public land.
(C) replace the Bank of the United States with an independent treasury.
(D) end the financial panic of 1837.
(E) establish the free coinage of silver.

86. The "Intolerable Acts" of 1774 included all of the following EXCEPT

(A) the closing of Boston harbor.
(B) new taxes on glass, tea, lead, and paper.
(C) making the Massachusetts council and judiciary appointive.
(D) allowing trials of accused colonial officials to be moved to England.
(E) authorizing the governor to limit town meetings to as few as one a year.

87. According to the Constitution, the president is chosen by

(A) the House of Representatives.
(B) popular vote of the people.
(C) the electoral college.

(D) the Senate.

(E) both Houses of Congress.

88. Which of the following did NOT take place during the Grant presidency?

(A) John Wesley Powell's exploration of the Grand Canyon

(B) Last federal troops removed from the South

(C) Settlement of the Alabama claims

(D) Completion of the first transcontinental railroad

(E) Credit Mobilier Scandal

89. The "Revolution of 1800" resulted in the election of

(A) John Adams.

(B) Thomas Jefferson.

(C) James Monroe.

(D) James Madison.

(E) John Quincy Adams.

90. The following table represents the amount of continental currency required to buy $1.00 in specie. In what year did the currency's value decline by the largest percentage?

1777	January	1.25	October	3.00
1778	January	4.00	October	5.00
1779	January	8.00	October	30.00
1780	January	42.50	October	77.50
1781	January	100.00	April	167.50

(A) 1777

(B) 1778

(C) 1779

(D) 1780

(E) 1781

91. The term "Middle Colonies" refers to which of the following groupings?

(A) New York, Pennsylvania, New Jersey, Delaware

(B) Georgia, South Carolina, Virginia, Maryland

(C) New Hampshire, New York, Virginia

(D) Massachusetts, New Hampshire, Connecticut, Rhode Island

(E) North Carolina, Virginia, Maryland, Delaware

92. Which of the following battles effectively ended the American Revolution?

    (A) Yorktown
    (B) Brandywine Creek
    (C) Saratoga
    (D) Princeton
    (E) King's Mountain

93. The Fourteenth Amendment to the Constitution

    (A) gave blacks federal and state citizenship.
    (B) disallowed any former Confederate officeholder from becoming a U.S. Senator under any circumstances.
    (C) repudiated federal war debts.
    (D) allowed a state to limit the voting of blacks.
    (E) required the former Confederate states to pay off their debts incurred during the Civil War.

94. Which of the following does NOT describe colonial government in America?

    (A) During the 1700s the assemblies became more powerful.
    (B) In royal colonies the governor could summon or dismiss the assembly.
    (C) Compared with England, the right to vote was limited to a few individuals.
    (D) The assemblies controlled the raising and spending of tax money.
    (E) In proprietary colonies the proprietor appointed the governor.

95. The War of 1812 resulted in which of the following?

    (A) New territory for the United States
    (B) Resumption of the status quo prior to the war
    (C) Defeat of the United States

(D) The strengthening of the Federalist party

(E) Loss of United States territory

96. Article I of the U.S. Constitution establishes

    (A) freedom of speech.

    (B) the powers of the presidency.

    (C) freedom of assembly.

    (D) the powers of Congress.

    (E) the powers of the Supreme Court.

97. In order for a treaty to become law, the _____ must ratify the treaty after it has been negotiated by the _____ .

    (A) House of Representatives ... Senate

    (B) Congress ... president

    (C) Supreme Court ... Senate

    (D) Senate ... president

    (E) president ... Senate

98. The first presidential election that relied upon the popular vote to select the electoral college was held in

    (A) 1789.

    (B) 1800.

    (C) 1824.

    (D) 1916.

    (E) 1928.

99. The American commitment to the "unalienable rights" of "life, liberty, and the pursuit of happiness" is most clearly expressed in

    (A) the U.S. Constitution.

    (B) the Declaration of Independence.

    (C) the Bill of Rights.

    (D) the Twenty-fifth Amendment.

    (E) *Plessy v. Ferguson.*

COTTON PRODUCTION AND SLAVE POPULATION, 1790-1860

Year	*Cotton Bales Produced*	*Number of Slaves*
1790	4,000	697,897
1820	73,222	1,538,098
1840	1,347,640	2,487,213
1860	3,841,416	3,957,760

100. The table above shows which of the following for the period 1790 to 1860?

(A) Cotton was the largest crop in the South.

(B) Slaves were efficient workers.

(C) Slavery was profitable.

(D) Cotton production was a primary cause for the growth of slavery.

(E) Northern textile mills required more Southern cotton.

101. The Mayflower Compact of 1620 established

(A) a land of religious freedom.

(B) the colony of Massachusetts.

(C) a royal colony.

(D) Plymouth colony.

(E) the colony of Rhode Island.

102. On the eve of Columbus' first arrival in 1492, the native Indian population of the Western Hemisphere is estimated at

(A) 1–5 million.

(B) 10–20 million.

(C) 25–40 million.

(D) 50–60 million.

(E) 80–100 million.

103. Columbus undertook his 1492 voyage to the Americas to

(A) Christianize the Indian population.

(B) prove that the Earth was round.

(C) discover new worlds.

(D) test the geographic theories of Ptolemy.

(E) secure wealth and power for himself and the Spanish throne.

104. Jamestown survived as the first permanent English settlement in America because

(A) the settlers followed the example of Roanoke.

(B) of the emergence of tobacco as a cash crop.

(C) of the religious convictions of its first settlers.

(D) of the mild climate of Virginia.

(E) of its use of Indian slaves as a labor force.

105. Roger Williams is best known in American history as

(A) advocating the uniting of church and state into a theocracy.

(B) an early champion of religious freedom.

(C) the chief justice at the Salem witch trials.

(D) the founder of New Hampshire.

(E) the first royal governor of Massachusetts.

106. Indentured servants in colonial America experienced

(A) great upward economic mobility.

(B) political power.

(C) racial harmony with black slaves.

(D) a high standard of living.

(E) low social status.

107. During the seventeenth century, black slaves in the Southern colonies

(A) came directly from East Africa.

(B) grew slowly as a labor force.

(C) were treated the same as slaves in the British West Indies.

(D) were allowed to set their children free.

(E) lived mostly in urban areas.

108. The Dominion of New England was

(A) the title of the first book published in America.

(B) the name given to Massachusetts by John Winthrop.

(C) an attempt to reorganize the British Empire by James II.

(D) the first American public school.

(E) the official name of the Puritan religion.

109. William Penn's plans for a Quaker colony in Pennsylvania included all of the following EXCEPT

(A) establishing peaceful relations with the Indians.

(B) allowing for religious freedom.

(C) establishing a democracy.

(D) the making of an economic profit.

(E) establishing a colony loyal to Great Britain.

110. At the close of the Seven Years' War in 1763, France ceded to Great Britain

(A) the French West Indies.

(B) Florida.

(C) Canada.

(D) the African slave trade.

(E) the Louisiana Territory.

111. England passed the Stamp Act in 1765 to

(A) punish Americans for protests to the Sugar Act.

(B) control the American press.

(C) raise money to reduce England's national debt.

(D) allow for illegal search-and-seizure of smugglers.

(E) allow Americans to settle the Ohio River Valley.

112. The eighteenth century population in British North America

(A) nearly doubled every 25 years.

(B) became increasingly more homogeneous.

(C) had a life expectancy of 45 years for males.

(D) was clustered inside the new cities of the colonies.

(E) was comprised of less than two percent African-Americans.

113. All of the following are major figures in the Enlightenment EXCEPT

(A) Benjamin Franklin.
(B) William Bradford.
(C) John Locke.
(D) Sir Isaac Newton.
(E) Thomas Jefferson.

114. After the American Revolution, the Loyalists did NOT

(A) return to Great Britain.
(B) emigrate to Canada.
(C) sue America for property loss.
(D) settle in the West Indies.
(E) create their own American colony in Ohio.

115. The Articles of Confederation created for the 13 states

(A) a strong national government.
(B) a sound national economy.
(C) a league of friendship among 13 independent countries.
(D) the Bill of Rights.
(E) interstate trade agreements.

116. During the winter of 1786, Shays' Rebellion indicated to most Americans

(A) the political dangers of the post-war recession.
(B) the weaknesses of state government.
(C) the need to reform the Articles of Confederation.
(D) the desperation of the yeoman farmer in America.
(E) All of the above.

117. In seventeenth century New England, married women were denied the right to

(A) vote for elected officials.

(B) divorce their husbands.

(C) arrange marriages for their children.

(D) own property.

(E) All of the above.

118. The passage of the Declaratory Act in 1766 by Parliament was greeted in America by

(A) the creation of the Continental Congress.

(B) mob violence against British merchants.

(C) refusal to pay these new taxes.

(D) little attention to its statement of parliamentary sovereignty.

(E) Tories fleeing to Canada.

119. During the Washington administration, the secretary of the treasury, Alexander Hamilton, proposed an economic program which included all of the following EXCEPT

(A) establishing close ties between the national government and American business.

(B) establishing a national bank.

(C) having the states pay off the total war debt.

(D) imposing new taxes through customs duties and excise taxes.

(E) retiring the full national debt but maintaining deficit government spending.

120. During the 1790s, Federalists and Republicans openly disagreed over

(A) the extent of popular control of government.

(B) foreign policy toward England and France.

(C) the activities of Citizen Genet.

(D) the fiscal policies of the national government.

(E) All of the above.

CLEP HISTORY OF THE UNITED STATES I TEST 2

ANSWER KEY

1.	(D)	31.	(C)	61.	(C)	91.	(A)
2.	(A)	32.	(B)	62.	(D)	92.	(A)
3.	(C)	33.	(C)	63.	(A)	93.	(D)
4.	(B)	34.	(D)	64.	(B)	94.	(C)
5.	(E)	35.	(C)	65.	(B)	95.	(B)
6.	(D)	36.	(C)	66.	(A)	96.	(D)
7.	(D)	37.	(B)	67.	(B)	97.	(D)
8.	(D)	38.	(A)	68.	(A)	98.	(C)
9.	(B)	39.	(C)	69.	(B)	99.	(B)
10.	(C)	40.	(B)	70.	(C)	100.	(D)
11.	(E)	41.	(D)	71.	(E)	101.	(D)
12.	(C)	42.	(D)	72.	(C)	102.	(E)
13.	(A)	43.	(D)	73.	(B)	103.	(E)
14.	(B)	44.	(C)	74.	(B)	104.	(B)
15.	(B)	45.	(D)	75.	(C)	105.	(B)
16.	(D)	46.	(B)	76.	(A)	106.	(E)
17.	(D)	47.	(A)	77.	(B)	107.	(B)
18.	(D)	48.	(A)	78.	(C)	108.	(C)
19.	(B)	49.	(A)	79.	(A)	109.	(C)
20.	(D)	50.	(D)	80.	(C)	110.	(C)
21.	(D)	51.	(D)	81.	(D)	111.	(C)
22.	(D)	52.	(D)	82.	(D)	112.	(A)
23.	(B)	53.	(C)	83.	(C)	113.	(B)
24.	(E)	54.	(A)	84.	(B)	114.	(E)
25.	(C)	55.	(C)	85.	(B)	115.	(C)
26.	(C)	56.	(B)	86.	(B)	116.	(E)
27.	(D)	57.	(A)	87.	(C)	117.	(A)
28.	(A)	58.	(A)	88.	(B)	118.	(D)
29.	(B)	59.	(B)	89.	(B)	119.	(E)
30.	(C)	60.	(B)	90.	(C)	120.	(E)

DETAILED EXPLANATIONS OF ANSWERS

TEST 2

1. **(D)** Francisco Pizarro explored Peru while Francisco Coronado travelled through the area of Texas, Oklahoma, and Kansas. Robert La Salle and Jacques Marquette pursued the Mississippi River, and Samuel de Champlain explored the New England coast, Lake Champlain, and the Great Lakes.

2. **(A)** Of the 400,000 slaveholders, about 200,000 owned five or fewer slaves. Only about 1 in 4 white Southerners belonged to a slaveholding family, but the percentage varied from region to region. Relatively few slaveholders lived in urban areas.

3. **(C)** Nonimportation (1806), embargo (1807), and nonintercourse (1809) all sought to force the British to recognize American rights on the sea.

4. **(B)** Turnpikes became popular in the 1790s and canals after the completion of the Erie Canal in 1825. The steamboat was introduced in 1807 and became particularly popular in the 1830s.

5. **(E)** The Missouri Compromise, engineered by Henry Clay, maintained the balance of slave and free states by bringing in Maine as a free state and Missouri as a slave state. It sought to diffuse slavery as an issue in westward expansion by prohibiting slavery north of latitude 36°30′, but it said nothing about popular sovereignty south of that line.

6. **(D)** The passage is from Jefferson's first inaugural address, March 1801. Coming after the extremely heated electoral campaign of 1800, it was followed immediately by Jefferson's famous statement, "We are all Republicans, we are all Federalists."

7. **(D)** Jefferson was trying to convince his audience that party strife should be forgotten once the will of the people has been expressed in an election (D). Jefferson recognized the inevitability of party politics in a democratic system, so he would not have argued against them (A), or that the strife caused by parties is foreign to the American character (B). Fundamental philosophical differences (C) are what give rise to different parties, and are not the topic of this passage, nor is Jefferson arguing that only his party acts in accordance with the Constitution (E).

8. **(D)** The Declaration argued that all men are created equal and are endowed with rights, that government is instituted for the purpose of preserving these rights and gains its powers from the governed, and that people have the right of revolution when government becomes despotism. It was Thomas Paine's *Common Sense* that argued that a small island should not rule a large continent. No taxation without representation was a popular phrase of Americans after the Stamp Act of 1765.

9. **(B)** The Treaty recognized Canada, Florida, and the Mississippi River as the boundaries of the United States. Florida went to Spain. The Missouri River lies west of the Mississippi while the Appalachians lay within the United States of 1783.

10. **(C)** In response to Lincoln's question of how he could support both popular sovereignty and the Dred Scott decision, Stephen Douglas said that slavery could be kept out of the territories if people there failed to pass laws to protect it. This became known as the Freeport Doctrine and lost Douglas support in the South.

11. **(E)** The passage is taken from a speech by U.S. Senator Albert Beveridge, an ardent imperialist, and represents a philosophy based on Manifest Destiny (I), American exceptionalism (II), and Social Darwinism (III). The doctrine of Manifest Destiny stated that it was the destiny of the United States to dominate and rule all of the American continent. It was based on the belief that the American people and American democracy were superior to other peoples and governments in the Americas. This is related to the concept of American exceptionalism (II), which stated that America was God's chosen nation and Americans were God's chosen people. The two concepts went hand-in-hand, because if Americans were God's chosen people, then it was God's will that they should someday dominate North America, if not the rest of the world. When Darwin's ideas were published, hypothesizing survival of the fittest, many Americans quickly embraced them because they were easily translated into So-

cial Darwinism, the belief that "superior" cultures will naturally come to dominate "inferior" cultures. This line of reasoning was used to establish "scientific" support for the concepts of Manifest Destiny and American exceptionalism. Together they provided a compelling, even if distorted, rationale for American imperialism.

12. **(C)** Cotton did not become a major product until the invention of the cotton gin in the 1790s. Sugar or molasses was purchased in the West Indies and taken to New England where it was manufactured into rum. The rum was then traded in Africa for slaves. In other forms of the triangular trade, tobacco was a major product.

13. **(A)** Those who supported the Constitution were called Federalists, while the Antifederalists opposed it. The Whigs, Republicans, and Democrats were political parties that emerged later in the country's history.

14. **(B)** Lee surrendered to Grant at the Appomattox Courthouse on April 9, 1865. Spotsylvania and Cold Harbor were battles between Lee and Grant that preceded the surrender. Joseph E. Johnston surrendered to William T. Sherman at Raleigh on April 17, 1865. Richmond was the capital of the Confederacy.

15. **(B)** The French and Indian War was the culmination of a series of wars between France and England: King William's War (1689–1697), Queen Anne's War (1700–1713), King George's War (1740–1748), and the French and Indian War (1754–1763). The American Revolution took place between 1776 and 1783.

16. **(D)** "Chattel" was the legal term for a piece of property. Black slaves were not considered human beings and therefore had no rights, nor were they employees. Servants who served for a limited period of time were called indentured servants. Individual masters might grant slaves freedom in their wills, but this happened infrequently.

17. **(D)** The Kentucky and Virginia Resolutions (1798) introduced the idea of nullification in response to the Alien and Sedition Acts (1798), which changed the years of residence necessary for naturalization and placed sharp limits on freedom of speech.

18. **(D)** The Judiciary Act of 1789 provided for a six-judge Supreme Court, 13 district courts, three circuit courts, and the office of attorney

general. It gave the Supreme Court the power to review state laws that conflicted with federal statutes.

19. **(B)** As secretary of the treasury, Hamilton was concerned with economic issues, thus he promoted the Bank of the United States, assumption of Confederation and state debts, excise taxes, and manufacturing, though the latter was unsuccessful in Congress. Congress passed the Judiciary Act in 1789, but it was not Hamilton's proposal.

20. **(D)** The paragraph summarizes the position taken by Abraham Lincoln during the Lincoln-Douglas debates in 1856. Lincoln was in a very difficult position throughout these debates and walked a political tightrope, opposing slavery on moral grounds while at the same time trying not to offend a sometimes violent racist electorate. Lincoln truly believed slavery to be a moral wrong that could not be allowed to expand. Hence, he adopted the inherently contradictory position of opposing slavery on moral grounds, but refusing to support efforts to eliminate it completely; claiming that blacks were equal to anybody, but refusing to support full citizenship for blacks. Stephen Douglas (A) never denounced slavery as immoral. Douglas never viewed blacks as the equal of whites and never argued for any rights for blacks. He openly stated during the Lincoln-Douglas debates that he wanted citizenship only for whites. John Brown (B) went to the other extreme. He was an ardent abolitionist who wanted not only an end to slavery and full rights for blacks, he wanted a military invasion of the South to force Southern slaveowners to release their slaves. His ill-conceived occupation of the Federal arsenal in Harpers Ferry, Virginia, was an attempt to begin a national insurrection that would lead to emancipation of the slaves. John Breckinridge (C) was the Kentucky lawmaker who ran as a Southern Democrat against Abraham Lincoln in the 1860 presidential election. As such he led the movement to protect states' rights and to preserve slavery as an institution. Dred Scott (E) was the center of the controversial Supreme Court decision of March 1857, in which the Court ruled that Scott, a freed slave, had no right to sue in the federal courts and could be returned to slavery.

21. **(D)** Benjamin Franklin made important discoveries regarding electricity. John Peter Zenger was a newspaper editor involved in a 1735 libel case. Jonathan Edwards was the New England preacher who probably started the Great Awakening. William Byrd was one of the leading Virginia planters of the early eighteenth century. George Whitefield was a British itinerant evangelist who preached throughout the American colonies during the Great Awakening.

22. **(D)** In most states women had no claim to money they earned; it was controlled by their husbands, as was their own property. Husbands could legally beat their wives "with a reasonable instrument." And the professions were largely closed to women. Women did not have the right to vote in federal elections until the passage of the Nineteenth Amendment in 1920.

23. **(B)** According to Lincoln's plan, the former Confederate states could resume their part in the Union after 10 percent of the voters as of 1860 took an oath of allegiance to the United States Constitution. The Wade-Davis Bill, which Lincoln killed by a pocket veto, required 50 percent of the voters as of 1860 to take an oath of allegiance. The Thirteenth Amendment was not adopted until after Lincoln's death, although Lincoln did require states to abolish slavery. Neither black voting rights nor Confederate debts were part of Lincoln's plan.

24. **(E)** This cartoon portrays a rather passive role for President Grant, suggesting that Southerners need only heed his advice to accept the new social realities and all will be well. There is no hint that the federal government might need to bring its weight to bear upon the situation.

25. **(C)** The population growth of pre-Civil War cities generally outdistanced the sewer systems. This contributed to the increasing death rate, especially in the growing slums. With the growth of slums came an increase in crime.

26. **(C)** The conflict at Lexington-Concord occurred April 19, 1775. Fort Ticonderoga was captured by the Americans on May 10, 1775 and the Battle of Bunker Hill took place on June 17. The British were forced to leave Boston in March 1776 and surrendered to Washington at Yorktown in 1781.

27. **(D)** By organizing Kansas-Nebraska on the basis of popular sovereignty, the Kansas-Nebraska Act repealed the Missouri Compromise of 1820 which had barred slavery north of 36°30′. The Wilmot Proviso was not passed by Congress. The Compromise of 1850 had nothing directly to do with slavery north of 36°30′. Dred Scott would not be decided until 1857. The Northwest Ordinance of 1787 had outlawed slavery in the western lands given up by the original 13 states.

28. **(A)** The first group of states to secede were Mississippi, Florida, Alabama, Georgia, Louisiana, Texas, and South Carolina. After Lincoln

called up troops in April 1861, Arkansas, Tennessee, North Carolina, and Virginia seceded. Missouri, Kentucky, Maryland, and Delaware were slave states that never seceded.

29. **(B)** England had returned Florida to Spain in 1783. In 1819 through the Adams-Onis Treaty, Spain ceded Florida to the United States in return for an American promise to pay $5 million to American citizens for claims against Mexico.

30. **(C)** The Louisiana Purchase effectively ended Napoleon's dream of power in the Western Hemisphere. He sold the territories, which he had purchased from Spain, because of difficulties in Haiti and need of money.

31. **(C)** Texas won independence from Mexico in 1836 through rebellion. California briefly became independent in 1846. The other territories never became independent.

32. **(B)** The 1794 Whiskey Rebellion opposed a 25 percent tax on whiskey proposed by Hamilton and passed by Congress; government regulation of whiskey production, import duties, and prohibition did not emerge as issues until much later.

33. **(C)** The First Bank of the United States was a joint private-public enterprise, with stock owned by both the federal government and private individuals and representatives of the government and private sector serving as directors.

34. **(D)** The Puritans, who established the Massachusetts Bay colony, sought to build a society based upon the will of God as revealed in the Bible according to their understanding. Rather than establishing religious toleration, they allowed only their Congregational church free exercise of religion. It was the founders of the Virginia colony who sought gold and later established tobacco as the basis of their economy.

35. **(C)** The Constitution in Article 1, Section 2 counted 3/5 of "other persons" than free persons for the purposes of representation. It otherwise ignored the issue of slavery, except for providing for the return of runaway slaves in Article 1, Section 9.

36. **(C)** The British trade regulations provided both advantages and disadvantages for the American colonies. For example, while guaranteeing

access to the British market, they prevented access to the markets of other countries. Individual laws often favored certain colonies over others, but as a whole they did not favor one section of the American colonies.

37. **(B)** While the Northwest Ordinance provided support for public education, prohibited slavery, and sought fair treatment of Indians, the only precedent it established was a procedure for a territory to become a state equal with all existing states. Popular sovereignty emerged later as a policy to allow states to decide for themselves whether to be slave or free.

38. **(A)** The Americans signed an alliance with France in 1778. Spain and the Netherlands came to American aid within the next year.

39. **(C)** The Jackson administration forced the tribes to be removed to the West. The Seminoles of Florida, however, resisted for several years. The Supreme Court had decided the issue in the Indians' favor but Jackson ignored the decision.

40. **(B)** The Germans, known as the Pennsylvania Dutch, settled heavily in Pennsylvania. The French Huguenots could be found in New York and South Carolina. The Scotch-Irish settled the frontier areas of the Middle and Southern colonies. The Dutch were concentrated in New York, although the English were the dominant ethnic group even in that colony. Spanish and Portuguese Jews could be found in the urban areas of New York, Rhode Island, and South Carolina.

41. **(D)** After 1832 there was little Southern criticism of the institution of slavery. The Nat Turner rebellion took place in 1831 and the Virginia legislature debated the abolition of slavery in 1832 but took no action.

42. **(D)** The Stamp Act Congress of 1765 established the nonimportation or boycott of British goods. The Paxton Boys marched on Philadelphia in response to Indian uprisings in 1763. The Boston Tea Party responded to the 1773 Tea Act, while the Battle of Lexington took place in 1775. The Boston Massacre occurred in 1770.

43. **(D)** The Jay Treaty of 1794 said nothing about British seizure of American vessels in the French West Indies, a major problem for Americans. Although the Treaty arranged to get British soldiers out of the Northwest posts, it obtained only limited trading rights with the West Indies and did nothing about compensation for slaves.

44. **(C)** William T. Sherman directed the "march to the sea" of 1864, capturing Savannah and splitting the Confederacy. Joseph Johnston served the Confederacy at the Battle of Seven Pines (1862) and Vicksburg (1862–1863). Thomas "Stonewall" Jackson played important roles for the Confederacy at the Second Battle of Bull Run (1862) and Chancellorsville (1863). Robert E. Lee commanded the Army of Virginia at such battles as Antietam (1862) and Gettysburg (1863). J.E.B. Stuart fought for the Confederacy at the Second Battle of Bull Run (1862), Chancellorsville (1863), and Gettysburg (1863).

45. **(D)** The central compromise was the agreement that all states would be represented equally in the Senate and by population in the House. There was general agreement that the Articles must be abandoned, that the federal government must be more powerful than the states, and that the legislative and executive powers must be balanced.

46. **(B)** The Missouri Compromise of 1820 brought Missouri into the Union as a slave state in 1821 and Maine as a free state in 1820.

47. **(A)** The United States still had a basically agricultural economy, hence factories had only a marginal effect on the total economy. The destruction of the Bank of the United States took away the major control over the state chartered banks and many of them became over-extended. Many banks failed after the 1836 Specie Circular. A poor wheat crop also forced the U.S. to use gold and silver to purchase grain from other countries.

48. **(A)** In this statement liberty is understood in terms of the group rather than the individual. Rather than being the primary value, liberty is subordinate to the good. In this sense, liberty is compatible with Puritan society and achievable in the present, although these ideas do not appear directly in the passage quoted.

49. **(A)** John Marshall served as chief justice from 1801 to 1835, during which the Court successfully claimed the power to determine the constitutionality of acts of Congress. John Jay served as chief justice from 1789 to 1794 and Roger B. Taney served from 1836 to 1864. Alexander Hamilton never served on the Supreme Court.

50. **(D)** Andrew Jackson vetoed in 1832 the rechartering of the Second Bank of the United States. Nicholas Biddle served as president of the

Second Bank of the United States, and Henry Clay and Daniel Webster supported its rechartering in Congress. John Marshall served as chief justice of the Supreme Court.

51. **(D)** Under the Articles of Confederation, Congress had the power to control foreign affairs, make war, settle disputes between the states, and coin or borrow money, but it did not have the power to tax.

52. **(D)** Although Lincoln won only 40 percent of the popular vote and none of the Southern or border states, he won the electoral votes of the Northern and Midwestern states as well as California and Oregon. He would have won even if all the votes against him had gone to a single candidate.

53. **(C)** Wealthy merchants, holders of government bonds, owners of large plantations, former officers of the Continental Army, Episcopal and Congregational ministers, important lawyers, and those involved in export and shipping tended to support the Federalists.

54. **(A)** The policy of "salutary neglect," described by Prime Minister Robert Walpole in the 1720s, made little attempt to enforce the Navigation Acts, passed in the 1660s to control colonial trade. The royal navy remained on the high seas and royal governors continued to be appointed by the king. Britain never encouraged the American colonies to establish their own parliament.

55. **(C)** Gabriel Prosser plotted a rebellion in Virginia in 1800 but was betrayed. Denmark Vesey similarly organized an uprising in South Carolina in 1822 but was discovered. Nat Turner led a rebellion in Virginia in 1831 that resulted in over 60 deaths.

56. **(B)** In *Marbury v. Madison* the Supreme Court claimed the power to determine the constitutionality of acts of Congress. In *Gibbons v. Ogden* (1824) it gave the federal government the power to regulate commerce. *Dartmouth College v. Woodward* (1819) extended federal protection to property rights under the contract clause, and *McCulloch v. Maryland* (1819) declared that a state could not block a federal agency. Nullification was the doctrine that a state could declare a federal law inoperative within its borders, a position advocated by South Carolina in the 1830s.

57. **(A)** The "right of deposit" meant that Americans could land their goods at New Orleans and ship them out again without paying taxes. The treaty also opened the Mississippi to American shipping for three years and settled the boundary with Florida.

58. **(A)** New York had two cities over 100,000 in population and three with between 35,000 and 100,000.

59. **(B)** Boss Tweed's moneybag and the dollar and cent signs indicate that political influence was up for sale. The cartoon does not say who was buying influence nor does it bring up the issue of efficiency.

60. **(B)** During the first half of the nineteenth century, American factory workers labored from 60 to 72 hours a week. Although some attempted to form unions, none were long-lasting. Working conditions allowed little concern for health and safety. Children made up a significant proportion of the work force. Socialism was not yet an important movement in the United States.

61. **(C)** *Pilgrim's Progress* was published by the English Puritan John Bunyan in 1678 and 1684. The Douay version of the Bible was used by Roman Catholics, while Nathaniel Hawthorne's *The Scarlet Letter*, Henry Thoreau's *Walden*, and Herman Melville's *Moby-Dick* were nineteenth century New England works.

62. **(D)** The Emancipation Proclamation of January 1, 1863, freed slaves in areas still in rebellion. The Thirteenth Amendment (1865) abolished slavery entirely.

63. **(A)** The Proclamation of 1763 ordered the ending of settlement west of the peaks of the Appalachians because of increasing problems with the Indians. The Peace of Paris (1763) ended the French and Indian War while the Sugar Act (1764) forbade trade with the non-English West Indies and required trials for those breaking the law to be held in Admiralty Courts, which had no juries. Numerous new taxes were placed on trade beginning in 1765.

64. **(B)** The Nullification Controversy arose in response to the Tariff of 1828 (Tariff of Abominations) and the Tariff of 1832. South Carolina declared the tariffs "null, void, and no law" in their state after February 1, 1833. A compromise tariff in 1833 diffused the situation. Popular sovereignty refers to the policy of having a state decide whether it would be slave or free.

65. **(B)** *The Federalist Papers* were written by John Jay, Alexander Hamilton, and James Madison to support ratification of the Constitution in New York state. Thomas Paine wrote *Common Sense* during the conflict with Great Britain and *The Age of Reason* to support rational religion. James Bryce, an Englishman, wrote *The American Commonwealth* in the late nineteenth century. John Adams's *Defense of the Constitutions of Government of the United States of America* was a history of republican government.

66. **(A)** Sacajawea was an Indian guide and interpreter for Lewis and Clark. Sitting Bull was a Sioux chief of the late nineteenth century. Zebulon Pike was an army officer who explored the West while James Wilkinson served as governor of the Louisiana Territory, and may have been involved in a plan to establish part of the region as a separate nation. Tecumseh led an Indian confederacy in revolt against the United States just prior to the War of 1812.

67. **(B)** A new fugitive slave law was adopted but the slave trade was abolished only in Washington, D.C. California was to enter the union as a free state while Utah and Mexico were left undetermined in regard to slavery. The western border of Texas was also settled.

68. **(A)** Thomas Paine published *Common Sense* in 1776. Thomas Jefferson drafted the "Declaration of Independence" that same year. Patrick Henry became famous for his "Give me liberty or give me death" speech in Virginia in 1775. All three men were indebted to the natural rights philosophy of the British writer John Locke. John Adams wrote *Defense of the Constitutions of Government of the United States of America* in the mid-1780s.

69. **(B)** Indentured servants sold their services for a limited period of time to repay their passage to America. In contrast, slaves were held in servitude for life. Both slaves and indentured servants were used for all types of manual labor but neither received wages for their work, except in

special circumstances. At the end of their indenturement, servants usually received 50 acres of land.

70. **(C)** Alexander Hamilton believed that the United States should assume the debts of both the Confederation and the states in order to draw people's loyalty from the states to the federal government, as explained in his *Report on Public Credit* (1790).

71. **(E)** The Bill of Rights, or first 10 amendments to the Constitution, placed limits on the power of the federal government, including freedom of religion, speech, press, and assembly, right to keep and bear arms, limits on the quartering of troops, limits on the right of government to search, various rights for accused persons, and nonenumerated rights and powers reserved by the states and people.

72. **(C)** The followers of Andrew Jackson established the Democratic party, whose roots could be loosely traced back to the Democratic-Republican (or Republican) party of Thomas Jefferson. The Federalists had died out since 1814 and the Whigs arose in the 1830s in opposition to Jackson and the Democrats. The Populists emerged in the 1880s.

73. **(B)** In 1831 William Lloyd Garrison called for immediate emancipation. He rejected colonization, free soil, and any other step-by-step emancipation as insufficient.

74. **(B)** The Great Awakening, which took place primarily in New England, split both the Congregational and Presbyterian churches between those who emphasized spiritual enthusiasm and those who preferred a more staid, rational approach. The Awakening was interdenominational in character, particularly through the evangelism of George Whitefield. The hanging of Quakers and the witchcraft trials both took place in the seventeenth century. The Church of England was not an established, or state supported, church in New England, where Congregationalism was established.

75. **(C)** Washington was dependent upon poorly trained militia to man his army. The British public was divided in its support of Britain's policy while about one-third of the American colonists opposed the war. Washington did not depend on conventional military tactics and began fighting in ways new to the English. The attention of the British government was also diverted by continuing conflict with France.

76. **(A)** Alexander Hamilton was arguing for "broad construction" of the Constitution, asserting that as long as the Constitution did not prohibit an action it was allowable when it carried out an end or goal of the Constitution. Thomas Jefferson argued for "strict construction," saying that the Constitution must specifically give the federal government a power in order for that power to be constitutional. Hamilton was saying nothing about the Supreme Court and rejected the idea that implied powers were reserved to the states.

77. **(B)** William Dean Howells emerged as a major writer after the Civil War. Irving, Emerson, Hawthorne, and Melville all wrote their major works before the Civil War, although Emerson and Melville lived beyond the war itself.

78. **(C)** In the 1857 Dred Scott decision, the Supreme Court decided that neither Congress nor the people living in a territory could bar slavery from that territory; therefore, the Missouri Compromise was unconstitutional. It also decided that slaves were not citizens, thus Scott had no right to bring his case to the Court.

79. **(A)** The North was fighting an offensive war, for it had to invade the South in order to win.

80. **(C)** The Monroe Doctrine of 1823 pledged that the U.S. would not intervene in European affairs. Because of previous discussions with the British, Monroe knew that the British navy would support the U.S. in opposing Russian or Spanish expansion in the Western Hemisphere.

81. **(D)** The French Revolution, beginning in 1789, made the maintenance of neutrality difficult for the United States for the next two decades.

82. **(D)** The Confederacy borrowed about $15 million from abroad and $100 million from its citizens, raised over $100 million through taxation, and printed over $1 billion in paper money. No income tax was established.

83. **(C)** The Constitutional Convention took place in 1787. The Declaration of Independence was signed in 1776, the Articles of Confederation ratified in 1781, and George Washington became president in 1789. Thomas Jefferson was elected to the presidency in 1800.

84. **(B)** The Great Plains refers to the trans-Mississippi West. The Tidewater refers to the area near the sea, the Piedmont includes the foothills on the eastern side of the Appalachians, while the backcountry lay in the Appalachians themselves and westward. The Fall Line is the dividing point between the Tidewater and the Piedmont where the water falls rapidly to the lower land.

85. **(B)** The Specie Circular of 1836 sought to slow down speculation in public land by requiring payment in gold and silver rather than bank notes. Sales of public lands were helping pay off the public debt. The Independent Treasury was not established until the 1840s.

86. **(B)** The Townshend Duties of 1767 placed new duties on glass, tea, lead, and paper. The "Intolerable" or "Coercive Acts" were passed in response to the Boston Tea Party and closed Boston Harbor until the tea was paid for, gave the governor greater powers, made the colony's council appointive rather than elective, and provided that colonial officials accused of capital crimes could have their trials moved to England.

87. **(C)** The electoral college is made up of electors, chosen by the people, and equal in number to the total number of representatives and senators from each state. These electors choose the president.

88. **(B)** Grant served as president from 1869 to 1877. Powell explored the Grand Canyon in 1869, the same year the transcontinental railroad was completed. The Alabama claims were settled in 1872. The Credit Mobilier scandal broke open in 1872. Federal troops were removed from the South in 1877, after Hayes became president.

89. **(B)** Thomas Jefferson was elected in 1800, John Adams in 1796, James Madison in 1808, James Monroe in 1816, and John Quincy Adams in 1824.

90. **(C)** Although the largest dollar amount that the currency declined was $67.50 between January and April, 1781, the largest percentage was in 1779 when it declined 375 percent.

91. **(A)** The "Middle Colonies" include New York, Pennsylvania, New Jersey, and Delaware. "New England" refers to Massachusetts, New Hampshire, Connecticut, and Rhode Island. The "Southern Colonies" were Georgia, South Carolina, North Carolina, Virginia, and Maryland.

92. **(A)** The British won the Battle of Brandywine Creek (1777), while the Americans won at Princeton (1776) and Saratoga (1777), the turning point of the war, and King's Mountain (1780). But it was the British surrender at the Battle of Yorktown (1781) that effectively ended the fighting.

93. **(D)** The Fourteenth Amendment promised that federal war debts would be paid but forbade the payment of Confederate war debts by the United States or any states. It allowed limitations on black voting but provided for a reduction in representation in such cases. It gave blacks federal and state citizenship.

94. **(C)** The right to vote was more widespread in the American colonies than in England because ownership of land was more open. The assemblies gained in power throughout the 1700s because they controlled the "purse strings." Royal governors had the power to summon or dismiss these assemblies, but the assemblies controlled the payment of the governor's salary.

95. **(B)** The Treaty of Ghent (1814) restored the antebellum status quo. Although the United States had attempted to take Canada, it had failed. Despite defeats in many battles and the burning of Washington, D.C., the U.S. was not defeated in the war. The Federalists, who opposed the war and were moving toward supporting secession of the Northeast, were seriously weakened when the war ended.

96. **(D)** Article I of the Constitution deals exclusively with Congress, the legislative branch of government. In this section of the Constitution, the powers and duties of Congress are carefully enumerated in detailed fashion. The most famous section of this article is Article I, Section 8, the "necessary and proper clause," which allows for a broad expanse of Congress' powers to make law. The powers of the presidency are covered in Article II, while those of the Supreme Court in Article III. Guarantees of freedom of speech and assembly are to be found in the first 10 amendments to the Constitution, the Bill of Rights.

97. **(D)** According to Article II, Section 2 (II, 2) of the United States Constitution, the Senate is granted the sole authority to ratify a treaty while the president, or any delegated representative he appoints, alone can negotiate treaties with a foreign nation. This division of power is part of the elaborate checks and balances established in our Constitution by the founding fathers in 1788. This principle is one of the key characteristics of a

republican form of government. The system was utilized to prevent one branch of government from becoming too powerful and dictatorial. Neither the Supreme Court nor the House of Representatives was included in this process. In recent years, American presidents have utilized increasingly the device of "executive agreements" with foreign nations to bypass the requirement of Senate approval of treaties. In 1937, the Supreme Court ruled in *United States v. Belmont* that although executive agreements are approved only by the president, they enjoy the same legal status as treaties.

98. **(C)** In the election of 1824, the members of the electoral college were selected by popular vote for the first time. Despite the public's misconceptions, the American president is selected by the electoral college and not the popular vote. Prior to 1824 members of the electoral college were selected by some agency of state government and as a result, the American electorate had little direct say in presidential elections. Today, a candidate requires 270 out of 535 electoral votes to become president. Members of the electoral college are chosen on a state-by-state basis according to party affiliation with the candidate. Each state is granted the same number of electors as its membership in Congress. In a winner-take-all format, a vote for a presidential candidate really is a vote for his party's state candidates to the electoral college and an indication to the electors from your state as to your candidate of choice. The November presidential election really is an election of the electoral college who meet in December to select the president.

99. **(B)** It is in the Declaration of Independence that Thomas Jefferson expressed the American devotion to these rights. The rights are considered "unalienable" in that they are afforded every human by birth and can be neither given away nor taken away. Jefferson adapted these three rights of life, liberty, and the pursuit of happiness from the seventeenth century English philosopher John Locke, who listed the rights as life, liberty, and prosperity. Jefferson prudently left the task of applying the specific meaning of these rights for every future generation of Americans to determine for themselves. The U.S. Constitution adds to these rights in its first ten amendments or Bill of Rights. The Twenty-fifth Amendment deals only with the disability of a president, while the Supreme Court decision of 1896 in *Plessy v. Ferguson* established a doctrine of "separate but equal" and sanctioned de jure racial segregation.

100. **(D)** The only relationship established by the table is between cotton production and slave laborers. As a result, we do not know from the table if the South produced more wheat than cotton. Nor do we know if slavery was

profitable as we do not see statistics on the cost of slaves and profits from the sale of cotton over time. We do not know from the table how many slaves were actually used to grow cotton and thus cannot judge labor efficiency. Finally, we do not know from the table where the cotton was exported. The only correlation that is revealed is that cotton production increases always were accompanied by increases in the number of slaves, thus directing one toward the conclusion that slavery grew along with the demand for increased cotton production.

101. **(D)** The original settlers of the Plymouth colony actually had purchased a tract of land in northern Virginia from the Virginia Company. They lost their course in crossing the Atlantic and upon arriving at Cape Cod decided to stay. The settlers feared that because they were occupying land not legally granted to them they would be forced to return to England. As a result, they drew up a contract among all the settlers called the Mayflower Compact to legally establish their existence. The Pilgrim settlers in Plymouth did not establish religious freedom as they only desired freedom for their religion and came to America to erect a religious utopia. In addition, Plymouth did not become part of Massachusetts until 1692 and indeed Puritans and Pilgrims had much dislike for each other and lived as separate, often hostile, colonies until 1692. Rhode Island was founded in 1644 by Roger Williams.

102. **(E)** In recent years, students of population analysis, demographers, have greatly revised the long accepted population estimates of James Mooney in 1925 for the Amerindian in pre-Colombian times. Mooney has estimated that less than 25 million Indians resided in the Americas around the year 1500. The main problem with Mooney's figures is that they were based primarily upon white European eyewitness accounts of the sixteenth and seventeenth centuries. Today archaeological findings and sophisticated demographic analysis using the computer have established the Indian population of the Western Hemisphere at nearly 100 million prior to Columbus' arrival. It should be noted that the Indian population stood at its lowest ebb in America in 1886 when there were less than 250,000 Amerindians. In the 1980 census, the Amerindian population had grown to 1.2 million.

103. **(E)** In his contract with the Spanish monarchy, Columbus established that he and his heirs would receive 40 percent of all wealth taken from the lands he was about to sail to; he would receive the title, Admiral of the Ocean Seas; and he would be named governor of any unchartered areas he came into contact with. Columbus' motives are clear from this contract as power, glory, and wealth. Few educated people in Europe believed that the

Earth was flat and Columbus had no desire to serve as a missionary for Christianity. Columbus did not come to America as an explorer; he came as a colonizer, seeking wealth and power. Once he landed in the Americas in 1492, he had proven Ptolemy wrong; a fact little mentioned by Columbus during the remainder of his lifetime.

104. **(B)** The establishment of Jamestown in 1607 as the first permanent English settlement in North America came dangerously close to failure. England had already failed in its initial venture in the 1580s at Roanoke, Virginia. Upon the first arrival of the Jamestown settlers, they indicated they had learned little from Roanoke and repeated the myopic quest for gold and silver rather than plant and secure a food supply. As with Roanoke, during the first harsh winter more than half the settlers perished. Hostile Indians did not bode well for the colony either. It was the combination of the efforts of John Smith and the discovery of tobacco as a cash crop for export to Europe that made the colony able to be economically profitable. According to most historians, the Anglican faith played a minimal role in Virginia throughout the seventeenth century.

105. **(B)** Roger Williams was forced to flee Massachusetts because of his unorthodox religious beliefs. Although a Puritan minister, Williams warned the ministry in Massachusetts that they exerted too much political power and were being corrupted by their theocracy. He was to be put on trial for heresy when he fled to Rhode Island, not New Hampshire. Williams allowed complete religious toleration to all settlers. He died well before the Salem witch trials of 1692–1694. He never served as governor of Massachusetts.

106. **(E)** Recent historical research has indicated that indentured servants, popular myths to the contrary, remained for the most part in the lower sections of colonial society throughout their lives. The low social status was especially true in the Southern colonies throughout the colonial period. Indentured servants generally signed a contract with their masters, trading their labor for room and board, and the learning of a skilled craft for a set number of years (usually seven years). The servants were in many cases treated harshly by their masters and emerged from their servitude impoverished with few skills mastered. Although servants supported Bacon in his rebellion in Virginia, they never gained political power throughout the colonial period. Most servants were very hostile toward black slaves in the South and showed little sympathy for the slave's loss of legal status as a human, a condition never applied to the indentured servant. In sum, the

indentured generally arrived in America on the edge of poverty and remained there for the bulk of their lives.

107. **(B)** Slavery as an institution grew very slowly in America, unlike in the British West Indies. Although the first American slaves arrived in 1619 in Jamestown, it was not until the 1790s that slavery as an institution grew substantially. Throughout the 1600s, most Southerners had yet to determine if they would seek their labor pool through white servants or black slaves. The incident of Bacon's Rebellion convinced many Southern planters that slaves ultimately were easier to control. Few Americans imported their slaves directly from East Africa, preferring their slaves from this region to have been seasoned a few years in the British West Indies. Unlike North American slavery, the slave system in the West Indies was exceptionally brutal, often working slaves to death within seven years of purchase. The children of slaves were always born slaves in the American slave system.

108. **(C)** Upon taking the crown of England in 1686, James II sent Edmund Andros to Boston with a master plan to unite Massachusetts, New Hampshire, New York, New Jersey, and Connecticut into a single colony with Andros as its governor. James was seeking to administer the colonies more closely and hoped to unify the growing empire under this system of consolidation. Andros ruled in such a tyrannical fashion in Massachusetts that he caused an uprising known as the Glorious Revolution where he was imprisoned. A similar uprising took place a year later in 1690 and is known as Leisler's revolt. During this period, James was removed from the throne by Parliament in a separate affair also called the Glorious Revolution. In England, growing fears of James' Catholic leanings led the Protestant Parliament to granting the throne to William and Mary of the Netherlands. All other answers to this question simply are not relevant.

109. **(C)** William Penn established a frame of government that granted the bulk of power to the Penn family and their advisors. Only reluctantly, and after much difficulty with the settlers, did Penn allow them a small voice in government in the colony. Indeed, the term "democracy" was used as a pejorative term throughout the colonial and Revolutionary periods. For the most part, democracy was a nineteenth and twentieth century political development in America. Few colonials believed the people capable of self-rule without some elite guidance and most used the term synomously with "mobocracy." Penn did establish religious toleration under Quaker control in Pennsylvania and during his lifetime the colony enjoyed peaceful relations with the Indians. Penn always envisioned the colony as part of the

British Empire and was adamant about making the colony a financial success, which was achieved.

110. **(C)** In 1763, William Pitt had led England to a great victory over France. As he entered the peace talks, Pitt was debating the French offer of all of Canada OR the West Indies sugar islands of Martinique and Guadaloupe as his fruits of victory. Although Pitt knew England was on the verge of bankruptcy and needed the revenue of the islands, he opted for Canada. This combination of a removed French menace from the North and a growing concern over the British national debt would ultimately prove two long-term causes of the American Revolution. France controlled neither Florida, Louisiana, nor the slave trade at the time of the peace.

111. **(C)** The primary purpose behind all of England's measures to raise a tax in America after 1763 was to reduce England's national debt. During the Seven Years' War with France, England was put on the verge of bankruptcy and could not tax its own subjects any higher. As a result, England turned to its colonies to raise the sorely needed revenue. The colonies had enjoyed the fruits of the empire and a policy of salutary neglect where they evaded taxes openly. The Stamp Act required all legal and published documents to bear a stamp issued from England with a small fee attached. Unlike the mild and sporadic protests against the Sugar Act earlier, Americans responded to the new tax with determined and forceful protests, led by merchants, lawyers, and printers. England had already angered the colonists by refusing their settlement west of Pennsylvania in the Ohio Territory by the Proclamation Line Act of 1763 and allowed illegal searches through the Writs of Assistance in 1760. The Stamp Act was not designed to control the American press.

112. **(A)** The health of the American colonies in the eighteenth century was proven to most Americans by the evidence of their explosive population growth that doubled every generation. In the eighteenth century, a rapidly growing population was considered the ultimate sign of a healthy nation. Along with its rapid growth, the colonies were growing more diverse as a people. New arrivals to America from areas other than England (Germans, Scotch-Irish, and Africans) made the middle and Southern colonies more pluralistic. The African-American population now comprised about 20 percent of the total population, indicating the South's increased reliance upon slaves as a labor source. The five American cities in the eighteenth century held less than 10 percent of the total population but enjoyed a major role in colonial affairs. Life expectancies for men still remained at or about 70 years of age throughout the colonies.

113. **(B)** William Bradford was one of the earliest settlers in Plymouth colony and was a major political force among the Pilgrims into the 1620s. He earned great fame in America for his history of the Pilgrims, *Of Plimouth Plantation.* The Enlightenment as a movement had its genesis in 1686 with the publication of Sir Isaac Newton's *Principia.* Both Franklin and Jefferson were considered the leading American examples of the Enlightenment figure, as was John Locke in England. The Enlightenment placed great faith in a rational universe and natural laws. Its followers believed that through the use of human reason man could discover the laws of nature and achieve perfection through a rational ordering of life. The Enlightenment placed great faith in human progress and believed that a science of human affairs was possible.

114. **(E)** The Loyalists for the most part emigrated out of America. Many returned to England during the war rather than suffer political and economic persecution by the colonials. Some Loyalists founded new settlements during the Revolution and its aftermath in Canada and the West Indies. It is estimated that Loyalists comprised about 20% of the American population during the Revolution. For those who fled the country, England offered modest pensions. These pensions could not replace the loss of their confiscated property by the patriots, an issue of long standing difference between England and America after the Revolutionary War. There was no Loyalist settlement in the Ohio Territory.

115. **(C)** The Articles of Confederation existed as the government of the United States from 1781 through 1788 when it was replaced by the United States Constitution. The Articles existed as a unicameral legislature in which each state had one vote. It was granted no coercive powers over the states and cannot be considered a national government, as it could not act directly on citizens. Because it could not raise taxes directly, but could only request moneys from the states, the Articles had little control over the states' finances. It paid for the war through an inflationary currency that at times was nearly worthless. After the war, the Articles proved unable to control interstate trade conflicts that led indirectly to the writing of the Constitution. The Bill of Rights was not ratified until 1791, two years after the Articles had expired. At best, it kept the 13 states from dividing through the use of a common enemy, England, during the war.

116. **(E)** In the immediate aftermath of the Revolutionary War in 1783, the British sought to do economically what they had been unsuccessful at militarily. British merchants indebted Americans heavily by extending credit and then in 1785 demanding full payment in gold. American merchants

demanded full payment from yeoman farmers and would not accept barter payment as tender. The result was that by 1786, 35 percent of American farmers were in danger of losing their farms through mortgages. The farmers of western Massachusetts requested aid from the state government and when none came took matters into their own hands. The angry farmers closed down the courts to stop foreclosure proceedings against farmers. Massachusetts requested aid from the Articles but the central government was unable to assist Massachusetts. Massachusetts eventually put down the rebellion with a show of force and the rebels scattered. Shays' Rebellion shocked most conservatives in America into recognizing that the Articles were sorely in need of reform. A convention was called for the summer of 1787 to meet in Philadelphia. The 55 delegates to that convention produced the Constitution of the United States.

117. **(A)** Seventeenth century married and single women were denied the right to vote in colonial elections. According to seventeenth-century law, married women (*feme coverts*) did retain the authority to divorce their husbands by proving just cause (i.e., extreme physical cruelty, abandonment, impious behavior). Also, mothers were considered equal partners with fathers in following the New England practice of parental arrangements of marriage for their children as a means of socioeconomic mobility. Finally, women were allowed to own personal property while married, and in many cases land and businesses as well. The denial of political rights to women in colonial America was based on the belief that women were unable to know public affairs as they were restricted in their affairs to the private domain of the household.

118. **(D)** The Declaratory Act was largely ignored by Americans because of their rejoicing over the repeal of the hated Stamp Act of 1765. As its title indicates, the Declaratory Act simply stated that although the notorious Stamp Act had been repealed, Parliament still retained its sovereignty over the American colonies. As a result, the Declaratory Act did not add new taxes, resulted in the temporary "end" of American protests, and actually strengthened the position of the Tories who were loyal to British authority in America. The creation of America's first Continental Congress, as the creation of an extralegal form of government, was an extremely radical act and did not occur until 1774.

119. **(E)** Although Hamilton publicly advocated retirement of the bulk of America's wartime debt to restore faith, he desired to retain a portion of the debt to cement creditors closer to the national government out of their self-interest. As a result, Hamilton supported the notion of deficit spending as a

means of attracting creditors to the national government. It was imperative to Hamilton that business interests be attracted to the national and not state governments. As a result, Hamilton demanded that the new national government assume the war debt of each individual state. In order to pay this sum, he proposed the raising of a revenue through customs duties and excise taxes. To conclude his plan, Hamilton sought to create a national bank with business leaders and government officials in the controlling interest. By these means, Hamilton sought to achieve his goal of uniting business leaders to the new national government during the 1790s. His program was directly opposed by Jefferson and Madison.

120. **(E)** Political parties burst across the nation's political horizon in the 1790s. The existence of political parties had been denounced by the Revolutionary War generation as evil and opposed to the common good of the republic. As a result, political parties virtually were non-existent prior to 1790. However, with the emergence of the Hamiltonian economic program and the start of war between England and France, two viewpoints of the "common good" of America emerged: the Federalists who supported Hamilton, favored England over France, and desired a government dominated by an elite group of politicians; the Democratic-Republicans who supported a nation of small farmers rather than business class, supported Revolutionary France over England, and expressed deep faith in democracy. The two parties openly split over the arrival of the new French minister to the United States in 1793, Edmund "Citizen" Genet. Genet sought to use American public opinion to swing support to France rather than maintain the course of neutrality under Washington.

PRACTICE TEST 3

This test is also on CD-ROM in our special interactive CLEP History of the United States I TEST*ware*®. It is highly recommended that you first take this exam on computer. You will then have the additional study features and benefits of enforced timed conditions, individual diagnostic analysis, and instant scoring. See page 2 for guidance on how to get the most out of our CLEP History of the United States I book and software.

CLEP HISTORY OF THE UNITED STATES I
Practice Test 3

(Answer sheets appear in the back of this book.)

TIME: 90 Minutes
120 Questions

DIRECTIONS: Each of the questions or incomplete statements below is followed by five possible answers or completions. Select the best choice in each case and fill in the corresponding oval on the answer sheet.

1. In 1786, Thomas Jefferson wrote the following:

   "Our present federal limits are not too large for good government, nor will the increase of votes in Congress produce any ill effect. On the contrary it will drown the little divisions at present existing there. Our confederacy must be viewed as the nest from which all America, North and South, is to be peopled. We should take care too not to think it for the interest of that great continent to press too soon on the Spaniards. Those countries cannot be in better hands. My fear is that they are too feeble to hold them till our population can be sufficiently advanced to gain it from them piece by piece. The navigation of the Mississippi we must have. This is all we are as yet ready to receive."

   In this private letter Jefferson is saying all of the following EXCEPT

   (A) the American political structure could survive in a larger territory.

   (B) the United States is not yet ready to take territory away from the Spanish.

   (C) a large territory will enable the political structure to overcome its divisions.

(D) it is possible that the United States might advance too quickly into Spanish territory.

(E) Spain provides good government for its territories.

2. Those who opposed ratification of the Constitution were called

(A) Democrats.

(B) Whigs.

(C) Antifederalists.

(D) Federalists.

(E) Republicans.

3. Which of the following events is placed in the INCORRECT year?

(A) 1854 — Kansas-Nebraska Act

(B) 1857 — Dred Scott decision

(C) 1858 — Lincoln-Douglas debates

(D) 1859 — John Brown's raid on Harper's Ferry

(E) 1861 — South Carolina secedes from the Union

4. Patroons were which of the following?

(A) A religious group that settled in the Carolinas

(B) An Indian tribe involved in the Pequot War

(C) The founders of Pennsylvania

(D) A colonial farm implement

(E) Owners of large tracts of land in New Netherlands

5. This engraving of the Nat Turner revolt takes what point of view?

HORRID MASSACRE IN VIRGINIA.

The Scenes within the above plate are designed to represent –Fig. 1. a Mother intreating for the lives of her children –2. Mr. O'Reilly murdered by his own slaves.–3. Mr Barrow, who bravely defended himself until his wife escaped.–4. A comp. of mounted Dragoons in pursuit of the Blacks. Library of Congress

(A) The revolt of the slaves was justified.

(B) Northern abolitionists were responsible for the revolt.

(C) The revolt was an attack upon innocent victims.

(D) The slaves were ineffective revolutionaries.

(E) The slave revolt was successful.

6. The largest city in the Southern colonies was

(A) Williamsburg.

(B) Baltimore.

(C) Savannah.

(D) Wilmington.

(E) Charleston.

7. The American colonists were able to control the power of the Royal governors through what means?

(A) The assemblies controlled all grants of money to be spent by the colonial governments.

(B) The assemblies appointed the governor.

(C) The assemblies could dismiss the governor.

(D) The assemblies established the constitutions that defined the governor's powers.

(E) The assemblies could pass laws over the governor's veto.

8. "Popular sovereignty" meant that

(A) slavery would not be allowed north of 36°30′.

(B) all territories would be permanently open to slavery.

(C) the states would decide themselves whether to be slave or free.

(D) no territories from the Mexican Cession would be open to slavery.

(E) slavery would be banned in the Southern states.

9. Which of the following served as president of the Confederate States of America?

(A) Robert E. Lee

(B) John C. Calhoun

(C) Robert Y. Hayne

(D) Jefferson Davis

(E) Alexander H. Stephens

10. Which of the following did NOT experience a Gold Rush after 1859?

(A) Nevada

(B) Alaska

(C) South Dakota

(D) California

(E) Colorado

11. What nationality group introduced the log cabin to the American colonies?

(A) English

(B) French

(C) Dutch

(D) Swedes

(E) Spanish

12. The Treaty of Paris was signed in

(A) 1781.

(B) 1789.

(C) 1776.
(D) 1783.
(E) 1787.

13. Which of the following correctly describes the attitude of Lincoln and Johnson toward Reconstruction?

(A) They regarded the South as conquered provinces.

(B) They regarded the South as unorganized territory.

(C) They saw the Civil War as a rebellion of individuals.

(D) They supported the establishment of Black Codes.

(E) They believed that Congress had the responsibility for Reconstruction.

14. According to the Constitution as passed in 1787 and ratified in 1789, a slave was equal to what fraction of a citizen for purposes of representation?

(A) 3/5
(D) 1/2
(B) 1/4
(E) 3/4
(C) 2/5

15. What Union general emerged to prominence in the Western theatre of the Civil War?

(A) George B. McClellan

(B) Ulysses S. Grant

(C) Irving McDowell

(D) John Pope

(E) George G. Meade

16. Which of the following was NOT a prominent critic of slavery?

(A) Hinton Rowan Helper
(D) John C. Calhoun
(B) Harriet Beecher Stowe
(E) Frederick Douglass
(C) William Lloyd Garrison

17. The most influential of the organized religious philosophies produced by eighteenth century rationalism and humanism was

    (A) deism.
    (B) unitarianism.
    (C) transcendentalism.
    (D) Presbyterianism.
    (E) Congregationalism.

18. The Alien and Sedition Acts included all of the following EXCEPT

    (A) increasing the residency requirements for U.S. citizenship.
    (B) extended presidential powers to remove foreign residents of the United States.
    (C) a threat to the jury system.
    (D) restriction of an opposition press.
    (E) the curtailment of free speech in America.

19. In response to the passage of the Alien and Sedition Acts by the Federalist Congress, Thomas Jefferson and James Madison

    (A) drafted the Kentucky and Virginia Resolutions which supported the concept of states' rights.
    (B) violated the Sedition Act in an effort to test its constitutionality.
    (C) demanded that the Alien Acts be submitted to a national referendum.
    (D) proposed a constitutional amendment limiting the president's power to enforce the acts.
    (E) urged the Republican members of Congress to boycott its sessions until the acts were repealed.

20. At the Hartford Convention the

    (A) Republicans strongly reaffirmed the states' right doctrine of the Kentucky and Virginia Resolutions.
    (B) governors of the New England states presented a resolution criticizing the Southern states for failing to support the war.
    (C) "war hawks" demanded the immediate invasion of Canada.

(D) Federalists proposed a constitutional amendment which would restrict the president to a single term and would prohibit successive presidents from the same state.

(E) Republicans agreed to accept higher tariffs in return for the Federalists accepting the Embargo Acts.

21. The doctrine of nullification put forth by John C. Calhoun in *The South Carolina Exposition and Protest*, published anonymously in 1828, held that

    (A) federal laws could be nullified only by amending the Constitution.

    (B) the Supreme Court had the sole power to nullify state and federal laws through the process of judicial review.

    (C) state and federal laws could be nullified only by the legislative bodies passing them.

    (D) the citizens of a state in a called convention could nullify state laws if these laws contradicted federal policies.

    (E) if a state judged a federal law to violate the Constitution, the state could declare the law null and void within its borders.

22. Which of the following authors is correctly paired with the work that he wrote?

    (A) Herman Melville: *The Sketch Book*

    (B) James Fenimore Cooper: *Conspiracy of Pontiac*

    (C) Nathaniel Hawthorne: *The Scarlet Letter*

    (D) Washington Irving: "The Raven"

    (E) Edgar Allen Poe: *The House of the Seven Gables*

23. Gabriel Prosser, Denmark Vesey, and Nat Turner were leaders of

    (A) the post-Revolutionary movement to establish separate and independent churches for the nation's free blacks.

    (B) unsuccessful slave revolts in the Southern states.

    (C) the efforts to provide educational opportunities for free blacks during the antebellum period.

    (D) the movement to return freed slaves to Africa.

(E) the American Anti-Slavery Society, the American Colonization Society, and the Knights of Liberty, respectively.

24. In general, most Europeans considered the Indians to be

(A) descendants of one of the lost tribes of Israel.

(B) survivors of the ancient civilization of Atlantis.

(C) heathens who were inferior beings.

(D) equal to the Europeans.

(E) innocent "children" who should not be contaminated by European civilization.

25. In the cartoon shown below, Ulysses Grant is presented as

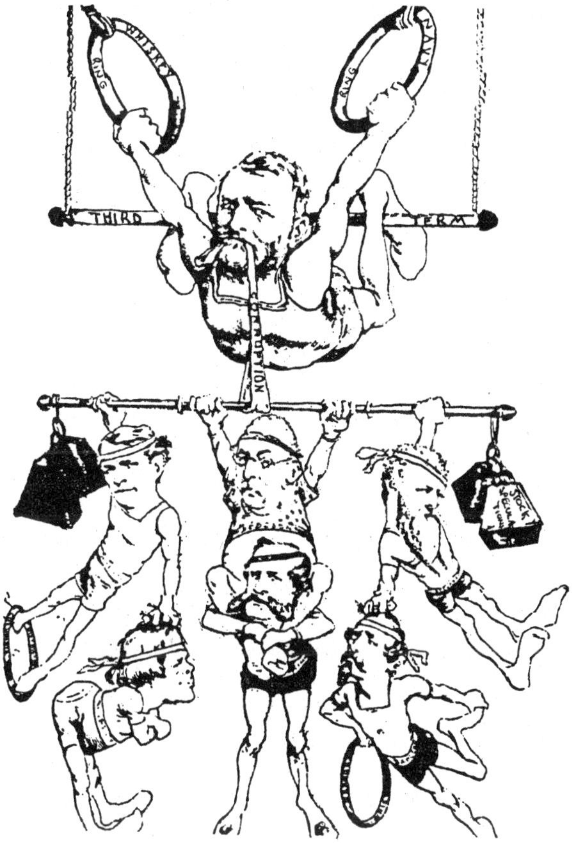

(A) adequately prepared for a third term.

(B) honest and competent.

(C) caught up in several types of corruption.

(D) weeding out corruption.

(E) a powerful president.

26. The completion of the Erie Canal in 1825 resulted in all of the following EXCEPT

(A) increased profitableness of farming in the Old Northwest.

(B) encouraging the emigration of European immigrants and New England farmers to the Old Northwest.

(C) forcing many New Englanders either to abandon their farms or to switch to dairy, fruit, and vegetable farming.

(D) a weakened political alliance between the farmers of the Old Northwest and the planters of the South.

(E) strengthening the dependency of farmers in the Old Northwest on the Mississippi River system for access to markets.

27. Pocahontas

I. was taken captive by an English trader and held as a hostage at Jamestown.

II. was converted to Christianity at her own request.

III. married John Rolfe.

IV. died in England.

(A) I only.

(B) II only.

(C) I and III only.

(D) II and IV only.

(E) I, II, III, and IV.

28. The trial of John Peter Zenger in 1735 for seditious libel

(A) established the government's right to censor the press.

(B) encouraged editors to be more critical of public officials.

(C) resulted in a "hung jury" and a dismissal of the charges.

(D) determined that government censorship of the press was unconstitutional.

(E) found Zenger guilty.

29. Thomas Paine's pamphlet *Common Sense* introduced a new element into the debate with Britain by

(A) calling for complete independence of the colonies and attacking not only King George III but also the idea of monarchy.

(B) emphasizing that both internal and external taxes could be levied on the colonies by the Parliament in London.

(C) rejecting John Locke's contract theory of government.

(D) arguing that taxation for the purpose of paying the government debt contracted during the French and Indian War was acceptable.

(E) suggesting that the colonies reconcile their difference with the government in London.

30. New York was an English colony because the

(A) English conquered the area from the Dutch.

(B) English settlers in the area gradually overwhelmed the French and Swedes.

(C) England laid claim to the area by right of colonization.

(D) Dutch and Swedes of the area petitioned the English to annex the colony.

(E) Treaty of Tordesillas gave the area to the English.

31. The Scotch-Irish immigrants to the English colonies in North America

I. felt little loyalty to either the English government or the Anglican church.

II. came in large numbers in the century due to deteriorating conditions in the Irish woolens industry.

III. generally settled on the frontier where they demonstrated a remarkable degree of resourcefulness, rugged individuality, and self-reliance.

IV. were predominantly Roman Catholics.

(A) I only.

(B) II only.

(C) I, II, and III only.

(D) II, III, and IV only.

(E) I, II, III, and IV.

32. Most of the slaves who came to the 13 mainland colonies in British North America

    (A) were from the southern part of Africa in what is today South Africa.

    (B) were granted their freedom after a specified period of service.

    (C) never made up more than five percent of the population of any colony.

    (D) were considered to be property and as such could be used as collateral for loans.

    (E) were protected from physical harm by the Roman Catholic church's *Canon Law*.

33. The Battle of Saratoga resulted in

    (A) Spain entering into a military alliance with the British in order to protect the Spanish colonies in the Americas.

    (B) the French formally recognizing American independence and making an open treaty of alliance with the Americans.

    (C) convincing the Indians to join the Americans in their struggle against the British.

    (D) isolating New England from the other colonies.

    (E) the Americans accepting British offers of reconciliation.

34. The new state constitutions adopted during the American Revolution

    (A) eliminated all property qualifications for voting.

    (B) generally did not contain a bill of rights.

    (C) abolished the office of governor.

    (D) provided for unicameral legislatures.

    (E) generally protected the people's civil liberties with a bill of rights.

35. In responding to Senator Robert Y. Hayne's defense of the *South Carolina Exposition*, who rebutted: "When my eyes shall be turned to behold for the last time, the sun in heaven, let their last feeble glance behold the gorgeous ensign of the republic not a stripe erased nor a single star obscured, bearing for its motto, that sentiment dear to

every true American heart — Liberty and Union, now and forever, one and inseparable!"?

(A) Henry Clay
(B) Thomas Jefferson
(C) John C. Calhoun
(D) Daniel Webster
(E) Stephen A. Douglas

36. The Connecticut Compromise advocated by Roger Sherman proposed settling the issue of representation in Congress by

(A) giving each state two senators, with the vote in the Senate to be by individuals and not states.

(B) having the members of both houses of Congress chosen by the state legislatures.

(C) providing for the popular election of both houses of Congress.

(D) apportioning representation in the House of Representatives according to population.

(E) Both (A) and (D).

37. While Chief Justice John Marshall presided over the Supreme Court, its decisions

(A) were generally protective of states' rights.

(B) showed no clear leaning toward either a "broad" or "strict" interpretation of the Constitution.

(C) laid the groundwork for a "broad" interpretation of the Constitution.

(D) reflected the impact of Thomas Jefferson's Kentucky Resolutions.

(E) were hostile to the development of business.

38. George Washington responded to the Whiskey Rebellion in the western counties of Pennsylvania by

(A) ignoring it until it died out.

(B) dispatching Alexander Hamilton, Secretary of the Treasury, to negotiate a reduced tax with the protesters.

(C) calling a special session of Congress to deal with the problem.

(D) sending an army larger than any he had ever commanded in the Revolution to put down the revolt.

(E) requesting an advisory opinion from the Supreme Court on the constitutionality of the excise tax.

39. The purchase of the Louisiana territory

I. doubled the size of the United States.

II. guaranteed Western farmers access to the Mississippi River as an avenue of trade.

III. presented Jefferson with a constitutional dilemma since he was a "strict" constructionist.

IV. gave the United States control of the port of New Orleans.

(A) I and II only.

(B) I and III only.

(C) I, II, and III only.

(D) I, II, and IV only.

(E) I, II, III, and IV.

40. The Webster-Ashburton Treaty of 1842

(A) forced the United States to give up the Mesabi iron range.

(B) was concerned in part with joint Anglo-American efforts to suppress the African slave trade.

(C) settled the dispute over the Oregon boundary.

(D) was not ratified by the Senate.

(E) led to Daniel Webster's resignation as secretary of state.

41. The Kansas-Nebraska Act (1854)

(A) repeated the basic ideas of the Missouri Compromise.

(B) ended the controversy over slavery in Kansas.

(C) did not allow the use of popular sovereignty in either Kansas or Nebraska.

(D) reopened the intense sectional controversy over the question of slavery in the territories.

(E) was supported by Abraham Lincoln.

42. The ultimate goal of Andrew Jackson's policy toward the Indians during his presidency was to

    (A) advocate their complete assimilation into white society.

    (B) extend citizenship and the franchise to adult Indian male property owners.

    (C) remove them to lands in the trans-Mississippi West.

    (D) preserve their culture as a vital part of American civilization.

    (E) encourage the peaceful coexistence of Indians and whites in an atmosphere of trust.

43. Andrew Jackson defended his policy of "rotation in office" which became known as the "spoils system" by asserting that

    I. a man should serve a term in office then return to the status of private citizen.

    II. men who held office too long became corrupted by a sense of power.

    III. the duties of government were too complex for the average citizen.

    IV. political appointments by newly elected officials promoted democracy.

    (A) I and II only.

    (B) II and III only.

    (C) III and IV only.

    (D) I, II, and IV only.

    (E) I, II, III, and IV.

44. "For abolishing the free System of English Laws in a neighbouring Province, establishing therein an Arbitrary government, and enlarging its Boundaries so as to render it at once an example and fit instrument for introducing the same absolute rule into these Colonies."

    In the above passage, Thomas Jefferson indicts King George III and Parliament for the

    (A) Quartering Act.

    (B) Prohibitory Act.

    (C) Quebec Act.

    (D) Stamp Act.

    (E) Townshend Acts.

45. William Lloyd Garrison persuaded the American Anti-Slavery Society to endorse the concept of

(A) compensated emancipation.

(B) gradual emancipation.

(C) immediate emancipation.

(D) colonization.

(E) violent revolution.

46. In the presidential election of 1860,

I. the Democratic party factionalized and nominated two candidates.

II. the election evolved into a contest between Abraham Lincoln and Stephen A. Douglas in the North, and John C. Breckinridge and John Bell in the South.

III. Abraham Lincoln won less than 50 percent of the popular vote.

IV. no candidate received a majority of the popular vote.

(A) I and II only.

(B) II and III only.

(C) III and IV only.

(D) II, III, and IV only.

(E) I, II, III, and IV.

47. When the Civil War started, Abraham Lincoln's primary objective was

(A) to abolish slavery.

(B) to promote the growth of industry in the North.

(C) to preserve the Union.

(D) to expand presidential powers.

(E) to punish the South.

48. The radical abolitionists who appeared in the early 1830s viewed slavery as

(A) a great moral evil.

(B) an economic problem.

(C) a problem with no solution.

(D) a dying institution.

(E) a problem whose solution should be left to the slave states.

49. Both President Andrew Johnson's plan for Reconstruction and that of Congress required the former Confederate states to

(A) enfranchise the freed slaves.

(B) extend civil and political equality to the freed slaves.

(C) ratify the Thirteenth, Fourteenth, and Fifteenth Amendments.

(D) draft new state constitutions.

(E) compensate the slaveowners for the loss of their slaves.

50. Most of the decimation of the Indian population in the Americas during the sixteenth century resulted from

(A) tribal warfare.

(B) famine.

(C) European diseases.

(D) enslavement by the Europeans.

(E) wars with the Europeans.

51. All of the following were responsible for the development of Western European expansion in the fifteenth century EXCEPT

(A) the desire to break the monopoly of the Italian states on trade with Asia.

(B) advances in navigational knowledge and ship design.

(C) the emergence of nation-states.

(D) an ideology that claimed superiority for the Europeans and inferiority for other peoples.

(E) Thomas Malthus' theory that the population of Western Europe would eventually outstrip its food supply.

52. The first permanent English colony in North America was

    (A) on Roanoke Island in North Carolina, developed by Sir Walter Raleigh.

    (B) the Massachusetts Bay colony, developed by the Puritans.

    (C) the Jamestown colony, developed by the Virginia Company.

    (D) the Avalon colony in Newfoundland, developed by Lord Baltimore.

    (E) the Plymouth colony on Cape Cod Bay, developed by the settlers from the *Mayflower*.

QUESTIONS 53 and 54 refer to the following passage.

The proposed Constitution, so far from implying an abolition of the State governments, makes them constituent parts of the national sovereignty, by allowing them a direct representation in the Senate, and leaves in their possession certain exclusive and very important portions of sovereign power.

53. The above passage is most likely to be found in which of the following?

    (A) Washington's *Farewell Address*

    (B) Jefferson's *Kentucky Resolutions*

    (C) Montesquieu's *Spirit of the Laws*

    (D) Tocqueville's *Democracy in America*

    (E) Hamilton, Madison, and Jay's *The Federalist Papers*

54. The author wants primarily to convince readers that

    (A) a balanced government is the best form of government.

    (B) the U.S. Constitution would preserve the rights and powers of the states.

    (C) the U.S. Constitution is a form of government uniquely suited to the American character.

    (D) the U.S. Constitution would effectively eliminate state governments.

    (E) the United States should keep itself free from entangling alliances with European countries.

55. The Maryland Toleration Act of 1649 provided for

    (A) the tolerance of most Christian churches.
    (B) freedom of conscience for those not accepting the Trinity.
    (C) an end to tax support for any church.
    (D) a complete separation of church and state.
    (E) the extension of the vote to Jews and non-Christians.

56. The colony founded as a haven for Quakers was

    (A) New Jersey.
    (B) Maryland.
    (C) Rhode Island.
    (D) Pennsylvania.
    (E) Virginia.

57. The French and Indian War resulted in all of the following EXCEPT

    (A) new lands in the trans-Mississippi West were opened to the colonists.
    (B) colonists began thinking of themselves as Americans rather than English or British.
    (C) Spain gained control of Louisiana.
    (D) the treaty ending the war eliminated the French from the American colonial frontier.
    (E) the myth of British invincibility was shattered.

58. The important staple for export in colonial Virginia was

    (A) tobacco.
    (B) cotton.
    (C) hemp.
    (D) indigo.
    (E) sugar cane.

59. The colony established by James Oglethorpe as a refuge for honest people imprisoned for debt was

(A) South Carolina.
(B) Georgia.
(C) Pennsylvania.
(D) North Carolina.
(E) Delaware.

60. The fundamental goal of mercantilism in the seventeenth and eighteenth centuries was

(A) to eliminate the obstacles to free trade among the countries of Europe.

(B) to have "mother" countries serve as a source of raw materials and the colonies as a source of manufactured goods.

(C) to limit foreign imports and to encourage a favorable balance of trade.

(D) to encourage wealthy nations to provide economic assistance to the developing areas of the world.

(E) to discourage the growth of economic nationalism.

61. At the close of the American Revolution, a group of American writers and artists sought to establish a distinctly American national culture. Which of the following artists does not belong to this movement?

(A) Noah Webster
(B) Philip Freneau
(C) Hector St. Jean Crèvecoeur
(D) Cotton Mather
(E) Joel Barlow

62. President John Adams' "Midnight Appointments" was the primary issue in the Supreme Court's ruling in

    (A) *Marbury v. Madison.*
    (B) *Gibbons v. Ogden.*
    (C) *Martin v. Hunter's Lessee.*
    (D) *Dartmouth v. Woodward.*
    (E) *Fletcher v. Peck.*

63. Chief Justice John Marshall established the power of judicial review for the Supreme Court in 1803. This doctrine grants

    (A) the Court the power of original jurisdiction.
    (B) the power of strict constructionalism.
    (C) the power of the government to regulate big business.
    (D) the power of the Court to determine what the laws of America are.
    (E) the power of the Court to select its own members.

64. "We prefer war to the putrescent pool of ignominous peace," best represents the attitudes of which group during the War of 1812?

    (A) Oliver Ellsworth and New England merchants
    (B) Henry Clay and Westerners
    (C) British nobility
    (D) James Madison and the Republicans
    (E) Harrison Gay Otis and the Federalists

65. The primary goal of the Hartford Convention was to

(A) have New England secede from the United States.

(B) assert a doctrine of states' rights.

(C) establish a public school system in the nation.

(D) establish direct trade with Japan.

(E) plan the invasion of Cuba.

66. The fragility of the Era of Good Feelings was shattered by the

(A) War of 1812.

(B) Chesapeake Affair.

(C) Missouri Compromise.

(D) Non-Intercourse Act.

(E) Jay Treaty.

67. The American population grew from _____ million in 1820 to _____ million in 1850.

(A) 1 … 6

(B) 20 … 40

(C) 9 … 23

(D) 62 … 88

(E) 40 … 44

68. During the 1820s, the ideal American family was portrayed as a family in which

(A) the home served as a refuge from a hostile world.

(B) the children were the center.

(C) there existed separate spheres for men and women.

(D) the mother primarily was responsible for raising the children.

(E) All of the above.

69. The Tariff Act of 1832 resulted in

(A) near war between the United States and South Carolina.

(B) a rift between President Jackson and Vice President Calhoun.

(C) the revival of a states' rights doctrine.

(D) a compromise solution proposed by Henry Clay.

(E) All of the above.

70. The American Colonization Society was an antislavery organization that

(A) advocated racial equality.

(B) sought full political rights for blacks.

(C) favored immediate emancipation.

(D) advocated the forced shipment of freed slaves to Africa.

(E) relied upon governmental action to end slavery.

71. The vast majority of Southern slaves lived on plantations holding

(A) less than 20 slaves.

(B) 50–100 slaves.

(C) 200–500 slaves.

(D) 500–1,000 slaves.

(E) more than 1,000 slaves.

72. The doctrine of Manifest Destiny argued that

(A) it was America's natural right to occupy all lands to the Pacific coast.

(B) the American economy needed new lands for new markets.

(C) America should remain first and foremost a nation of farmers.

(D) the nation needed new lands to safeguard democracy.

(E) All of the above.

73. Which of the following events occurred first?

(A) Kansas-Nebraska Act

(B) Nat Turner Rebellion

(C) Seneca Falls Convention

(D) Lincoln-Douglas debates

(E) Homestead Act

74. "I wish to speak today, not as a Massachusetts man, nor as a Northern man, but as an American for the preservation of the Union." Daniel Webster delivered this speech in defense of

(A) Dartmouth College.

(B) the Charles River Bridge.

(C) Abraham Lincoln.

(D) the Compromise of 1850.

(E) the Second Bank of the United States.

75. Stephen Douglas' advocacy of popular sovereignty in the Kansas-Nebraska Act ignited rather than dispelled the flames of sectionalism. Popular sovereignty sought to

(A) allow blacks to vote in the Kansas-Nebraska territories.

(B) let the residents of Kansas-Nebraska areas determine their own laws on slavery through elections.

(C) force the Supreme Court to rule on slavery's constitutionality.

(D) remove the slavery issue from politics.

(E) None of the above.

76. The "Secret Six" were the financial supporters of

(A) the attack on Fort Sumter.

(B) John Brown's raid on Harper's Ferry.

(C) Lincoln's presidential candidacy.

(D) Southern secession.

(E) King Cotton Diplomacy.

77. The final four states to secede from the United States after the firing on Fort Sumter were

(A) Alabama, Georgia, South Carolina, and North Carolina.

(B) Virginia, Arkansas, Tennessee, and North Carolina.

(C) Georgia, Mississippi, South Carolina, and Texas.

(D) South Carolina, Kentucky, Maryland, and Delaware.

(E) Florida, Georgia, Maryland, and South Carolina.

78. During the Civil War, the Copperheads were

(A) anti-Lincoln Republicans.

(B) Northern pro-war Democrats.

(C) pro-Union Southerners.

(D) Northern anti-war Democrats.

(E) None of the above.

79. The Southern strategy of gaining a European ally against the North was attempted through a policy referred to as

(A) the Stars and Bars.

(B) the war of attrition.

(C) King Cotton Diplomacy.

(D) nullification.

(E) mercantilism.

80. The Great Plains Indian culture can best be described in the 1840s as

(A) nomadic.

(B) centered around the buffalo.

(C) at its zenith.

(D) animistic in its reverence for the spiritual power of nature.

(E) All of the above.

81. Lincoln's Reconstruction plan for the defeated Southern states included all of the following EXCEPT

(A) abolition of slavery.

(B) free education for the ex-slaves.

(C) republican state governments.

(D) a required 10 percent of all voters in a state to take a loyalty oath to the United States.

(E) citizenship for the ex-slaves.

82. The Wade-Davis Bill best represents the views of

(A) President Andrew Johnson.

(B) the Radical Republicans.

(C) the carpetbaggers.

(D) the scalawags.

(E) the Democratic party.

83. The Thirteenth Amendment established

(A) the legal end of slavery in America.

(B) the two-term presidency.

(C) the right to vote for ex-slaves.

(D) the income tax.

(E) female suffrage.

84. In trying to impeach President Andrew Johnson, Congress used the

(A) Morrill Act.

(B) Tenure of Office Act.

(C) Civil Rights Act.

(D) *Ex Parte* Milligan.

(E) None of the above.

85. Thomas Nast achieved fame and influence as a

(A) radio commentator.

(B) newspaper publisher.

(C) photographer.

(D) film producer.

(E) political cartoonist.

86. Which of the following is true of the Stamp Act Congress?

(A) It was the first unified government for all the American colonies.

(B) It provided an important opportunity for colonial stamp agents to discuss methods of enforcing the act.

(C) It was attended only by Georgia, Virginia, and the Carolinas.

(D) It provided an important opportunity for colonial leaders to meet and establish ties with one another.

(E) It rejected the assertion that the colonies ought to protest acts of Parliament deemed to be unconstitutional.

87. The map below depicts the United States immediately after which of the following events?

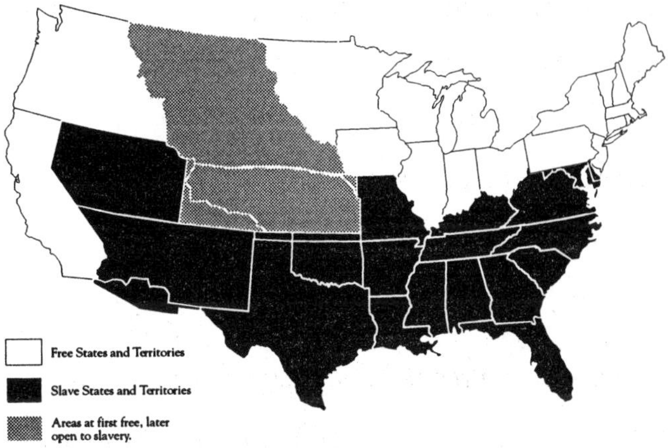

(A) Passage of the Compromise of 1850

(B) Negotiation of the Webster-Ashburton Treaty

(C) Passage of the Northwest Ordinance

(D) Settlement of the Mexican War

(E) Passage of the Missouri Compromise

88. The principle of "popular sovereignty" was

(A) first conceived by Senator Stephen A. Douglas.

(B) applied as part of the Missouri Compromise.

(C) a central feature of the Kansas-Nebraska Act.

(D) a policy favored by the Whig party during the late 1840s and early 1850s.

(E) successful in solving the impasse over the status of slavery in the territories.

89. In issuing the Emancipation Proclamation, one of Lincoln's goals was to

(A) gain the active aid of Britain and France in restoring the Union.

(B) stir up enthusiasm for the war in such border states as Maryland and Kentucky.

(C) please the Radicals in the North by abolishing slavery in areas of the South already under the control of Union armies.

(D) please Russia, one of the Union's few overseas friends, where the serfs had been emancipated the previous year.

(E) keep Britain and France from intervening on the side of the Confederacy.

90. The most common form of resistance on the part of black American slaves prior to the Civil War was

(A) violent uprisings in which many persons were killed.

(B) attempts to escape and reach Canada by means of the "Underground Railroad."

(C) passive resistance, including breaking tools and slightly slowing the pace of work.

(D) arson of plantation buildings and cotton gins.

(E) poisoning of the food consumed by their white masters.

91. Which of the following best describes the attitudes of Southern whites toward slavery during the mid-nineteenth century (ca. 1835–1865)?

(A) Slavery was a necessary evil.

(B) Slavery should be immediately abolished.

(C) Slavery was a benefit to both whites and blacks.

(D) Slavery should gradually be phased out and the freed slaves colonized to some place outside the United States.

(E) Slavery was a national sin.

92. For farmers and planters in the South, the 1850s was a period of

(A) low prices for agricultural products.

(B) rapid and violent fluctuations in crop prices.

(C) high crop prices due to repeated crop failures.

(D) high crop prices and sustained prosperity.

(E) desperate poverty, culminating in the Panic of 1857.

93. The economic theory of mercantilism would be consistent with which of the following statements?

(A) Economies will prosper most when trade is restricted as little as possible.

(B) A government should seek to direct the economy so as to maximize exports.

(C) Colonies are of little economic importance to the mother country.

(D) It is vital that a country imports more than it exports.

(E) Tariff barriers should be avoided as much as possible.

94. In seeking diplomatic recognition from foreign powers during the War for Independence, the American government found it necessary to

(A) make large financial payments to the governments of France, Spain, and Holland.

(B) promise to cede large tracts of American territory to France upon a victorious conclusion of the war.

(C) demonstrate its financial stability and self-sufficiency.

(D) demonstrate a determination and potential to win independence.

(E) agree to grant France a specially favored trading status.

95. William Lloyd Garrison, in his publication *The Liberator,* was outspoken in calling for

(A) the gradual and compensated emancipation of slaves.

(B) colonization of slaves to some place outside the boundaries of the United States.

(C) repeal of the congressional "gag rule."

(D) immediate and uncompensated emancipation of slaves.

(E) the strict maintenance of the constitutional doctrine of states' rights.

96. The immediate issue in dispute in Bacon's Rebellion was

(A) the jailing of individuals or seizure of their property for failure to pay taxes during a time of economic hardship.

(B) the under-representation of the backcountry in Virginia's legislature.

(C) the refusal of large planters to honor the terms of their contracts with former indentured servants.

(D) the perceived failure of Virginia's governor to protect the colony's frontier area from the depredations of raiding Indians.

(E) the colonial governor's manipulation of tobacco prices for the benefit of himself and a small clique of his friends.

97. The Newburgh Conspiracy was concerned with

(A) betrayal of the plans for the vital fort at West Point, New York.

(B) the use of the Continental Army to create a more centralized Union of the states.

(C) resistance to the collection of federal excise taxes in western Pennsylvania.

(D) New England's threat to secede should the War of 1812 continue.

(E) Aaron Burr's plot to detach the western United States as an empire for himself.

98. The Wilmot Proviso stipulated that

(A) slavery should be prohibited in the lands acquired as a result of the Mexican War.

(B) no lands should be annexed to the United States as a result of the Mexican War.

(C) California should be a free state while the rest of the Mexican Cession should be reserved for the formation of slave states.

(D) the status of slavery in the Mexican Cession should be decided on the basis of "popular sovereignty."

(E) the Missouri Compromise line should be extended through the Mexican Cession to the Pacific, lands north of it being closed to slavery.

99. The Whig party turned against President John Tyler because

(A) he was felt to be ineffective in pushing the Whig agenda through Congress.

(B) he spoke out in favor of the annexation of Texas.

(C) he opposed the entire Whig legislative program.

(D) he criticized Henry Clay's handling of the Nullification Crisis.

(E) he aggressively favored the expansion of slavery.

100. In coining the phrase "Manifest Destiny," journalist John L. O'Sullivan meant that

(A) the struggle for racial equality was the ultimate goal of America's existence.

(B) America was certain to become an independent country sooner or later.

(C) it was the destiny of America to overspread the continent.

(D) America must eventually become either all slave or all free.

(E) America should seek to acquire an overseas empire.

101. All of the following were causes of the Mexican War EXCEPT

(A) American desire for California.

(B) Mexican failure to pay debts and damages owed to the U.S.

(C) U.S. annexation of the formerly Mexican-held Republic of Texas.

(D) Mexican desire to annex Louisiana.

(E) the disputed southern boundary of Texas.

102. The primary motive of those who founded the British colony in Virginia during the seventeenth century was the

(A) desire for economic gain.

(B) desire for religious freedom.

(C) desire to create a perfect religious commonwealth as an example to the rest of the world.

(D) desire to recreate in the New World the story of feudalistic society that was fading in the Old.

(E) desire to increase the power and glory of Great Britain.

103. Which of the following statements is true of Lincoln's Ten Percent Plan?

(A) It stipulated that at least ten percent of former slaves must be accorded the right to vote within a given Southern state before that state could be readmitted to the Union.

(B) It allowed the rights of citizenship only to those Southerners who could take an oath that they had never been disloyal to the Union.

(C) It allowed high-ranking rebel officials to regain the right to vote and hold office by simply promising future good behavior.

(D) It was silent on the issue of slavery.

(E) It provided for the restoration of loyal governments for the erstwhile Confederate states now under Union control.

104. All of the following were parts of Andrew Johnson's plan for Reconstruction EXCEPT

(A) recommending to the Southern states that the vote be extended to the recently freed slaves.

(B) requiring ratification of the Thirteenth Amendment.

(C) requiring payment of monetary reparations for the damage caused by the war.

(D) requiring renunciation of secession.

(E) requiring repudiation of the Confederate debt.

105. The term "Seward's Folly" referred to Secretary of State William Seward's

(A) advocacy of a lenient policy toward the defeated Southern states.

(B) break with the majority radical faction of the Republican party in order to back President Andrew Johnson.

(C) belief that the Civil War could be avoided and the Union restored by provoking a war with Britain and France.

(D) negotiation of the purchase of Alaska from Russia.

(E) ill-fated attempt to gain the presidency in 1860.

106. In response to southern intransigence in the face of President Andrew Johnson's mild Reconstruction plan, Congress did all of the following EXCEPT

(A) exclude Southern representatives and senators from participating in Congress.

(B) pass the Civil Rights Act of 1866.

(C) order the arrest and imprisonment of former Confederate leaders.

(D) approve and send on to the states the Fourteenth Amendment.

(E) divide the South into five districts to be ruled by military governors with almost dictatorial powers.

107. When President Andrew Johnson removed Secretary of War Edwin M. Stanton without the approval of the Senate, contrary to the terms of the recently passed Tenure of Office Act, he

(A) was impeached and removed from office.

(B) came within one vote of being impeached.

(C) was impeached and came within one vote of being removed from office.

(D) resigned to avoid impeachment and was subsequently pardoned by his successor.

(E) was impeached, refused to resign, and his term ended before a vote could be taken on his removal from office.

108. The purpose of the Treaty of Tordesillas was

(A) to divide the non-European world between Spain and Portugal.

(B) to specify which parts of North America should be French and which parts Spanish.

(C) to create an alliance of France, Holland, and England against Spanish designs in the New World.

(D) to divide the New World between France and Spain.

(E) to exclude any Portuguese colonization from the Western Hemisphere.

109. During the 1760s and 1770s the most effective American tactic in gaining the repeal of the Stamp and Townshend Acts was

(A) tarring and feathering British tax agents.

(B) sending petitions to the king and Parliament.

(C) boycotting British goods.

(D) destroying private property, such as tea, on which a tax was to be levied.

(E) using death threats to intimidate British tax agents.

110. One of the purposes of the 1773 Tea Act was to

(A) prevent overconsumption of tea in America.

(B) lower the price of tea in Great Britain by decreasing the demand for it in America.

(C) save the British East India Company from financial ruin.

(D) create a long-term shift in wealth from Britain's North American colonies to its colony in India.

(E) calm labor unrest in India.

111. During the American War of Independence, the Battle of Saratoga was most significant because it

(A) left the British with inadequate resources to carry on the war.

(B) prevented the British from ever mounting another successful invasion of American territory.

(C) allowed American forces to seize large portions of Canada.

(D) persuaded France to begin openly supporting the Americans.

(E) caused Holland to delay its decision to enter the war on the side of the British.

112. Besides mass production through the use of interchangeable parts, Eli Whitney also influenced American history by his invention of the

(A) practical river steamboat.

(B) cotton gin.

(C) incandescent light bulb.

(D) telegraph.

(E) steam locomotive.

113. The Republican response to the 1798 Alien and Sedition Acts included

(A) South Carolina's nullification of the acts.

(B) the Virginia and Kentucky Resolutions.

(C) the Hartford Convention.

(D) the Ostend Manifesto.

(E) the Mulligan Letters.

114. The Puritans who settled the Massachusetts Bay colony wanted their settlement to be primarily

(A) a place where they could get away from persecution.

(B) an example to the rest of the world.

(C) a place where they would have the opportunity to prosper free from government regulation.

(D) a society that practiced complete separation of church and state.

(E) a pluralistic society in which all would be free to practice and teach their beliefs.

115. The Missouri Compromise provided that Missouri be admitted as a slave state, Maine be admitted as a free state, and

(A) all of the Louisiana Territory north of the northern boundary of Missouri be closed to slavery.

(B) all of the Louisiana Territory north of 36°30′ be closed to slavery.

(C) the entire Louisiana Territory be open to slavery.

(D) the lands south of 36°30′ be guaranteed to slavery and the lands north of it negotiable.

(E) all of the Louisiana Territory north of the southern boundary of Missouri be closed to slavery for 30 years.

116. The Morrill Land Grant Act provided

(A) 160 acres of free land within the public domain to any head of household who would settle on it and improve it over a period of five years.

(B) large amounts of federal government land to states that would establish agricultural and mechanical colleges.

(C) 40 acres of land to former slaves.

(D) that the land of former Confederates should not be confiscated.

(E) large reservations for the Indians of the Great Plains.

117. All of the following reflect the views of Americans expressed by Alexis de Tocqueville and other early nineteenth century European visitors EXCEPT

(A) daily life in America was highly politicized.

(B) Americans exhibited a strong sense of national pride.

(C) Americans were highly individualistic.

(D) Americans exhibited a strong sense of social deference.

(E) Americans valued personal freedom.

118. Noah Webster, Ralph Waldo Emerson, and James Fenimore Cooper were all significant as

(A) literary figures of the Transcendentalist movement.

(B) pioneers in the development of the American novel.

(C) the compilers of a well-known dictionary.

(D) contributors to a more distinctly American literature.

(E) trendsetters in American popular culture.

119. Which of the following was most responsible for the change shown between 1815 and 1830?

Average Inland Freight Rates in the U.S.
1800–1830

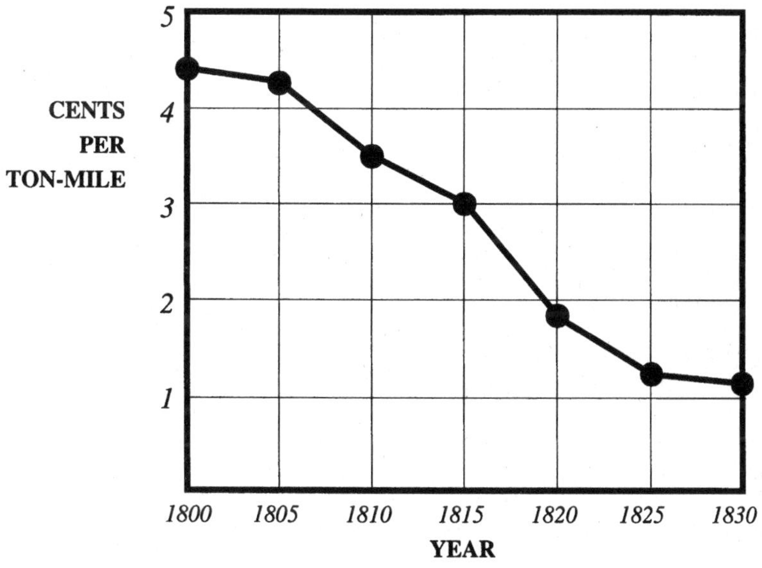

(A) The development of practical steam-powered railroad trains

(B) The development of a network of canals linking important cities and waterways

(C) The growth in the nation's mileage of improved roads and turnpikes

(D) Improvements in the design of keelboats and flatboats

(E) The development of steamboats

120. The Molasses Act was intended to enforce England's mercantilist policies by

(A) forcing the colonists to export solely to Great Britain.

(B) forcing the colonists to buy sugar from other British colonies rather than from foreign producers.

(C) forbidding the colonists to engage in manufacturing activity in competition with British industries.

(D) providing a favorable market for the products of the British East India Company.

(E) creating an economic situation in which gold tended to flow from the colonies to the mother country.

CLEP HISTORY OF THE UNITED STATES I
TEST 3

ANSWER KEY

1.	(E)	31.	(C)	61.	(D)	91.	(C)
2.	(C)	32.	(D)	62.	(A)	92.	(D)
3.	(E)	33.	(B)	63.	(D)	93.	(B)
4.	(E)	34.	(E)	64.	(B)	94.	(D)
5.	(C)	35.	(D)	65.	(B)	95.	(D)
6.	(E)	36.	(E)	66.	(C)	96.	(D)
7.	(A)	37.	(C)	67.	(C)	97.	(B)
8.	(C)	38.	(D)	68.	(E)	98.	(A)
9.	(D)	39.	(E)	69.	(E)	99.	(C)
10.	(D)	40.	(B)	70.	(D)	100.	(C)
11.	(D)	41.	(D)	71.	(A)	101.	(D)
12.	(D)	42.	(C)	72.	(E)	102.	(A)
13.	(C)	43.	(D)	73.	(B)	103.	(E)
14.	(A)	44.	(C)	74.	(D)	104.	(C)
15.	(B)	45.	(C)	75.	(B)	105.	(D)
16.	(D)	46.	(E)	76.	(B)	106.	(C)
17.	(B)	47.	(C)	77.	(B)	107.	(C)
18.	(C)	48.	(A)	78.	(D)	108.	(A)
19.	(A)	49.	(D)	79.	(C)	109.	(C)
20.	(D)	50.	(C)	80.	(E)	110.	(C)
21.	(E)	51.	(E)	81.	(E)	111.	(D)
22.	(C)	52.	(C)	82.	(B)	112.	(B)
23.	(B)	53.	(E)	83.	(A)	113.	(B)
24.	(C)	54.	(B)	84.	(B)	114.	(B)
25.	(C)	55.	(A)	85.	(E)	115.	(B)
26.	(E)	56.	(D)	86.	(D)	116.	(B)
27.	(E)	57.	(A)	87.	(A)	117.	(D)
28.	(B)	58.	(A)	88.	(C)	118.	(D)
29.	(A)	59.	(B)	89.	(E)	119.	(E)
30.	(A)	60.	(C)	90.	(C)	120.	(B)

DETAILED EXPLANATIONS OF ANSWERS

TEST 3

1. **(E)** Jefferson was fearful that the Spanish government was too weak to hold on to its territories long enough for orderly expansion of the United States.

2. **(C)** Those who opposed the Constitution became known as Antifederalists because supporters of the Constitution had adopted the name Federalists. Democrats, Whigs, and Republicans were names of political parties to emerge later in American history.

3. **(E)** South Carolina seceded from the Union in December 1860, prior to Lincoln's inauguration as president.

4. **(E)** Patroon was the term for the owners of large tracts of land in the Dutch colony of New Netherlands, which was taken over by the English in 1664. The Pequot War took place in 1635–67 between the Puritans and the Pequots. The French Huguenots settled in the Carolinas in the seventeenth century, while William Penn founded Pennsylvania in 1681 as a haven for Quakers. Colonial farm implements included such items as the mould board plow, hoe, rake, and grain cradle.

5. **(C)** This engraving emphasizes the innocence and helplessness of the victims.

6. **(E)** The Southern colonies were largely rural in character. Charleston, South Carolina, was the largest city, with a population of about 10,000 in the 1750s. Baltimore, the second largest city, had a population of 5,000 at this time.

7. **(A)** The colonial assemblies controlled the purse strings of colonial government, including the governor's salary, and therefore were in a strong bargaining position vis-à-vis the royal governor.

8. **(C)** "Popular sovereignty," as put forward by Stephen A. Douglas and embodied in the Compromise of 1850 and the Kansas-Nebraska Act of 1854, gave to the states themselves the power to decide whether they were to be slave or free.

9. **(D)** Jefferson Davis served as president of the Confederacy, while Alexander H. Stephens served as vice president. Robert E. Lee was commander of the Confederate forces. Robert Y. Hayne and John C. Calhoun were outspoken supporters of Southern interest while representing South Carolina in the U.S. Senate prior to the Civil War.

10. **(D)** California experienced its Gold Rush in 1849. In 1859 both Colorado and Nevada had Gold Rushes, followed by South Dakota in 1874, and Alaska in 1880 and 1896.

11. **(D)** The log cabin was introduced by the Swedes who settled in Delaware between 1638 and 1655.

12. **(D)** The Treaty of Paris was signed in 1783. The Declaration of Independence was signed in 1776. Cornwallis surrendered in 1781. The Constitutional Convention took place in 1787 and the Constitution was ratified in 1789.

13. **(C)** Lincoln and Johnson saw the Civil War as a rebellion of individuals. Therefore, they emphasized use of the presidential pardon. The Radical Republicans saw the South as either conquered provinces or unorganized territory and believed that Congress had power over Reconstruction. The Southern states passed Black Codes in the aftermath of the War.

14. **(A)** Three-fifths of the slaves were to be counted for purposes of both representation and taxation. This was a compromise between Southerners who wanted to count the slaves for representation but not taxation and Northerners who took the opposite position.

15. **(B)** General Ulysses S. Grant emerged to prominence in battles along the Mississippi, including Fort Donelson, and Vicksburg. In 1864, Grant became the supreme commander of all the Union armies.

16. **(D)** John C. Calhoun defended the interests of the South, including slavery, while representing South Carolina in the United States Senate between 1832 and 1850. Hinton Rowan Helper published *The Impending Crisis* in 1857, arguing that slavery caused the South to be economically inferior to the North. Harriet Beecher Stowe published her graphic novel of slavery, *Uncle Tom's Cabin*, in 1851–52. William Lloyd Garrison was a leading white abolitionist and Frederick Douglass a leading black abolitionist.

17. **(B)** With its roots in the eighteenth century Enlightenment, Unitarianism was formally organized by William Ellery Channing in 1825. Although it rejected the Trinity, it had no doctrine beyond the universal brotherhood of God and man. Deism was a widespread religious belief among the educated classes in the eighteenth century, but was not an organized movement. Transcendentalism was a philosophical and literary movement, involving several former Unitarians, such as Ralph Waldo Emerson, that emerged in the 1830s. Presbyterianism and Congregationalism were orthodox Christian denominations with roots deep in the colonial period.

18. **(C)** The Alien and Sedition Acts of 1797–1798 were a direct and bold attempt by President Adams to crush the opposition party of Madison-Jefferson, the Democratic-Republicans. Adams feared that Jefferson's party was bent on establishing a French-styled class revolution in America. To ensure that his party, the Federalists, remained in power, Adams pushed through the Federalist Congress a series of laws known as the Alien and Sedition Acts. These Acts increased the residency requirement for citizenship from five to 14 years. (Thus, new immigrants to America, who tended to support Jefferson, would be disenfranchised for 14 years.) In addition, the president was granted broad powers to remove "undesirable" aliens, thus putting a political muzzle on aliens. In addition, the laws established large monetary fines and sentences to prison for anyone who attacked the American government (the Adams administration) in print or speech. The laws never included an attack on the jury system and indeed relied upon juries to determine guilt or innocence in all seditious libel cases.

19. **(A)** Thomas Jefferson anonymously drafted resolutions protesting the Alien and Sedition Acts, and the legislature of Kentucky adopted these resolutions. During its 1789–99 session James Madison drafted the resolutions adopted by the Virginia legislature in 1789. The Kentucky and Virginia Resolutions invoked the compact theory of the Constitution. Jefferson and Madison asserted in their resolutions that the federal government was

an agent of the states and the states were the final judges of the limits of federal power.

20. **(D)** The Hartford Resolutions demanded a series of constitutional amendments. These proposed amendments would: 1) require a two-thirds vote of Congress to declare war, to impose commercial restrictions, and to admit new states; 2) omit slaves from the census used to apportion representation in Congress; and 3) restrict presidents to a single term in office and prohibit successive presidents from the same state.

21. **(E)** The doctrine of nullification was based on the contention that the Constitution was a compact among the sovereign states. When the states entered into the compact, they retained their essential sovereignty and delegated limited and clearly specified powers to the federal government. If a state judged a federal law to violate the compact, it could nullify the law within its borders.

According to the doctrine of nullification/interposition, each state could be the judge of the legality or constitutionality of national action and could "interpose" its sovereignty to nullify invalid federal action. Southern leaders reactivated the theory in opposition to the desegregation rulings of the Supreme Court. The federal courts have rejected the doctrine as contrary to the national supremacy clause of Article VI of the Constitution.

22. **(C)** *The Scarlet Letter* (1850) and *The House of the Seven Gables* (1851) were Nathaniel Hawthorne's two greatest novels. *The Scarlet Letter* was a grim yet sympathetic analysis of adultery. In this novel, Hawthorne did not condemn the woman, Hester Prynne, but the people who judged her.

23. **(B)** Gabriel Prosser organized and led a rebellion of slaves in Henrico County, Virginia in 1800. Denmark Vesey, a free black, inspired a group of slaves in Charleston, South Carolina, with the idea of seizing their freedom in 1822. Nat Turner planned and led a slave uprising in 1831 in Southampton County, Virginia. These slave rebellions failed and Prosser, Vessey, and Turner were executed.

24. **(C)** Most Europeans assumed that since the Indians were non-European they were inferior beings. Likewise, the Europeans dismissed the Indians as being heathens since they were not Christian. The colonists also considered the Indians to be the epitome of savagery and barbarism.

25. **(C)** This cartoon shows Ulysses Grant caught within several strands of corruption, including the Whiskey Ring and corruption in the Navy Department.

26. **(E)** Prior to the completion of the Erie Canal, farmers in the Old Northwest depended on the Mississippi River system to get their produce to market. The completion of the Erie Canal resulted in the shifting of the commerce of the Old Northwest from the Mississippi River system to the Great Lakes and the Erie Canal.

27. **(E)** Pocahontas was the daughter of the powerful Indian chieftain Powhatan. While being held as a hostage at Jamestown, she converted to Christianity and was baptized Rebecca. In 1614, she married John Rolfe and accompanied him to England. As Pocahontas was preparing to return to Virginia, she died suddenly.

28. **(B)** John Peter Zenger was accused of seditious libel for publishing criticisms of New York's governor. Zenger was imprisoned for ten months and brought to trial in 1735. Ignoring the established rule in English common law that one might be punished for criticism which fostered "an ill opinion of the government," the jury considered the attack on the governor to be true and found Zenger innocent. Although the libel law remained the same, the jury's verdict emboldened editors to criticize officials more freely.

29. **(A)** Thomas Paine published his pamphlet *Common Sense* in January 1776. Written at a time when others were debating the issue of home rule, *Common Sense* called on the American colonies to declare their independence from Great Britain. Paine refocused the hostility previously vented on Parliament and directly attacked allegiance to the king.

30. **(A)** The Dutch founded the colony of New Netherlands on the Hudson River. Despite this, Charles II bestowed a large tract of land south of the Massachusetts Bay colony upon his brother in 1664. Although it took three Anglo-Dutch wars to secure it, New Netherlands was under British control by the end of 1664.

31. **(C)** Although the Scotch-Irish spoke English, they felt little loyalty to either the English government or the Anglican church. Most of the Scotch-Irish were Presbyterian and had been treated badly by the English government. They came to America because of the deteriorating economic

conditions in the Irish woolens industry and generally settled on the frontier.

32. **(D)** Slavery was recognized in the laws of all the colonies, but it flourished in the Tidewater South. South Carolina had a black majority through most of the eighteenth century. About half the slaves imported into the mainland colonies came from Congo-Angola and the Bight of Biafra. Nearly all the rest of the slaves came from the Atlantic coast of Africa up to Senegambia. Although the slave codes varied from colony to colony, they were essentially the same. These codes legally transformed the slaves into property.

33. **(B)** After being defeated at the Battle of Brandywine Creek, the American patriots, led by Horatio Gates and Benedict Arnold, forced General John Burgoyne to surrender his entire army at Saratoga in October 1777. This was one of the most significant military victories of the war for the Americans. The victory at Saratoga prevented the isolation of the New England states and convinced the French that the Americans might well make good their claim to independence. In December 1777, the French recognized the United States as an independent country.

34. **(E)** The first state constitutions varied mainly in detail. These constitutions formed governments much like the colonial governments with elected governors and senates instead of appointed governors and councils. The first state constitution generally embodied a separation of powers and included a bill of rights protecting the rights of petition, freedom of speech, trial by jury, etc.

35. **(D)** The Webster-Hayne debate grew out of the Foot Resolution. Senator Samuel Foot of Connecticut proposed that the sale of public lands be restricted to those surveyed and already on the market. This stemmed from the Eastern manufacturer's alarm over the great migration to the West. The Western senators, as might have been expected, sprang to the defense of their section's interests. The South, needing sectional allies in its controversies with the Northeast, promptly sided with the West. Its most outstanding orator was Senator Robert Hayne of South Carolina. Hayne condemned the New England states for their disloyalty during the War of 1812 and for their insistence on a protective tariff. He then acclaimed Calhoun's doctrine of nullification as the only means of safeguarding the minority interests of the South. Hayne, like Calhoun, did not advocate a breakup of the Union, but his arguments were remembered by nullifiers and secessionists for future use.

36. **(E)** The Connecticut Compromise, advanced by Oliver Ellsworth and Roger Sherman, was submitted to the Constitutional Convention to break the deadlock created by the rejection of the Randolph Plan and Patterson Plan. The compromise provided for a bicameral legislature. One chamber of the legislature was to have equal representation from each state, and the other chamber was to be based on proportional representation.

37. **(C)** Chief Justice John Marshall viewed the Constitution as an instrument of national unity, a document that created its own sanctions by its implied powers. Marshall's decisions affirmed the constitutional power of the Court to engage in judicial review of federal and state legislation, gave judicial sanction to the doctrine of centralization of powers at the expense of the states, and erected barriers against attacks upon property rights.

38. **(D)** Alexander Hamilton's revenue proposals included an excise tax on whiskey. The backcountry farmers resisted this tax, and this resistance culminated when the farmers of western Pennsylvania took up arms to prevent the collection of the tax. Washington responded to this challenge by sending a force of 13,000 militiamen to put down the Whiskey Rebellion.

39. **(E)** While the Louisiana Purchase more than doubled the size of the United States, it also guaranteed Western farmers access to the Mississippi River as an avenue of trade. Importantly, the purchase of this territory gave the United States control of the port of New Orleans. Jefferson was troubled by the fact that according to his oft-repeated "strict" interpretation of the Constitution, the United States technically lacked the constitutional power to purchase the Louisiana territory. Nevertheless, Jefferson approved its purchase.

40. **(B)** The Webster-Ashburton Treaty (1842) fixed the present northeastern Maine-Canada border and provided for a joint Anglo-American effort to suppress the African slave trade.

41. **(D)** After the discovery of gold in California in 1848 and the admission of California to the Union in 1850, the West began to fill up rapidly. Consequently, there arose a demand for a transcontinental railroad to connect the East with the Pacific Coast. The bone of contention was the location of the eastern terminus. Should it be in the North or the South? The favored section would reap rich rewards in wealth, population, and influence.

Those supporting a southern route argued that (a) it would be easier to build because the mountains were less high; (b) unlike the proposed northern lines, it would not pass through unorganized territory. Texas was already a state. New Mexico, with the Gadsden Purchase added, was an organized territory with federal troops available to give protection against the Indians; and (c) any northern or central line would have to be built through the unorganized territory of Nebraska. The advocates of a northern route countered with the argument that if organized territory was the test, then Nebraska should be given organized status. Thousands of land hungry pioneers were already poised on the Nebraska border; and if the area were given territorial status, it would rapidly fill up.

At this point in 1854, Stephen A. Douglas, Senator from Illinois, entered the fray. Douglas had invested heavily in Chicago real estate and railway stock, and he was anxious to have Chicago become the eastern terminus of the proposed Pacific Railroad. Douglas would thus (a) endear himself to the voters of Illinois, (b) benefit his own section, and (c) enhance the value of his private holdings. He knew that the South would never favor the creation of a new territory without some concession to slavery. In order to secure Southern votes for the northern route, he pushed through Congress the Kansas-Nebraska bill. This legislation provided that

1. instead of one territory, two would be organized. Kansas, to the west of Missouri, would presumably be slave, and Nebraska, to the west of Iowa, would presumably be free;
2. the Missouri Compromise would be repealed; and
3. the status of slavery in the two territories would be settled by "popular sovereignty."

The Southern members of Congress, who at first had not thought of Kansas as slave soil, rose to the bait. Here was a chance to get one more desperately needed slave state. They voted almost unanimously for the bill. Most of the Northern members of Congress voted against it. They regarded the repeal of the Missouri Compromise, which prohibited slavery in all the Nebraska Territory which lay north of the 36°30' line, as a breach of faith.

42. **(C)** Andrew Jackson believed that Indians were better off out of the way. By the time of his election as president in 1828, he was fully in agreement with the view that the Indians should be moved onto the plains west of the Mississippi. In response to Jackson's request, Congress approved the Indian Removal Act.

43. **(D)** Andrew Jackson advanced the principle of rotation in office. He held that "no man has any more intrinsic right to official station than

another." According to Jackson's reasoning, "those holding government jobs for a long time are apt to acquire a habit of looking with indifference upon the public interests and of tolerating conduct from which an unpracticed man would revolt." To Jackson, rotation in office meant that more citizens could participate in running the government; and in a democracy, this was an advantage since it made government more responsive to the electorate.

44. **(C)** The act Jefferson was attacking in this passage of the Declaration of Independence was the 1774 Quebec Act, establishing Roman Catholicism and authoritarian government in that province and extending it to embrace all of what is now the United States west of the Appalachians, north of the Ohio River, and east of the Mississippi. The Quartering Act (A), also of 1774, provided for the quartering of British troops in America at the expense of the colonists. The Prohibitory Act (B), issued late in 1775, declared the Americans to be no longer under the protection of King George III and amounted to a virtual declaration of war. The Stamp Act (D) of 1765 and the Townshend Acts (E), issued three years later, were attempts by Parliament to tax the American colonies.

45. **(C)** William Lloyd Garrison was the most vehement of the Massachusetts abolitionists. From 1831 to 1865, he advocated the immediate and complete emancipation of slaves. Garrison edited a militantly abolitionist weekly paper, *The Liberator*. In its pages, he attacked moderate abolitionists, advocated Northern secession, and castigated slaveholders. On July 4, 1854, Garrison publicly burned a copy of the Constitution and informed the holiday gathering: "So perish all compromises with tyranny."

46. **(E)** In April 1860, at their nominating convention in Charleston, South Carolina, the Democrats failed to nominate a candidate. Eventually, at a convention in Baltimore, the Northern Democrats nominated Stephen A. Douglas. The Southern Democrats held a separate convention at Richmond and nominated John C. Breckinridge. When the Republicans met in Chicago, they nominated Abraham Lincoln on the third ballot. A fourth party, the Constitutional Union party, entered the presidential contest and nominated John Bell. In the election, Lincoln garnered only 39 percent of the popular vote, but he received a clear majority in the electoral college. Lincoln carried every free state except New Jersey. Although Douglas received the second highest popular vote, he gained only 12 electoral votes.

47. **(C)** When the Civil War broke out, Abraham Lincoln made it clear that his primary objective was to preserve the Union. In calling for volunteers, Lincoln made no mention of abolishing slavery.

48. **(A)** The radical abolitionists viewed slavery as a moral, not a political, issue. Accordingly, they debated slavery in terms of morality and not political expediency. The radical abolitionists wanted the immediate emancipation of the slaves.

49. **(D)** Andrew Johnson's plan for Reconstruction called for the loyal white citizens in the former Confederate states to draft and ratify new constitutions and to elect state legislatures, which were to repeal the ordinance of secession, repudiate the Confederate state debts, and ratify the Thirteenth Amendment. The Congressional plan for Reconstruction called for new lists of registered voters, including former slaves, to be compiled. In each of the states, the newly registered voters would elect a constitutional convention. The new state constitutions were required to provide guarantees of universal manhood suffrage. When a state had adopted a constitution acceptable to Congress and had ratified the Fourteenth Amendment, its senators and representatives would be admitted to Congress.

50. **(C)** European diseases, smallpox and measles, to which the Indians had no resistance, decimated the Indian population of the Americas. When Cortez invaded Mexico, its Indian population numbered at least 20 million. A century later it had declined to 2 million.

51. **(E)** Thomas Malthus published his *Essay on Population* in 1789. In it, he contended that, since population increased by a geometric ratio and food supply increased only by an arithmetic ratio, it was basic natural law that population would outstrip food supply. Malthus did not have an impact on fifteenth century Western Europe.

52. **(C)** After several unsuccessful efforts, the English established a permanent settlement in North America in 1607. This settlement, Jamestown, was located on a peninsula near the mouth of the James River in Virginia.

53. **(E)** *The Federalist Papers* were a series of 85 letters written to newspapers by Hamilton, Madison, and Jay. The passage comes from *Federalist* number 10, written by Alexander Hamilton. Its purpose was to explain, and ease people's minds about, the proposed U.S. Constitution.

54. **(B)** In order to set people's minds at ease about the proposed U.S. Constitution and thus secure its ratification, Hamilton sought to demonstrate that the Constitution would preserve the rights and powers of the states, the opposite of (D). Hamilton, along with the other Federalists, did believe that a balanced government was the best form of government (A) and that the U.S. Constitution offered a form of government especially suited to the American character (C), but these facts are not the point of the argument presented here. That the United States should keep itself free from entangling alliances with European countries (E) was the advice of George Washington in his *Farewell Address.*

55. **(A)** Although Maryland was founded as a haven for Roman Catholics, there existed from the beginning a large Protestant majority. Lord Baltimore solved this problem by accepting a Toleration Act (1649) that gave freedom of religion to anyone "professing to believe in Jesus Christ."

56. **(D)** William Penn secured proprietary rights in 1681 to the region north of Maryland and west of the Delaware River. He was a devout Quaker who viewed his colony as a holy experiment. In 1682, Penn constructed a "Frame of Government" that guaranteed complete religious freedom to the colonists.

57. **(A)** The Peace of Paris (1763) gave Britain all French North American possessions east of the Mississippi River and all of Spanish Florida. France ceded Louisiana to Spain in compensation for Spain's loss of the Floridas. Therefore, the trans-Mississippi West was not open to the colonists.

58. **(A)** Although the settlers of Virginia tried to produce things that were needed in England, tobacco became the staple crop. Tobacco plants could be set on semi-cleared land and cultivated with a hoe.

59. **(B)** Georgia was the last colony to be founded. It was established to provide a new start in life for Englishmen imprisoned for debt and to erect a military barrier against the Spaniards on the southern border of English America.

60. **(C)** Mercantilism, the pursuit of economic power through national self-sufficiency, was the dominant economic doctrine in Western Europe by 1660. This doctrine encouraged the state to stimulate manufacturing, to develop and protect its own shipping, and to make use of colonies as sources of raw materials and markets for its manufactured goods.

61. **(D)** Cotton Mather was a leading Puritan minister and intellectual who died a half-century prior to the American Revolution. Mather was a leading figure in the Salem witch trials of 1692–1694 and earned great fame for the publication of his book *Magnalia Christi Americana*, a homage to great Puritan Americans, in 1704. Noah Webster was one of the greatest champions of an American culture in late eighteenth century America and designed his dictionary to create a national language. Freneau, Crèvecoeur, and Barlow all sought to exalt a new American culture at the close of the Revolution. Through their essays, poems, and plays, each supported the view of a special historical mission for America and its people for the cause of freedom and liberty in world history.

62. **(A)** After losing the election of 1800 to Thomas Jefferson and the Democratic-Republicans, President John Adams sought to use the national courts to block Jefferson from radical programs over the next four years. On the night before Jefferson's inaugural, Adams appointed several new federal judges from the Federalist party. Upon learning of this later, Jefferson sought to remove the midnight appointments through a test case of one appointment, William Marbury. In 1803, Marbury sued Secretary of State James Madison for his judgeship and petitioned the Supreme Court. In *Marbury v. Madison*, Chief Justice John Marshall correctly ruled that the issue was not a matter for the Supreme Court but Congress. In so doing, however, Marshall declared the Judiciary Act of 1789 unconstitutional and granted the Supreme Court the power of judicial review. (This power allows the Court to be the final arbiter on the constitutionality of all laws enacted by Congress.) In *Fletcher* (1810), Marshall extended the Court's power of judicial review over state governments; in *Gibbons* (1824), Marshall extended governmental power over commerce; in *Martin* (1816), Marshall extended judicial review to the state courts; in *Dartmouth* (1819), Marshall offered views of contracts and corporations that would greatly influence the economy throughout the nineteeth century.

63. **(D)** The power of judicial review allows the Supreme Court as the last voice on the constitutionality of law in America. Only the U.S. Constitution grants the Court the power of original jurisdiction in Article III. "Strict constructionialism" is a judicial viewpoint of recent years that argues one cannot liberally interpret pre-existing laws to decide a case. As a result, it is a theory and not a power. The Court does not select its own members; the Article provides that presidents nominate justices upon the advice and consent of the U.S. Senate's approval of a nominee. Finally, the Court's ability to regulate big business was never granted; the regulation of big

business comes under the domain of congressional and Executive Department regulatory agencies (Federal Trade Commission, Environmental Protection Agency; Federal Communications Commission, etc.).

64. **(B)** The speech cited was delivered by Henry Clay to his Western supporters in Congress in 1811. Clay and his group, nicknamed the "war hawks," supported American war with Great Britain to advance the westward push of the country to enhance their land speculations in this region and end the "Indian menace." The Federalists and New England merchants were both vehemently opposed to the War of 1812, while President Madison sought to negotiate a peaceful settlement with England and reluctantly went to war in 1812. The British nobility generally were opposed to the war as well.

65. **(B)** New England dissatisfaction with the War of 1812 was evident from the start. Because of the trade embargoes of Jefferson and Madison, the New England merchant community was suffering from a depression that affected the entire region economically. New Englanders called for a meeting in Hartford, Connecticut in 1814 to discuss the region's options. Few delegates supported a movement to secede from the nation. Instead, the delegates, under the leadership of the Federalist party, advanced a view of states' rights identical to the position of the South during the Civil War. Tired of being treated as a neglected minority in the nation under Republican presidents, the New England delegates accomplished little at the Convention. The news of the Treaty and the Battle of New Orleans doomed the Convention and the Federalists in the eyes of most Americans as unpatriotic. Neither Japanese trade nor a Cuban invasion were ever discussed at the Convention.

66. **(C)** In 1819, the cooperative nationalism that America had enjoyed since the end of the War of 1812 was ended when the issue of slavery and the statehood of Missouri came before Congress. From 1815 through 1819, the nation had focused on programs of public improvements and advanced views of a monolithic patriotism. When Missouri applied for statehood in 1819, however, the Northern states feared the growing power of the South and the institution of slavery. As debates heated and sectionalism dominated nationalism in the Congress, Henry Clay of Kentucky formed a compromise that allowed the sectional balance of slave and free states to continue. Clay allowed Missouri to enter as a slave state with Maine

arriving as a free state; thus, there were 12 slave and 12 free states. Secondly, the Compromise divided the issue of slavery along the 36°30' line: all territories north of the line would be free while areas south could enter as slave areas. The War of 1812 occurred prior to the Era of Good Feelings; the Chesapeake affair took place in 1807 and involved the British navy's impressment of American sailors; the Non-Intercourse Act occurred in 1807 and was Jefferson's feeble effort to avoid war with England. The Jay Treaty occurred in 1794 prior to the Era of Good Feelings.

67. **(C)** The period from 1820 through 1850 marked one of tremendous population growth for the United States. As the figures indicate, the nation's population more than doubled during this single generation from both new waves of immigration and natural increases.

68. **(E)** During the 1820s, the image of the American family underwent a major transformation from that of a work force based on discipline to an agency that was child centered and based upon love. Historians have labeled this process of change the domestification of the family. In the seventeenth and eighteenth centuries, the family was a reflection of society at large and seen primarily as a working unit on the farm. Strict discipline and adult domination were its mainstays. However, in the 1820s, Americans now viewed the home as a refuge from the outside world where one could escape from societal demands. In addition, love replaced discipline as the bonds of the family, with children now occupying center stage in familial matters. Finally, women were seen as operating in separate spheres from their husbands: the woman raised the children and ran the home; the males made money in the outside world. What emerged was a kind of separate but equal doctrine for female roles.

69. **(E)** The Tariff Act of 1832 led directly to the Nullification Crisis between South Carolina and the United States. The Tariff Act established high import fees for all European manufactured goods in an effort to protect Northern industries. South Carolina balked at the policy which offered no protection for Southern farmers and forced them to pay higher prices as consumers. Under the leadership of Vice President John C. Calhoun, South Carolina re-established the states' rights view (the doctrine argues the states and not the national government is sovereign and therefore each state can decide which national laws to obey) and refused to pay the tariff by nullifying it. President Jackson threatened to force South Carolina to obey by armed invasion and South Carolina threatened to secede from the nation. Speaker of the House of Representatives, Henry

Clay, intervened in the matter averting war with a compromise solution that effectively allowed South Carolina to avoid paying the tariff duties without advancing states' rights doctrines.

70. **(D)** In 1817, Benjamin Lundy formed the American Colonization Society as the first antislavery organization in America. The group advocated gradual emancipation of slaves on an individual basis and refused to see abolition of slavery as a political affair. Comprised mostly of ministers, the Society sought to appeal to the Christian conscience of each slave owner to emancipate their slaves. Once freed, the ex-slaves would then be shipped back immediately to Africa as the Society was extremely racist in its views of the inherent inferiority of blacks to whites. The Society believed there was no place for African-Americans in the nation and sought to remove all blacks from American soil rather than promote racial equality and full political rights for blacks.

71. **(A)** Despite the images of large plantations in novels and movies, the vast majority of slaves in the nineteenth century lived on farms that held less than 20 slaves. In 1860, 80 percent of all Southern slaves lived on such farms. The notion of a large plantation relying on the labor of hundreds and even thousands of slaves is not supported by historical fact.

72. **(E)** The rise of the doctrine of Manifest Destiny in the 1820s and 1830s championed the viewpoint that it was America's natural God-given destiny to create a mighty nation stretching from the Atlantic to the Pacific shores. The advocates of this view contended that the health of the American economy demanded new markets from this push westward and that an expanding frontier guaranteed that the nation would remain a democracy of small, independent yeoman farmers. This belief remained powerful in the country throughout the nineteenth century.

73. **(B)** The Nat Turner Rebellion occurred in 1831 as the bloodiest slave uprising in American history when 55 whites were killed by about 15 slaves in Virginia. The Kansas-Nebraska Act was passed in 1854 and sought to establish the principle of popular sovereignty in the two territories on the issue of slavery to promote the presidential ambitions of Senator Stephen Douglas of Illinois. The Seneca Falls Convention convened in 1848 as a militant expression of women's rights led by Lucretia Mott and Elizabeth Cady Stanton. The Lincoln-Douglas debates took place in 1858 as both candidates vied for the Senate seat in Illinois. The Homestead Act was passed by Congress in 1862 and granted a free 160-acre farm in the

Far West (Great Plains region) to any American citizen 21 years of age or older who would work the land for five years.

74. **(D)** This speech by Daniel Webster delivered in defense of the Compromise of 1850 on the floor of the House of Representatives is considered one of the most famous speeches in American history. As Webster was closing out his illustrious political career, he ushered forth all his political and rhetorical skills to combat the growing spirit of sectionalism that was threatening his beloved America. Webster used all his power to gain passage of the act and completed his efforts with this brilliant appeal to patriotic nationalism. His defense of Dartmouth College before the Supreme Court gave rise to a rhetorical flourish of "only a small college, but there are, sirs, those who love it." Webster never delivered major addresses on Lincoln, the Bank, or the Bridge case.

75. **(B)** In 1854, Stephen Douglas harbored ambitions for the presidency in 1856. In order to attract the Southern votes required for his victory, Douglas proposed an act to amend the Missouri Compromise line of 36°30' in the case of the Kansas-Nebraska territories. Although both areas were north of the line, Douglas argued the settlers of the regions should decide for themselves on slavery. The result was civil war in the two regions as pro-Southern settlers openly battled with antislavery forces over the next two years. Douglas never was a champion of the black vote and believed Congress, not the Supreme Court, could solve the slave crisis.

76. **(B)** The Secret Six were a group of New York millionaires who provided the financial backing for John Brown's raid on Harper's Ferry, Virginia in 1859. Brown, a militant abolitionist, sought to seize a federal arsenal in the South and distribute weapons to slaves to lead a massive slave uprising. When information about Brown's ties to the Secret Six surfaced during his trial, the South began to seriously consider secession as its only course of action against the abolitionists. The Secret Six felt Lincoln much too soft on slavery in 1860 to offer him support. In fact, their support of Brown's raid displays their view that violence and not politics would end slavery in America.

77. **(B)** On April 12, 1861, the Confederate forces began their bombardment on Fort Sumter. With the Fort's surrender and Lincoln's proclamation that an insurrection existed, the states of the Upper South (Virginia, Arkansas, Tennessee, and North Carolina) joined the Lower South

(South Carolina, Alabama, Mississippi, Florida, Georgia, Louisiana, and Texas) who had seceded in February 1861 to form the Confederate States of America.

78. **(D)** The American Civil War was an unpopular war in the North. Lincoln constantly was troubled by draft riots and the threats of Northern anti-war Democrats, called the Copperheads. Anti-Lincoln Republicans adopted the name Radical Republicans and pro-Union Southerners were labeled scalawags after the war. Lincoln masterfully was able to maintain control over his Party during the war and narrowly was re-elected in 1864, in large part owing to some eleventh-hour Northern military victories. At the close of the war, the Copperheads were treated with severe hatred in the North, especially after Lincoln's assassination.

79. **(C)** King Cotton Diplomacy was the sole foreign policy strategy of the Confederacy. The South refused to export cotton to Europe in the hopes that this embargo would lead to a depression in the European textile industry and force Western Europe to ally with the South because of their dependance upon cotton. This strategy failed because Europeans had been stockpiling American cotton since 1855 in anticipation of the Civil War and found a new source of cotton in Egypt. The Stars and Bars was the nickname for the Confederate flag, while a war of attrition was General Grant's military strategy for ending the Civil War. Mercantilism was Great Britain's economic policy toward its American colonies in the seventeenth and eighteenth centuries, while nullification was the attempt by South Carolina not to pay new tariff rates in 1831.

80. **(E)** In the 1840s, the Indians of the Great Plains were at their height as a civilization. Not yet in close contact with whites, the Plains Indians lived a nomadic existence hunting the plentiful buffalo who provided the Indians with food, clothing, and shelter. The Plains tribes were noted for their deep reverence of the forces of nature and believed all natural elements held a soul and were to be treated with respect.

81. **(E)** In 1864, Lincoln announced his plan to allow the South to re-enter the Union. The plan, known as his Reconstruction Plan, was extremely lenient to the defeated South. Lincoln proposed the South re-enter on a state-by-state basis after having agreed to abolish slavery, educate the ex-slaves, establish republican state governments, and have 10 percent of Southern citizens take an oath of loyalty to the Union. The Radical Republicans in Congress opposed Lincoln's plan as too lenient and criticized the

plan for not allowing for the citizenship of the ex-slaves which the Radicals established under the Fourteenth Amendment in 1867.

82. **(B)** In 1864, the Radical Republicans openly broke from President Lincoln's Reconstruction plans with the passage of the Wade-Davis Act. This Act presented the Radicals' Reconstruction plans and sought to treat the South as a conquered territory under military rule. Rather than the quick readmission of Southern states that Lincoln envisioned, the Act demanded readmission only after 50 percent of the voters of each state could prove their loyalty to the Union during the Civil War. Lincoln vetoed the Act. President Johnson did not support Wade-Davis, nor did the Democratic party. Both the scalawags and carpetbaggers had little association with the measure as Southerners who cooperated during Reconstruction with the North and carpetbaggers who went down South to work on rebuilding the devastated South after the war.

83. **(A)** Slavery was ended by Congress' ratification of the Thirteenth Amendment to the U.S. Constitution in 1865. The Radical Republicans were in control of Congress and passed the amendment in the aftermath of Lincoln's assassination by John Wilkes Booth. The Fifteenth Amendment (1867) extends the vote to ex-slaves, who were granted citizenship under the Fourteenth amendment in 1867. The Nineteenth Amendment (1920) extends the vote to women, while the Sixteenth Amendment (1913) established the federal income tax. The Twenty-second Amendment in 1951 established the two-term limit on the presidency.

84. **(B)** In the impeachment proceedings against President Johnson, Congress cited his violation of the Tenure of Office Act in removing Secretary of War Stanton without Senate approval. Of the 11 charges of impeachment brought by the House against Johnson, nine were based on the Tenure of Office Act. The Morrill Act was passed in 1862 to establish publicly financed land grant colleges in the states. The Civil Rights Act was passed in 1866 and directed against the black codes in Southern governments, not Johnson. *Ex Parte* Milligan (1866) ruled that civilian courts should have been allowed to function during the Civil War rather than the military tribunals Lincoln established. The case was a decision by the Supreme Court of the United States.

85. **(E)** Thomas Nast was a famous political cartoonist of the late nineteenth century.

86. **(D)** One of the most important aspects of the Stamp Act Congress was the opportunity it provided for colonial leaders to meet and establish acquaintances with one another. Nine colonies — not merely Georgia, Virginia, and the Carolinas (C) — were represented at it, but far from being a unified government for all the American colonies (A), it simply passed mild resolutions protesting the Stamp Act. It was not, therefore, either a vehicle for enforcing the act (B) or opposed to American protests against the act (E).

87. **(A)** The map depicts the United States after the Compromise of 1850. The states of Texas and California as well as the Utah and New Mexico Territories were not part of the United States at the time of the 1842 Webster-Ashburton Treaty (B), dealing with the Maine-New Brunswick boundary; the 1787 Northwest Ordinance (C), organizing what was to become the states of Ohio, Indiana, Illinois, Michigan, and Wisconsin; and the 1820 Missouri Compromise (E), regulating the status of slavery in the territory gained by the Louisiana Purchase. California and the two territories were gained as a result of the Mexican War (D), but California statehood, as well as territorial status for Utah and New Mexico, had to await the Compromise of 1850.

88. **(C)** The principle of popular sovereignty was a central feature of the Kansas-Nebraska Act. Though championed by Senator Stephen A. Douglas (A), it had previously been put forward by 1848 Democratic presidential candidate Lewis Cass. A favorite policy of Democrats — not Whigs (D) — during the late 1840s and early 1850s, it proved a failure in solving the impasse over the status of slavery in the territories (E). It differed from the system of congressionally specified free and slave areas used in the Missouri Compromise (B).

89. **(E)** One of Lincoln's reasons for issuing the Emancipation Proclamation was to keep Britain and France from intervening on the side of the Confederacy. Lincoln neither needed, wanted, nor could have obtained the active aid of these countries in restoring the Union (A), and Russia, which had indeed freed its serfs the previous year, would have been a U.S. ally regardless (D). The Radicals in the North would indeed have been pleased had Lincoln freed the slaves in areas of the South already under the control of Union armies (C), but it was precisely that which the Emancipation Proclamation did not do, largely out of concern for the more-or-less loyal slaveholding border states such as Maryland and Kentucky, who were not at all enthused about Lincoln's action even as it was (B).

90. **(C)** Blacks most commonly resisted slavery passively, if at all. The Underground Railroad (B), though celebrated in popular history, involved a relatively minute number of slaves. Arson (D), poisoning (E), and violent uprising (A), though they did sometimes occur and were the subject of much fear on the part of white Southerners, were also relatively rare.

91. **(C)** During the period from 1835-1865 Southerners generally defended slavery as a positive benefit to society and even to the slaves themselves. That slavery was a necessary evil (A) and should be gradually phased out as the slaves were colonized outside the United States (D) was the attitude of an earlier generation of white Southerners, including Thomas Jefferson. That slavery was a national sin (E) and should be immediately abolished (B) was the view of the Abolitionists, a minority even in the North during this period.

92. **(D)** Farmers and planters in the South enjoyed high crop prices and sustained prosperity during the 1850s. Crops were large (C) and prices were high and steady (A) and (B). Southerners saw this as a sign of the superiority of their slave economy over that of the North, hard hit as it was by the Panic of 1857 (E).

93. **(B)** Mercantilists believed the government should seek to direct the economy so as to maximize exports. Mercantilists DID, however, believe in government interference in the economy (A), high tariff barriers (E), and the possession of colonies (C). Exports, they asserted, must exceed imports, not the other way around (D).

94. **(D)** In order to gain foreign recognition during the War for Independence, it was necessary for the United States to demonstrate a determination and potential to win independence. The U.S. could not have demonstrated financial stability (C) at this time, nor could it have made financial payments (A). It did not prove necessary to make either territorial (B) or trade (E) concessions to France.

95. **(D)** Garrison called for the immediate and uncompensated emancipation of all slaves. He was not particularly in favor of states' rights (E), and he definitely opposed either gradualism or compensation (A). He also opposed colonization (B). Though he opposed the congressional gag rule, its repeal was not his main issue of concern.

96. **(D)** Bacon's followers were disgruntled at what they saw as the governor's refusal to protect their frontier area from Indian raids. The jailing of individuals or seizure of their property for failure to pay taxes during a time of economic hardship (A) was the source of Massachusetts' 1786 Shays' Rebellion. The under-representation of the backcountry areas in colonial legislatures (B) was an ongoing source of irritation in the colonial South. The mistreatment of former indentured servants by large planters (C) and the favoritism of Virginia's governor Berkeley to his clique of friends — though he almost certainly could not have manipulated tobacco prices himself (E) — may have been underlying causes but were not the immediate issue in dispute in Bacon's Rebellion.

97. **(B)** The Newburgh Conspiracy was composed of army officers disgusted with a central government too weak to collect taxes to pay them and their troops. Betrayal of the plans for the fort at West Point (A) was Benedict Arnold's treason. Resistance to the collection of federal excise taxes in western Pennsylvania (C) took the form of the Whiskey Rebellion of 1791. New England's threat to secede should the War of 1812 continue (D) was made at the 1814 Hartford Convention. Burr's strange plot (E) came to nothing.

98. **(A)** The Wilmot Proviso was intended to prohibit slavery in the area acquired through the Mexican War. Congress generally agreed that the United States would acquire some territory from the war (B). That California should be a free state while the rest of the Mexican Cession was reserved for slavery (C), that the status of slavery in the Mexican Cession should be decided on the basis of "popular sovereignty" (D), and that the Missouri Compromise line should be extended to the Pacific (E) were all suggestions for a compromise that might calm the furor aroused by the Wilmot Proviso.

99. **(C)** The Whigs turned on Tyler because he opposed their entire legislative program. He did speak out in favor of Texas annexation (B) and he seemed to favor expansion of slavery (E); but these offenses would have been relatively minor in Whig eyes by comparison.

100. **(C)** O'Sullivan spoke of America's "manifest destiny to overspread the continent." The idea that America must eventually become either all slave or all free (D) was expressed by Lincoln in his "House Divided" speech and was called by William H. Seward the "Irrepressible Conflict." Racial equality (A) was still not a popular idea when O'Sullivan wrote in

the first half of the nineteenth century. By that time, of course, America was already an independent country (B), but the desire for overseas possessions (E) was still half a century off.

101. **(D)** Mexico did expect to win the war, invade the U.S., and dictate a peace in Washington, but whatever desire, if any, the Mexicans may have had for the state of Louisiana was not a factor in the coming of the war. The U.S. did, however, desire to annex California (A) and did annex Texas (C); Mexico did refuse to pay its debts (B) and did claim Texas (C); and the southern boundary of Texas was in dispute (E). All of these contributed to the coming of the war.

102. **(A)** The colony at Jamestown was founded primarily for economic gain, though a secondary motive was a desire to increase the power and glory of Great Britain (E). Desire for religious freedom in some form (B) was the motivation of the settlers of Plymouth and some of those who settled Maryland and Pennsylvania. Desire to create a perfect religious commonwealth as an example to the rest of the world (C) was the motive for the Massachusetts Bay colony; and desire to recreate in the New World the sort of feudalistic society that was fading in the Old (D) was probably a motive of some of the colonial proprietors such as those of the Carolinas.

103. **(E)** Lincoln's Ten Percent Plan provided for the restoration of loyal government in states formerly in rebellion. It did not require that any of the former slaves be given the right to vote (A). It allowed Southerners to participate in the political process provided they would take an oath of future, not past (B), loyalty to the Union and acceptance of the abolition of slavery (D). High-ranking Confederates were excepted from this provision (C) and had to apply separately to the president for pardon.

104. **(C)** Johnson did not require former Confederate states to pay reparations. He did, however, recommend they extend the franchise to blacks (A), and he did require them to ratify the Thirteenth Amendment (B), renounce secession (D), and repudiate the Confederate debt (E).

105. **(D)** "Seward's Folly" was the name given to the purchase of Alaska. Seward had indeed believed that the Civil War could be avoided and the Union restored by provoking a war with Britain and France (C) — a foolish belief but not well known enough to gain a label. He had attempted to gain the presidency in 1860 and failed (E), though no one would have labeled his campaign a folly. Seward also favored a lenient policy toward

the defeated South (A) and broke with the majority wing of his party to support President Andrew Johnson (B), though whether that was folly or courage remains debatable.

106. **(C)** Congress did not order the arrest and imprisonment of former Confederate leaders, often because many of them were protected by presidential pardons or the terms of their surrenders. It did, however, exclude Southern representatives (A), pass the Civil Rights Act (B), approve and send on to the states the Fourteenth Amendment (D), and put the South under army occupation and military rule (E).

107. **(C)** Johnson was impeached but was never removed from office (A) and (B). He did not resign, was not pardoned, and was never charged with a criminal offense (D). The vote on his removal from office was in fact taken (E) but fell short by one vote.

108. **(A)** The Treaty of Tordesillas (1494) was intended to divide the non-European world between Spain and Portugal. The French, English, and Dutch were left entirely out in the cold (B) and (D). As a result (though certainly not an intent!) of the treaty between Spain and Portugal, they did sometimes form a common cause against the Spanish who dominated the New World (C). The Portuguese half of the world was mainly in the Eastern Hemisphere, but Portugal also received Brazil in the Western Hemisphere (E).

109. **(C)** Boycotting British goods, known as nonimportation, was the most effective American method of gaining repeal of undesirable acts of Parliament. Tarring and feathering tax agents (A), sending petitions to the king and Parliament (B), and even a certain amount of destruction of private property (D), and intimidation by threats (E) were tried, with more-or-less unsatisfactory results.

110. **(C)** One purpose of the Tea Act was to save the financially troubled East India Company, not so much for the sake of India (D) and (E) as for the sake of wealthy East India Company stockholders who also happened to be members of Parliament. Of course, with this purpose in mind, the British were anxious to increase the demand for and consumption of tea in America as much as possible (A) and (B).

111. **(D)** The greatest significance of the Battle of Saratoga was that it persuaded France to give its open backing to the United States. Naturally,

the British were still quite capable of carrying on the war (A) and mounting further invasions (B), and the Americans were still quite incapable of taking any part of Canada (C). Holland would never have considered entering the war on the side of the British in any case (E).

112. **(B)** Eli Whitney had an enormous influence on American history through his invention of the cotton gin. The steamboat (A) was invented by Whitney's contemporary Robert Fulton, the steam locomotive (E) and the telegraph (D) somewhat later in the nineteenth century, and the incandescent light bulb (C), by Thomas Edison, near the end of the century.

113. **(B)** The Virginia and Kentucky Resolutions were the centerpiece of the Republican response to the Alien and Sedition Acts. The 1814 Hartford Convention (C), on the other hand, was a Federalist response to Republican policies. South Carolina's nullification (A) was aimed at the highly protective Tariff of 1828. The 1854 Ostend Manifesto (D) dealt with U.S. desires to acquire Cuba from Spain, and the Mulligan Letters (E) incriminated 1884 Republican presidential candidate James G. Blaine in an unsavory stock scheme.

114. **(B)** The Puritans wanted to make Massachusetts an example to the rest of the world of what a true Bible commonwealth could be. Escaping persecution (A) was at most a secondary motivation, and desire for prosperity (C) would have come some place behind that. The Puritans, had they thought of such things, would have rejected the idea of separation of church and state (D) or the pluralistic society (E).

115. **(B)** As part of the 1820 Missouri Compromise, all of the Louisiana Territory north of 36°30′— that is, the southern (A) boundary of most of Missouri — was closed (C) to slavery. According to the compromise, this was to be permanent, though subsequent behavior on the part of some politicians — the 1854 Kansas-Nebraska Act — might lead one to believe the free areas had been left negotiable (D) or closed to slavery only for 30 years (E) — but such was not the case.

116. **(B)** The Morrill Land Grant Act provided large amounts of federal government land to states that would establish agricultural and mechanical colleges. It was the Homestead Act that granted 160-acre farms free to those who would settle on them (A). After the Civil War there was some talk of providing former slaves with "40 acres and a mule," but nothing came of it (C). Even without a special act of Congress to prevent it, in fact very little land of former Confederates was confiscated (D). Various acts

of Congress and decisions of presidents throughout the 1800s dealt with the disposition of the Great Plains Indians (E).

117. **(D)** De Tocqueville found the Americans had little or no sense of social deference. They were politicized (A) and individualistic (C), proud of their country (B), and placed a high value on personal freedom (E).

118. **(D)** Webster, Emerson, and Cooper were all contributors to a more distinctly American literature. Emerson was a literary figure of the Transcendentalist movement (A). Cooper was a pioneer in the development of the American novel (B). Webster was the compiler of a well-known dictionary (C) that introduced Americanized spellings. Of the three, only Cooper could be said to have been a part of the popular culture (E).

119. **(E)** The largest impact on the reduction of inland freight rates during this period was created by the introduction of steamboats. Railroads (A) came somewhat later. Keelboats, flatboats (D), turnpikes (C), and canals (B) were of less importance.

120. **(B)** The Molasses Act was intended to force the colonists to buy sugar from more expensive British colonial sources rather than from foreign producers. Forcing the colonists to export solely to Great Britain (A), forbidding them to engage in manufacturing activity in competition with British industries (C), and creating an economic situation in which gold tended to flow from the colonies to the mother country (E) were also goals of mercantilism. Providing a favorable market for the products of the British East India Company (D) was the purpose of the Tea Act.

CLEP HISTORY OF THE UNITED STATES I – TEST 1

1. (A) (B) (C) (D) (E)
2. (A) (B) (C) (D) (E)
3. (A) (B) (C) (D) (E)
4. (A) (B) (C) (D) (E)
5. (A) (B) (C) (D) (E)
6. (A) (B) (C) (D) (E)
7. (A) (B) (C) (D) (E)
8. (A) (B) (C) (D) (E)
9. (A) (B) (C) (D) (E)
10. (A) (B) (C) (D) (E)
11. (A) (B) (C) (D) (E)
12. (A) (B) (C) (D) (E)
13. (A) (B) (C) (D) (E)
14. (A) (B) (C) (D) (E)
15. (A) (B) (C) (D) (E)
16. (A) (B) (C) (D) (E)
17. (A) (B) (C) (D) (E)
18. (A) (B) (C) (D) (E)
19. (A) (B) (C) (D) (E)
20. (A) (B) (C) (D) (E)
21. (A) (B) (C) (D) (E)
22. (A) (B) (C) (D) (E)
23. (A) (B) (C) (D) (E)
24. (A) (B) (C) (D) (E)
25. (A) (B) (C) (D) (E)
26. (A) (B) (C) (D) (E)
27. (A) (B) (C) (D) (E)
28. (A) (B) (C) (D) (E)
29. (A) (B) (C) (D) (E)
30. (A) (B) (C) (D) (E)
31. (A) (B) (C) (D) (E)
32. (A) (B) (C) (D) (E)
33. (A) (B) (C) (D) (E)
34. (A) (B) (C) (D) (E)
35. (A) (B) (C) (D) (E)
36. (A) (B) (C) (D) (E)
37. (A) (B) (C) (D) (E)
38. (A) (B) (C) (D) (E)
39. (A) (B) (C) (D) (E)
40. (A) (B) (C) (D) (E)
41. (A) (B) (C) (D) (E)
42. (A) (B) (C) (D) (E)
43. (A) (B) (C) (D) (E)
44. (A) (B) (C) (D) (E)
45. (A) (B) (C) (D) (E)
46. (A) (B) (C) (D) (E)
47. (A) (B) (C) (D) (E)
48. (A) (B) (C) (D) (E)
49. (A) (B) (C) (D) (E)
50. (A) (B) (C) (D) (E)
51. (A) (B) (C) (D) (E)
52. (A) (B) (C) (D) (E)
53. (A) (B) (C) (D) (E)
54. (A) (B) (C) (D) (E)
55. (A) (B) (C) (D) (E)
56. (A) (B) (C) (D) (E)
57. (A) (B) (C) (D) (E)
58. (A) (B) (C) (D) (E)
59. (A) (B) (C) (D) (E)
60. (A) (B) (C) (D) (E)
61. (A) (B) (C) (D) (E)
62. (A) (B) (C) (D) (E)
63. (A) (B) (C) (D) (E)
64. (A) (B) (C) (D) (E)
65. (A) (B) (C) (D) (E)
66. (A) (B) (C) (D) (E)
67. (A) (B) (C) (D) (E)
68. (A) (B) (C) (D) (E)
69. (A) (B) (C) (D) (E)
70. (A) (B) (C) (D) (E)
71. (A) (B) (C) (D) (E)
72. (A) (B) (C) (D) (E)
73. (A) (B) (C) (D) (E)
74. (A) (B) (C) (D) (E)
75. (A) (B) (C) (D) (E)
76. (A) (B) (C) (D) (E)
77. (A) (B) (C) (D) (E)
78. (A) (B) (C) (D) (E)
79. (A) (B) (C) (D) (E)
80. (A) (B) (C) (D) (E)
81. (A) (B) (C) (D) (E)
82. (A) (B) (C) (D) (E)
83. (A) (B) (C) (D) (E)
84. (A) (B) (C) (D) (E)
85. (A) (B) (C) (D) (E)
86. (A) (B) (C) (D) (E)
87. (A) (B) (C) (D) (E)
88. (A) (B) (C) (D) (E)
89. (A) (B) (C) (D) (E)
90. (A) (B) (C) (D) (E)
91. (A) (B) (C) (D) (E)
92. (A) (B) (C) (D) (E)
93. (A) (B) (C) (D) (E)
94. (A) (B) (C) (D) (E)
95. (A) (B) (C) (D) (E)
96. (A) (B) (C) (D) (E)
97. (A) (B) (C) (D) (E)
98. (A) (B) (C) (D) (E)
99. (A) (B) (C) (D) (E)
100. (A) (B) (C) (D) (E)
101. (A) (B) (C) (D) (E)
102. (A) (B) (C) (D) (E)
103. (A) (B) (C) (D) (E)
104. (A) (B) (C) (D) (E)
105. (A) (B) (C) (D) (E)
106. (A) (B) (C) (D) (E)
107. (A) (B) (C) (D) (E)
108. (A) (B) (C) (D) (E)
109. (A) (B) (C) (D) (E)
110. (A) (B) (C) (D) (E)
111. (A) (B) (C) (D) (E)
112. (A) (B) (C) (D) (E)
113. (A) (B) (C) (D) (E)
114. (A) (B) (C) (D) (E)
115. (A) (B) (C) (D) (E)
116. (A) (B) (C) (D) (E)
117. (A) (B) (C) (D) (E)
118. (A) (B) (C) (D) (E)
119. (A) (B) (C) (D) (E)
120. (A) (B) (C) (D) (E)

CLEP HISTORY OF THE UNITED STATES I – TEST 2

1. (A) (B) (C) (D) (E)
2. (A) (B) (C) (D) (E)
3. (A) (B) (C) (D) (E)
4. (A) (B) (C) (D) (E)
5. (A) (B) (C) (D) (E)
6. (A) (B) (C) (D) (E)
7. (A) (B) (C) (D) (E)
8. (A) (B) (C) (D) (E)
9. (A) (B) (C) (D) (E)
10. (A) (B) (C) (D) (E)
11. (A) (B) (C) (D) (E)
12. (A) (B) (C) (D) (E)
13. (A) (B) (C) (D) (E)
14. (A) (B) (C) (D) (E)
15. (A) (B) (C) (D) (E)
16. (A) (B) (C) (D) (E)
17. (A) (B) (C) (D) (E)
18. (A) (B) (C) (D) (E)
19. (A) (B) (C) (D) (E)
20. (A) (B) (C) (D) (E)
21. (A) (B) (C) (D) (E)
22. (A) (B) (C) (D) (E)
23. (A) (B) (C) (D) (E)
24. (A) (B) (C) (D) (E)
25. (A) (B) (C) (D) (E)
26. (A) (B) (C) (D) (E)
27. (A) (B) (C) (D) (E)
28. (A) (B) (C) (D) (E)
29. (A) (B) (C) (D) (E)
30. (A) (B) (C) (D) (E)
31. (A) (B) (C) (D) (E)
32. (A) (B) (C) (D) (E)
33. (A) (B) (C) (D) (E)
34. (A) (B) (C) (D) (E)
35. (A) (B) (C) (D) (E)
36. (A) (B) (C) (D) (E)
37. (A) (B) (C) (D) (E)
38. (A) (B) (C) (D) (E)
39. (A) (B) (C) (D) (E)
40. (A) (B) (C) (D) (E)
41. (A) (B) (C) (D) (E)
42. (A) (B) (C) (D) (E)
43. (A) (B) (C) (D) (E)
44. (A) (B) (C) (D) (E)
45. (A) (B) (C) (D) (E)
46. (A) (B) (C) (D) (E)
47. (A) (B) (C) (D) (E)
48. (A) (B) (C) (D) (E)
49. (A) (B) (C) (D) (E)
50. (A) (B) (C) (D) (E)
51. (A) (B) (C) (D) (E)
52. (A) (B) (C) (D) (E)
53. (A) (B) (C) (D) (E)
54. (A) (B) (C) (D) (E)
55. (A) (B) (C) (D) (E)
56. (A) (B) (C) (D) (E)
57. (A) (B) (C) (D) (E)
58. (A) (B) (C) (D) (E)
59. (A) (B) (C) (D) (E)
60. (A) (B) (C) (D) (E)
61. (A) (B) (C) (D) (E)
62. (A) (B) (C) (D) (E)
63. (A) (B) (C) (D) (E)
64. (A) (B) (C) (D) (E)
65. (A) (B) (C) (D) (E)
66. (A) (B) (C) (D) (E)
67. (A) (B) (C) (D) (E)
68. (A) (B) (C) (D) (E)
69. (A) (B) (C) (D) (E)
70. (A) (B) (C) (D) (E)
71. (A) (B) (C) (D) (E)
72. (A) (B) (C) (D) (E)
73. (A) (B) (C) (D) (E)
74. (A) (B) (C) (D) (E)
75. (A) (B) (C) (D) (E)
76. (A) (B) (C) (D) (E)
77. (A) (B) (C) (D) (E)
78. (A) (B) (C) (D) (E)
79. (A) (B) (C) (D) (E)
80. (A) (B) (C) (D) (E)
81. (A) (B) (C) (D) (E)
82. (A) (B) (C) (D) (E)
83. (A) (B) (C) (D) (E)
84. (A) (B) (C) (D) (E)
85. (A) (B) (C) (D) (E)
86. (A) (B) (C) (D) (E)
87. (A) (B) (C) (D) (E)
88. (A) (B) (C) (D) (E)
89. (A) (B) (C) (D) (E)
90. (A) (B) (C) (D) (E)
91. (A) (B) (C) (D) (E)
92. (A) (B) (C) (D) (E)
93. (A) (B) (C) (D) (E)
94. (A) (B) (C) (D) (E)
95. (A) (B) (C) (D) (E)
96. (A) (B) (C) (D) (E)
97. (A) (B) (C) (D) (E)
98. (A) (B) (C) (D) (E)
99. (A) (B) (C) (D) (E)
100. (A) (B) (C) (D) (E)
101. (A) (B) (C) (D) (E)
102. (A) (B) (C) (D) (E)
103. (A) (B) (C) (D) (E)
104. (A) (B) (C) (D) (E)
105. (A) (B) (C) (D) (E)
106. (A) (B) (C) (D) (E)
107. (A) (B) (C) (D) (E)
108. (A) (B) (C) (D) (E)
109. (A) (B) (C) (D) (E)
110. (A) (B) (C) (D) (E)
111. (A) (B) (C) (D) (E)
112. (A) (B) (C) (D) (E)
113. (A) (B) (C) (D) (E)
114. (A) (B) (C) (D) (E)
115. (A) (B) (C) (D) (E)
116. (A) (B) (C) (D) (E)
117. (A) (B) (C) (D) (E)
118. (A) (B) (C) (D) (E)
119. (A) (B) (C) (D) (E)
120. (A) (B) (C) (D) (E)

CLEP HISTORY OF THE UNITED STATES I – TEST 3

1. (A) (B) (C) (D) (E)
2. (A) (B) (C) (D) (E)
3. (A) (B) (C) (D) (E)
4. (A) (B) (C) (D) (E)
5. (A) (B) (C) (D) (E)
6. (A) (B) (C) (D) (E)
7. (A) (B) (C) (D) (E)
8. (A) (B) (C) (D) (E)
9. (A) (B) (C) (D) (E)
10. (A) (B) (C) (D) (E)
11. (A) (B) (C) (D) (E)
12. (A) (B) (C) (D) (E)
13. (A) (B) (C) (D) (E)
14. (A) (B) (C) (D) (E)
15. (A) (B) (C) (D) (E)
16. (A) (B) (C) (D) (E)
17. (A) (B) (C) (D) (E)
18. (A) (B) (C) (D) (E)
19. (A) (B) (C) (D) (E)
20. (A) (B) (C) (D) (E)
21. (A) (B) (C) (D) (E)
22. (A) (B) (C) (D) (E)
23. (A) (B) (C) (D) (E)
24. (A) (B) (C) (D) (E)
25. (A) (B) (C) (D) (E)
26. (A) (B) (C) (D) (E)
27. (A) (B) (C) (D) (E)
28. (A) (B) (C) (D) (E)
29. (A) (B) (C) (D) (E)
30. (A) (B) (C) (D) (E)
31. (A) (B) (C) (D) (E)
32. (A) (B) (C) (D) (E)
33. (A) (B) (C) (D) (E)
34. (A) (B) (C) (D) (E)
35. (A) (B) (C) (D) (E)
36. (A) (B) (C) (D) (E)
37. (A) (B) (C) (D) (E)
38. (A) (B) (C) (D) (E)
39. (A) (B) (C) (D) (E)
40. (A) (B) (C) (D) (E)
41. (A) (B) (C) (D) (E)
42. (A) (B) (C) (D) (E)
43. (A) (B) (C) (D) (E)
44. (A) (B) (C) (D) (E)
45. (A) (B) (C) (D) (E)
46. (A) (B) (C) (D) (E)
47. (A) (B) (C) (D) (E)
48. (A) (B) (C) (D) (E)
49. (A) (B) (C) (D) (E)
50. (A) (B) (C) (D) (E)
51. (A) (B) (C) (D) (E)
52. (A) (B) (C) (D) (E)
53. (A) (B) (C) (D) (E)
54. (A) (B) (C) (D) (E)
55. (A) (B) (C) (D) (E)
56. (A) (B) (C) (D) (E)
57. (A) (B) (C) (D) (E)
58. (A) (B) (C) (D) (E)
59. (A) (B) (C) (D) (E)
60. (A) (B) (C) (D) (E)
61. (A) (B) (C) (D) (E)
62. (A) (B) (C) (D) (E)
63. (A) (B) (C) (D) (E)
64. (A) (B) (C) (D) (E)
65. (A) (B) (C) (D) (E)
66. (A) (B) (C) (D) (E)
67. (A) (B) (C) (D) (E)
68. (A) (B) (C) (D) (E)
69. (A) (B) (C) (D) (E)
70. (A) (B) (C) (D) (E)
71. (A) (B) (C) (D) (E)
72. (A) (B) (C) (D) (E)
73. (A) (B) (C) (D) (E)
74. (A) (B) (C) (D) (E)
75. (A) (B) (C) (D) (E)
76. (A) (B) (C) (D) (E)
77. (A) (B) (C) (D) (E)
78. (A) (B) (C) (D) (E)
79. (A) (B) (C) (D) (E)
80. (A) (B) (C) (D) (E)
81. (A) (B) (C) (D) (E)
82. (A) (B) (C) (D) (E)
83. (A) (B) (C) (D) (E)
84. (A) (B) (C) (D) (E)
85. (A) (B) (C) (D) (E)
86. (A) (B) (C) (D) (E)
87. (A) (B) (C) (D) (E)
88. (A) (B) (C) (D) (E)
89. (A) (B) (C) (D) (E)
90. (A) (B) (C) (D) (E)
91. (A) (B) (C) (D) (E)
92. (A) (B) (C) (D) (E)
93. (A) (B) (C) (D) (E)
94. (A) (B) (C) (D) (E)
95. (A) (B) (C) (D) (E)
96. (A) (B) (C) (D) (E)
97. (A) (B) (C) (D) (E)
98. (A) (B) (C) (D) (E)
99. (A) (B) (C) (D) (E)
100. (A) (B) (C) (D) (E)
101. (A) (B) (C) (D) (E)
102. (A) (B) (C) (D) (E)
103. (A) (B) (C) (D) (E)
104. (A) (B) (C) (D) (E)
105. (A) (B) (C) (D) (E)
106. (A) (B) (C) (D) (E)
107. (A) (B) (C) (D) (E)
108. (A) (B) (C) (D) (E)
109. (A) (B) (C) (D) (E)
110. (A) (B) (C) (D) (E)
111. (A) (B) (C) (D) (E)
112. (A) (B) (C) (D) (E)
113. (A) (B) (C) (D) (E)
114. (A) (B) (C) (D) (E)
115. (A) (B) (C) (D) (E)
116. (A) (B) (C) (D) (E)
117. (A) (B) (C) (D) (E)
118. (A) (B) (C) (D) (E)
119. (A) (B) (C) (D) (E)
120. (A) (B) (C) (D) (E)

INSTALLING REA's TEST*ware*®

SYSTEM REQUIREMENTS

Pentium 75 MHz (300 MHz recommended), or a higher or compatible processor; Microsoft Windows 95, 98, NT 4 (SP6), Me, 2000, or XP; 64 MB Available RAM; Internet Explorer 5.5 or higher (Internet Explorer 5.5 is included on the CD); minimum 100 MB available hard-disk space; VGA or higher-resolution monitor, 800x600 resolution setting; Microsoft Mouse, Microsoft Intellimouse, or compatible pointing device.

INSTALLATION

1. Insert the CLEP History of the United States I TEST*ware*® CD-ROM into the CD-ROM drive.
2. If the installation doesn't begin automatically, from the Start Menu, choose the RUN command. When the RUN dialog box appears, type d:\setup (where D is the letter of your CD-ROM drive) at the prompt and click OK.
3. The installation process will begin. A dialog box proposing the directory "Program Files\REA\CLEP_USHistoryI" will appear. If the name and location are suitable, click OK. If you wish to specify a different name or location, type it in and click OK.
4. Start the CLEP History of the United States I TEST*ware*® application by double-clicking on the icon.

REA's CLEP History of the United States I TEST*ware*® is **EASY to LEARN AND USE**. To achieve maximum benefits, we recommend that you take a few minutes to go through the on-screen tutorial on your computer. The "screen buttons" are also explained here to familiarize you with the program.

TECHNICAL SUPPORT

REA's TEST*ware*® is backed by customer and technical support. For questions about **installation or operation of your software**, contact us at:

Research & Education Association
Phone: (732) 819-8880 (9 a.m. to 5 p.m. ET, Monday–Friday)
Fax: (732) 819-8808
Website: http://www.rea.com
E-mail: info@rea.com

Note to Windows XP Users: In order for the TEST*ware* to function properly, please install and run the application under the same computer-administrator level user account. Installing the TEST*ware* as one user and running it as another could cause file access path conflicts.

USING YOUR INTERACTIVE TEST*ware*®

Exam Directions

The **Exam Directions** button allows you to review the specific exam directions during any part of the test.

Stop Test

At any time during the test or when you are finished taking the test, click on the **Stop** button. The program will advance you to the following screen.

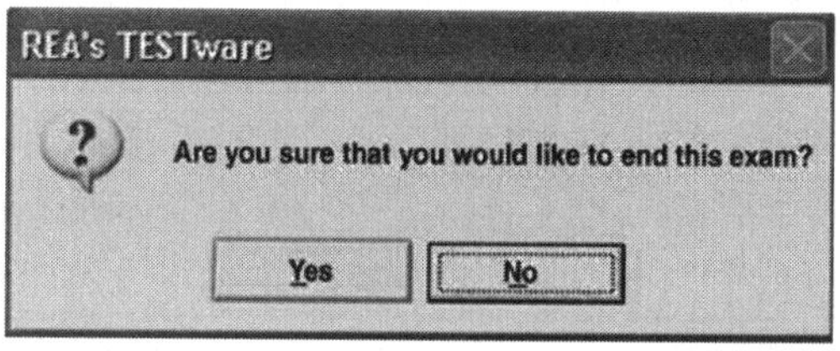

This screen allows you to quit the entire test, or return to the last question viewed prior to clicking the **Stop** button.

Back / Next Buttons

These two buttons allow you to move successfully between questions. The **Next** button moves you to the next question, while the **Back** button allows you to view the previous question.

Mark/Q's List

If you are unsure about an answer to a particular question, the program allows you to mark it for later review. Flag the question by clicking on the **Mark** button. The **Q's List** button allows you to navigate through the questions and explanations. This is particularly useful if you want to view marked questions in Explanations Mode.

View Scores

Three score reports are available: Chart, Summary and Detail (shown below). All are accessed by clicking on the **View Scores** button from the Main Menu.

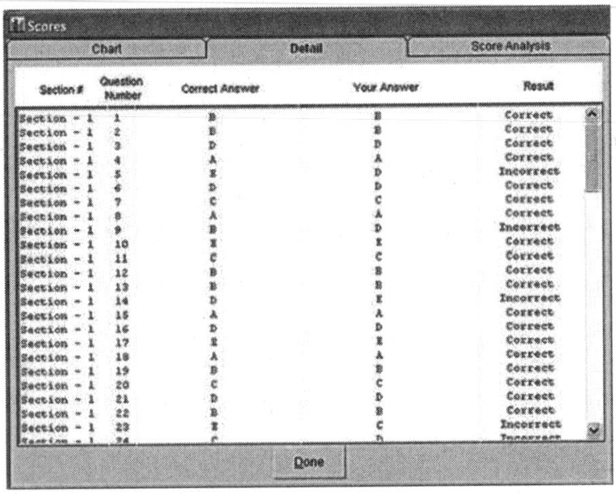

Explanations

In Explanations mode, click on the **Q & A Explanations** button to display a detailed explanation to any question. The split window shown below can be resized for easier reading.

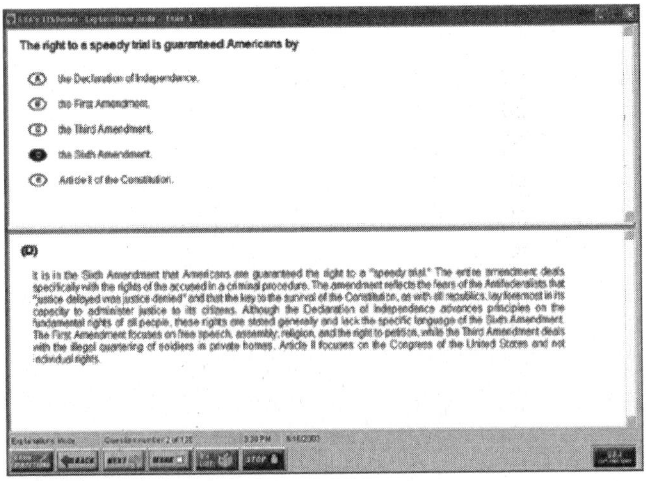

Congratulations!

By studying the reviews in this book, taking the written and computerized practice exams, and reviewing your correct and incorrect answers, you'll be well prepared for the CLEP History of the United States I exam. Best of luck from everyone at REA.